Understanding
Medical Research

From The Library of
PATRICK J. HOGAN M.D.
2121 Addison
HOUSTON, TEXAS 77030

Understanding Medical Research

A Practitioner's Guide

Jane L. Garb, M.S.
Research Biostatistician
Department of Surgery
Baystate Medical Center
Springfield, Massachusetts

Little, Brown and Company
Boston   New York   Toronto   London

Library of Congress Cataloging-in-Publication Data

Garb, Jane L.
    Understanding medical research : a practitioner's guide / Jane L. Garb.
        p.   cm.
    Includes bibliographical references and index.
    ISBN 0-316-29169-2
    1. Medicine—Research—Statistical methods.   I. Title.
    [DNLM: 1. Statistics—methods.   2. Research Design.
3. Bibliometrics.   4. Data Collection.   5. Publishing.   WA 950
G213u   1996]
R853.S7G37   1996
610'.72—dc20
DNLM/DLC
for Library of Congress   96-17216
                                                              CIP

Printed in the United States of America

SEM

Editorial: Jo-Ann T. Strangis
Production Editor: Katharine S. Mascaro
Production Services: Graphic World Publishing Services, Anne Gassett
Production Supervisor and Designer: Mike Burggren
Cover Designer: Deborah Azerrad Savona

To my children, Sarah and David,
for their patience in giving me the time to complete this book.
I give my weekends back to you now.

Contents

Preface

At a recent meeting of the Surgical Journal Club at our hospital, a resident raised doubts about the usefulness of statistics in clinical medicine. He felt each procedure takes us "one step further from the data" and clouds our understanding of the facts with statistical mystique. The purpose of *Understanding Medical Research: A Practitioner's Guide,* as well as my purpose in attending journal club meetings, is to "de-mystify" statistics. I intend to present the general statistical procedures used and the rationale for their use without a complete explanation of the mathematic theory that makes them appropriate. Each procedure we shall discuss has a solid mathematic justification. I ask you to accept this on faith, just as you might accept the validity of an MRI scan without a complete understanding of the physics involved in generating the image.

The purpose of statistics is not, as some would argue, to confuse the issue, but rather to objectify the conclusions we make from a body of data. The calculations of relative risk and confidence intervals allow us to objectively interpret the meaning of group differences or the size of a treatment effect. The calculations of statistical tests allow us to make objective decisions about whether these differences are "real."

I ask you, therefore, to approach this book with healthy skepticism in order to develop a critical eye toward reading the literature, so that together we can explore the ways in which statistics can be used to clarify and objectify the results of clinical studies, as well as the ways in which they can be misused. This is of primary importance to you as clinicians, so that you can sift through the ever-increasing volume of studies you encounter in medical literature. Some of these studies are good and worthy of adding to your clinical armamentarium. Others are poor, with conclusions not supported by the data, and should be ignored. Still others—possibly the majority—are worthwhile in some respects and poor in others; such studies should be accepted with reservations. This book will help you develop the judgment to decide into which of these categories a given study falls. To acquire good judgment in reading medical journals is as important for you, as a clinician, as it is to acquire good judgment in managing patients. What you read will shape your opinions about the elements of good patient care and will ultimately determine how you practice medicine.

I am grateful to Drs. Theodore Colton, James Garb, and Nicholas Coe, and to Mr. Steve Calderone for their helpful editorial suggestions. I also wish to convey a special thanks to Dr. Paul Friedmann, who suggested I write this book and encouraged me in the process.

J.L.G.

Introduction

The primary purpose of this book is to provide clinicians with the practical skills to evaluate studies in the medical literature or to conduct original studies for publication. The need for these skills by the practicing physician is increasing. With the vast number of studies published, the experienced clinician or resident-in-training is faced with the problem of picking-and-choosing. Each month, reading the dozens of journals in his or her area of interest, a physician must decide which articles provide usable results for clinical practice and which should be disregarded.

Alternatively, if a clinician is interested in doing original research in some area of practical interest, he or she may have difficulty finding a qualified expert outside the setting of a university medical center to assist in study design or statistical analysis. The clinician must develop these skills on his or her own.

In writing this book, I have made it short and to the point. Its treatment of statistical issues contrasts with elementary statistics texts in that it does not focus on the theory behind or methods for calculation of statistical tests, but rather on their practical application and interpretation. Let's face it, you, the clinician, are too busy for anything but bare essentials. I understand this, having worked as a research consultant with clinicians for more than 15 years. My approach in developing a study is to get my client to formulate the clinical question he or she is asking in one sentence, focus on the major clinical outcome to answer the question, define the groups to be compared, and work from there to build a study. When interpreting the results of a statistical test, I focus on the practical interpretation and relevance as they apply to the original clinical question.

My approach to reading the literature is essentially the same: discern the major clinical question asked by the study, identify the groups being compared and the basis on which they are compared, determine whether the choice of groups and comparisons made are appropriate, and decide whether statistical tests have been used appropriately. This will tell me if the clinical question has been adequately addressed, if the study is valid or invalid, and whether the results are clinically relevant or irrelevant.

The style of this book parallels the way I approach studies; it is logical, orderly, and concise. I explain the gist of the relevant concepts, with little elaboration or narrative, but with many practical illustrations. It is a manual, rather than a textbook. I will not veer into statistical theory, and use of mathematic formulas is kept to the barest minimum.

The first two sections of this book set forth the principles of good study design and analysis. They deal with the two major purposes of clinical studies: estimation and hypothesis testing. Chapters 1 and 2 deal with the use of statistics in estimation and evaluation of screening tests. Chapter 3 introduces a framework for looking at studies that test hypotheses: assessment of a causal relationship between a risk factor and an outcome. Chapter 4 presents and compares the major ways in which this relationship can be assessed—the major types of study design. Chapters 5 and 6 discuss the reasons why an association may not be causal: bias, confounding, and chance. Chapter 7 enumerates the criteria for concluding that an association between a risk factor and an outcome is causal. Chapter 8, which is an extension of Chap. 6, describes the most common types of statistical tests. Specific statistical tests and measures are also described in Appendix A, which provides details and examples of when and how they are used, what they measure, and what is involved in their computation. Chapter 9 describes how confidence intervals can be used in hypothesis testing.

The principles developed in the first two sections are applied in the next two sections. Section III concerns evaluating studies in the medical literature. To help guide the reader in this process, questions are applied to hypothetical studies of estimation and hypothesis testing.

Section IV offers guidelines for conducting an original study and seeing it through to publication. This includes advice on study design, choice, and use of computer programs in the conduct and analysis of the study, and writing and submitting a scientific paper. Appendixes B to E serve as adjuncts to Section IV.

Questions for evaluating the major types of studies and a flowchart for choosing a statistical test are reproduced as detachable pages at the end of this book. Each page, when photocopied at 135% magnification, will fill an 8-1/2 X 11 sheet of paper. You can reproduce the questions to answer each time you read a journal article, just as we do in the examples in this book. You can also use the questions to evaluate the design and write-up of your own study. Use the flowchart to decide if the statistical tests used in a study are appropriate, or to choose a test for your own study.

PRINCIPLES OF ESTIMATION

Describing Population Characteristics

One purpose of studies in the medical literature is to describe the characteristics of a particular population. This description process is referred to as **estimation.**

I. Estimates from a Sample

To describe a population, we usually take a sample from that population because it is often impractical to survey the entire population. Using the sample, we "estimate," or approximate, the true characteristics of the population. Population and sample characteristics can be divided into three classes, depending on how they are measured. They are **continuous** if they are measured on a numeric scale that represents a true quantity. Examples of continuous estimates include blood pressure in millimeters, weight in pounds or kilograms, hematocrit in millimeters, and height in inches or centimeters. Characteristics are **categorical, or discrete,** if they are measured in categories or classes. Examples are dis ease status (present/absent), sex (male/female), marital status (married/widowed/divorced), and eye color (blue/brown/hazel). Characteristics are **ordinal** if they are measured in categories that have a natural order, such as symptom severity (mild/moderate/ severe), job satisfaction (high/medium/low), and level of education (grade school/high school/college/graduate school). Numbers may be used to represent ordinal categories. For example, employees may be asked to rate their level of job satisfaction on a scale from 1 (completely dissatisfied) to 5 (completely satisfied). Patient functional status may be rated on a scale from 1 (total assistance required) to 7 (totally independent).

The values of sample characteristics are considered **estimates** of the values in the larger population. The estimates used to describe a population characteristic depend on how that characteristic is measured. To describe a continuous characteristic from a population, we usually use the **mean** and **standard deviation.** The mean is the average value of that characteristic in the population. The standard deviation is a measure of how much individual values in the population vary from the mean.

> For example, we wish to determine the mean age of surgical residents in U.S. teaching hospitals. To estimate this value, we take a sample of 100 residents across the country. The mean age of the sample is 28. This gives us an estimate of the mean age of all U.S. surgical residents.

To describe a categorical, or discrete, characteristic from a population, we usually use a **proportion:** the number of individuals in the population who possess that characteristic out of the total number of individuals in the population, expressed as a decimal or percent. When a proportion refers to the frequency of some event, such as mortality or the occurrence of disease, it is referred to as a **rate** and is expressed as a frequency per 100; per 1000; per 100,000; and so on.

> For example, we wish to determine the rate of staphylococcal infection in the neonatal intensive care unit (NICU) of a certain hospital. We determine that the proportion of positive cultures in the NICU at a given time is 0.003, so we report that the rate of staphylococcal infection in newborns is 3 per 1000.

When a rate refers to the proportion of **new** cases of disease in a given period of time, it is called the **incidence rate.** When a rate refers to the proportion of **existing** cases (both new and old) at a given point in time or during a certain period, it is called the **prevalence rate.** The preceding example describes a prevalence rate.

We can use a **median** or **mode** to describe an ordinal characteristic. The median is the halfway point in the population: the value of the characteristic above and below which 50% of the number of individuals in the population lie. The mode is the value most frequently attained in the population. Because these measures are not as affected by extreme low or high values, they are also useful for describing a continuous characteristic whose values are not "normally" distributed about the mean. (Normal distributions will be further discussed in Chap. 15, pages 176–177).

For example, we wish to describe how well 200 pediatric residents in a particular hospital perform oral examinations. The total score is measured on a scale from 1 (excellent) to 10 (poor). In this case, rather than taking a sample, we survey the entire population because it is relatively small. The residents' scores are reported in the following table:

Score	Frequency	Percent	Cumulative %
1	40	20	20
2	16	8	28
3	12	6	34
4	32	16	50
5	**52**	**26**	**76**
6	20	10	86
7	16	8	94
8	4	2	96
9	4	2	98
10	4	2	100

The median score is 4.5: 50% of the residents tested above 4.5, and 50% tested below. Note that because the median lies between 4 and 5 in this example, we took the midpoint of these two numbers as the median. The mode was 5 because 5 was the most common score.

The **accuracy** of a sample estimate (such as a mean or proportion) refers to how close that estimate is to the true value in the population from which the sample was obtained. There are two aspects of an estimate's accuracy: **bias and precision,** where **bias** refers to systematic error and **precision** refers to random error.

II. Bias

Bias is the systematic error in an estimate, in one direction or another. If bias is present, the estimate will consistently vary by some amount from the true population value. Fig. 1-1 is a graphic representation of bias.

Bias in an estimate can occur in the following ways:

1. **Selection bias** occurs when the subjects selected for study are not representative of the population from which they were chosen. Therefore, the results of the study cannot be applied to the broader population they are supposed to represent: They cannot be **generalized.**

    For example, suppose we wish to estimate the prevalence of chronic obstructive lung disease in people over age 65 in the United States.

Fig. 1-1.   Bias

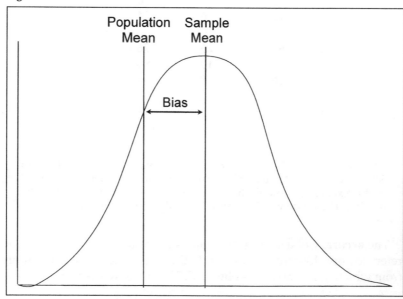

To do this, we choose a sample of retired mine workers and determine the proportion of people in this group with the disease. Our sample is not representative of the general U.S. population but instead represents a high-risk group for lung disease. Therefore, any prevalence estimate obtained from this group will be biased.

2. **Misclassification or information bias** resulting from a **systematic** defect or inaccuracy in the measuring device itself or in the observer obtaining or recording the measurements.

   For example, using a scale that is two pounds off will give a biased estimate of weight in any sample of subjects using that scale.

   As another example, some subjects will always choose the middle score on a five-point attitude scale. Their estimates will therefore be biased from their true attitudes.

If we can measure the amount of bias in a measuring instrument, we can correct for it when making estimates from our sample. This is true with many medical instruments that have a known bias determined from quality control studies. Before taking a measurement, we calibrate the instrument to correct for this bias. However, in most medical studies, it is impossible to measure the amount of bias that exists. We can only demonstrate that we minimized the possibility by taking a representative sample of the population, using measuring devices whose accuracy has been established, or training all observers in the consistent and accurate recording of data. In Chap. 5 we shall deal further with the subject of bias as it relates to hypothesis testing.

III. Precision

In contrast to bias, which refers to systematic error, precision refers to the degree of **chance,** or **random, error** or variability in an estimate. The greater its variability, the **less** precise an estimate will be. For a continuous measurement, it follows that the greater the standard deviation, the less precise an estimate the mean will be. Fig. 1-2 represents different levels of precision, ranging from the most precise (a) to the least precise (c).

The precision of an estimate is a function of the **inherent variability** among individuals in a population, in the measuring instrument itself, in the conditions under which the instrument is

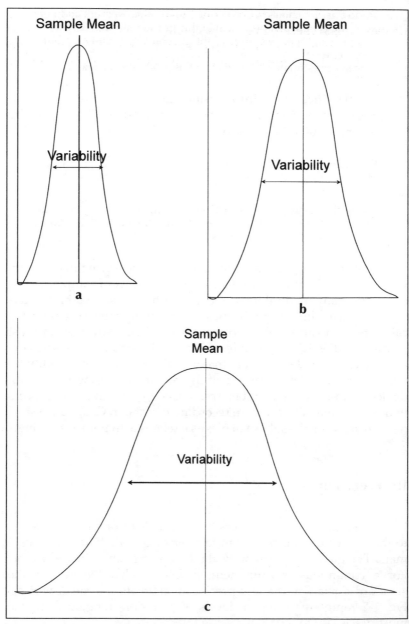

Fig. 1-2.   Different degrees of precision

used, among observers who record the measurements, or in the particular sample chosen. Even if the conditions and measuring instrument are extremely consistent, the estimates from different samples chosen from the sample population will inevitably vary owing to the sampling process itself.

For example, in a sphygmomanometer, an ill-fitting blood pressure cuff can decrease the precision of any blood pressure readings taken with this device.

As another example, environmental conditions such as room temperature, ventilation, or extraneous noise level during testing can affect the precision of intelligence tests.

Also, use of multiple observers of varying levels of experience can affect the precision of glucose tolerance tests.

Statistical bias and precision in a study are independent of each other. An estimate can be biased but precise, as illustrated in Fig. 1-3. On the other hand, an estimate can be unbiased but imprecise, as illustrated in Fig. 1-4.

Fig. 1-3. A biased but precise estimate

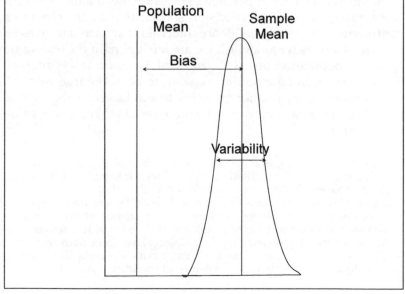

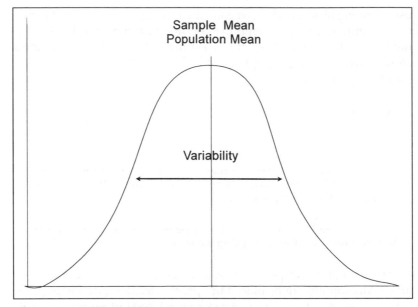

Fig. 1-4.   An unbiased but imprecise estimate

IV. Confidence Intervals

Although it is usually impossible to measure the amount of bias in
an estimate, its degree of precision is measured by the size of its
confidence interval. A confidence interval for an estimate gives us
a range of values within which we are fairly certain the true value
from the population lies. The width of the confidence interval,
then, depends on how certain we want to be of the true value. A
99% confidence interval for an estimate will be wider than a 95%
confidence interval, but we will be more certain that the true value
lies within it.

Refer to our example of estimating the mean age of surgical residents
in **I.** Suppose the 95% confidence interval for the sample mean were
20 to 28 years. That means we are 95% confident that the true mean
age of all surgical residents lies between 20 and 28 years. If we wanted
to be **more certain**—say 99% certain—our confidence interval would
be **wider** (in this case, 18 to 30 years). If we wanted to be **less certain**—
say only 90% certain—our confidence interval would be **narrower** (in
this case, 22 to 26 years). The investigator can choose the size of the
confidence interval based on the degree of confidence desired.

The confidence interval for many estimates can be computed using the **standard error,** which is a function of the variability in the sample, as measured by the standard deviation, and the sample size. **The 95% confidence interval for an estimate**—such as a mean, a difference in means, or a proportion—consists of the **estimate plus or minus twice its standard error.** For the 99% confidence interval, multiply the standard error by 2.58 instead of 2. For the 90% confidence interval, multiply the standard error by 1.64.

A. Confidence Interval for a Mean
Even if the standard error of the mean is not reported in a study, the standard deviation and sample size usually are. Obtain the standard error (SE) of the mean by dividing the standard deviation (SD) by the square root of the sample size ($\sqrt{n}$):

$$SE = SD \div \sqrt{n}$$

You can then use the standard error to compute the 95% confidence interval, as explained.

For example, if the mean systolic blood pressure for a group of 100 patients is 125 and the standard deviation is 40, we would compute a 95% confidence interval as follows:

1. Compute the standard error from the standard deviation and sample size.

$$SE = 40 \div \sqrt{100}$$
$$= 40 \div 10$$
$$= 4$$

2. Multiply the standard error by 2.

$$2 \times 4 = 8$$

3. Subtract 8 from and add 8 to the mean.

$$125 - 8 = 117$$
$$125 + 8 = 133$$

Considering the current sample, we are 95% confident that the true mean lies between 117 and 133. The 99% confidence interval for this example would be $125 \pm 2.58 \times 4$, which is 115 to 135 after rounding. The 90% confidence interval would be $125 \pm 1.64 \times 4$, or 118 to 132 after rounding.

B. Confidence Interval for a Proportion

To compute the standard error used in the confidence interval (CI) for a proportion (p) in large samples, we can use the following formula, where n is the sample size.

$$SE = \sqrt{\frac{p(1 - p)}{n}}$$

For example, suppose we want to find the 95% confidence interval for the admission rate of elderly patients (over age 65) for a given hospital in a particular year. We take a sample of 300 patients from the admission records of the hospital during that year and find that the admission rate of elderly patients is 100 in 300, or 0.33. The 95% confidence interval for the proportion of elderly patients is calculated as follows:

$$CI = p \pm (2 \times SE)$$

$$= 0.33 \pm \left(2 \times \sqrt{\frac{(0.33)(0.67)}{300}}\right)$$

$$= 0.33 \pm (2 \times \sqrt{.0007})$$

$$= 0.33 \pm (2 \times .027)$$

$$= 0.33 \pm 0.05, \text{ after rounding}$$

$$= 0.27 \text{ to } 0.38$$

We are thus 95% confident that the true admission rate of elderly patients falls between 0.27 and 0.38, or 27 and 38 per hundred.

The preceding formula is appropriate only for relatively large samples (when the proportion times the sample size is greater than or equal to 5). See the papers by Simon [1] and Gardner and Altman [2] for the calculation of confidence intervals for proportions with small samples. Alternatively, many statistical packages, such as the one we will discuss in Part IV, calculate both the usual confidence intervals for proportions or means and "exact" confidence intervals for use with a small sample size.

C. Confidence Interval for a Zero Proportion

When we find no cases of an event in a sample, resulting in a proportion or rate of zero, we should also derive a confidence interval, as we did for other proportions. However, the aforementioned formula will not work if the proportion is zero. In this case, we use the "rule of three" [3]:

> **The upper limit of the 95% confidence interval for 0 is $3/n$**

For example, in a sample of 20 children, none are found to be ill with measles. We can therefore be 95% confident that the true prevalence rate in the population of all children falls between 0 and $3/20$, or 15% or 15 per 100.

An approach to evaluating estimation studies in the literature will be given in Part III, Chaps. 10 and 11.

V. Summary

Estimation refers to the process of describing the characteristics of a population based on a sample from that population. The values obtained from the sample are called **estimates** of the values in the larger population.

1. Population and sample characteristics can be divided into three classes depending on how they are measured: continuous when measured on a numeric scale, categorical when measured in categories, and ordinal when the categories are ordered.
2. To describe a continuous characteristic from a population or a sample, we use the mean and standard deviation. The mean is the average, and the standard deviation is a measure of how much individuals vary from the mean.
3. To describe a categorical, or discrete, characteristic, we use a proportion. This is the number of individuals who possess a characteristic out of all individuals in a population or sample.

   a. A rate is the proportion of individuals in which some event occurs in a population in a specific period of time, stated per 100 or 1000 and so on.

b. The incidence rate is the rate of new cases of disease in a population.
c. The prevalence rate is the rate of existing cases (both new and old) in a population at one time or during a period.

4. To describe an ordinal characteristic, or a continuous one that is not normally distributed, we use the median or mode. The median is the value of the characteristic above and below which half the number of individuals lie. The mode is the most frequent value of the characteristic.

The accuracy of an estimate derived from a sample refers to how close that estimate is to the true population value. Accuracy is assessed in terms of bias and precision. Statistical bias is the degree of systematic error in an estimate. Two of the most frequent forms of bias are bias in the choice of subjects for study (selection bias) and in the measuring instrument or observer recording the data (misclassification bias). Bias usually cannot be measured. Precision refers to the degree of chance error in the estimate and refers to its internal consistency (i.e., the variability of the individual values that comprise the estimate). Precision can be measured by the width of the confidence interval. A confidence interval gives us a range of values within which we are fairly certain (e.g., 95% or 99%) the true population value lies. The greater the level of the confidence interval, the greater our certainty. Sections **IV. A** through **IV. C** give methods for calculating the confidence interval for a mean, proportion, and zero proportion.

VI. References

The *Mayo Clinic Proceedings* series "Statistics for Clinicians" [4, 5] gives additional detail on confidence intervals.

1. Simon R. Confidence intervals for reporting results of clinical trials. *Ann Intern Med* 105:429–435, 1986.
2. Gardner MJ, Altman DG. Confidence intervals rather than p-values: estimation rather than hypothesis testing. *Brit Med J* 292:746–750, 1986.
3. Hanley JA, Lippman-Hand A. If nothing goes wrong, is everything all right?" *JAMA* 249(13):1743–1745, 1983.
4. O'Brien PC, Shampo MA. Statistics for clinicians 4. Estimation from samples. *Mayo Clin Proc* 56:274–276, 1981.
5. O'Brien PC, Shampo MA. Statistics for clinicians 10. Normal values. *Mayo Clin Proc* 56:639–640, 1981.

Screening Tests

Evaluating a diagnostic test is actually a special instance of estimation. Many diagnostic tests are used as "screening tests," or diagnostic tests that are easy and inexpensive to use on a large number of people. Screening tests give a **presumptive** diagnosis when definitive testing of the entire population is unfeasible or impractical. A screening test has two purposes:

1. To identify people who are **likely** to have a disease, so they can be more definitively evaluated to determine if they actually have the disease.
2. To identify people who are **unlikely** to have the disease and in whom no further testing is warranted.

Use of screening tests reduces the cost of detecting disease in a large population by subjecting only a small proportion to expensive, rigorous diagnostic testing.

I. Validity

We can evaluate the accuracy of a screening test in detecting disease by comparing its results with the established "gold standard" for detecting the same disease: true disease status. First we give both the screening test and the "standard" test to the same group of people (test population). Then we compare the results of the screening test (positive or negative) for all subjects with their disease status (diseased or nondiseased) as determined by the standard test. The results of this comparison can be represented in a table:

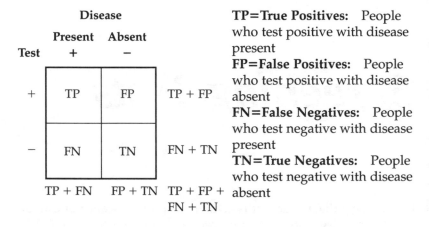

TP=True Positives: People who test positive with disease present

FP=False Positives: People who test positive with disease absent

FN=False Negatives: People who test negative with disease present

TN=True Negatives: People who test negative with disease absent

Several measures are important in evaluating the validity of a screening test. The **sensitivity** of a test is a measure of how accurate the test is in detecting **diseased** individuals:

$$\text{Sensitivity} = \frac{TP}{TP + FN}$$

The **specificity** of a test is a measure of how accurate the test is in detecting **nondiseased** individuals:

$$\text{Specificity} = \frac{TN}{FP + TN}$$

The **overall accuracy** of a test is the percent correct classification of **all individuals:**

$$\text{Overall accuracy} = \frac{TP + TN}{TP + FP + FN + TN}$$

For example, suppose a new test is developed for the early detection of duodenal ulcer. We compare the results of the screening test with the results of gastroscopy in 100 subjects and present our findings in the following table:

Disease

	Present +	Absent −	
Test			
+	TP 9	FP 18	27
−	FN 1	TN 72	73
	10	90	100

The screening test correctly identified 9 of the 10 subjects with duodenal ulcer for a sensitivity of 90%. The test correctly identified 72 of the 90 normal subjects, for a specificity of 80%.

When evaluating a screening test, how do we decide which measures of accuracy are important? Sensitivity, specificity, and overall accuracy measure different aspects of a test's validity. The purpose of our screening program will determine which measure is most important in evaluating one screening test or in choosing among several screening tests.

For example, suppose our primary concern is to detect as many individuals as possible with a disease that is fatal, but curable if found in the early stages. We would look for the screening test with the highest sensitivity, even if its specificity and overall accuracy are somewhat lower.

Suppose, on the other hand, that the disease in question is more benign and that the standard testing for disease is extremely expensive and uncomfortable for the patient. In this instance we would want to limit the number of individuals unnecessarily subjected to the standard test, even if it meant that we might fail to detect some individuals with the disease. We would then choose a test with high specificity, even if its sensitivity were lower.

The overall accuracy of the test would be the most important measure if the purpose of the screening program were to estimate the number of diseased and nondiseased individuals for public health planning purposes.

As a general rule, **to confirm the presence of disease we want a test with high specificity. To screen for disease or to exclude a diagnostic possibility, we want a test with high sensitivity.**

A. Use of Cutoffs to Alter Sensitivity and Specificity

Many screening tests are measured on a continuous scale and can therefore have arbitrary cutoff points to define a positive and negative test. These cutoffs can then be manipulated to increase or decrease the sensitivity and specificity, depending on whether it is more important for the test to be sensitive or specific.

> For example, in a study by Gumaste et al. [1], the researchers compared serum lipase and serum amylase levels as screening tests to distinguish patients with acute pancreatitis from those with non-pancreatic abdominal pain. The lower the level chosen as a cutoff, the more certainty that patients with acute pancreatitis would be classified as "positive" on the screening test (i.e., the higher the sensitivity). Conversely, the higher the level chosen as a cutoff, the more certainty that patients without acute pancreatitis would be classified as "negative" on the screening test (i.e., the higher the specificity). The authors chose a level of three times normal as the cutoff for detecting acute pancreatitis which resulted in high specificity of the serum amylase test (99%), but low sensitivity (72%). Sensitivity and specificity of the serum lipase test were 100% and 99% respectively.

> Example 1 in Chap. 10 provides a second example using cutoff points for positive and negative values of a screening test. It is a study to determine admission criteria for predicting a positive CT scan in patients with head trauma. The implications of using various cutoffs for this test are discussed in the questions following the example.

Specificity and sensitivity are inversely related—when one is increased, the other is decreased. To determine an optimum cutoff point that results in sufficiently high sensitivity while maintaining an acceptably low false positive rate (1 minus the specificity), we can plot the sensitivity and false positive rate resulting from various cutoffs for the screening test. A graph of this type is called an *ROC*, or receiver operating characteristic graph, because sensitivity and specificity are referred to as the operating characteristics of a screening test. Although it was not used in the previously cited study by Gumaste, an ROC graph for serum amylase in duodenal ulcer might look something like Fig. 2-1.

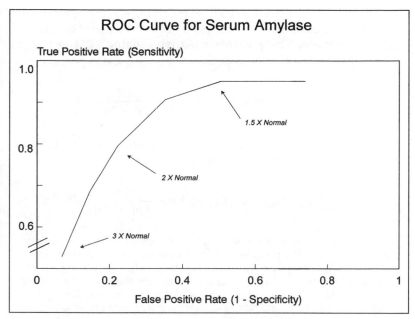

Fig. 2-1.   Receiver operating characteristics (ROC)

As Fig. 2-1 shows, as the cutoff for serum amylase is lowered the true positive rate (sensitivity) increases, but the false positive rate increases (lowering the specificity).

Although not based on the actual data from the Gumaste study, the maximum level of sensitivity in this example would be reached using a cutoff for serum amylase of 1.5 times normal, at which point the curve reaches a plateau. Lower cutoffs would provide no gain in sensitivity but would increase the false positive rate (further lowering the specificity).

II. Predictive Value

The sensitivity, specificity, and overall accuracy are measures of the validity of a screening test, and their values remain constant **whatever population is tested.** Another measure that evaluates the usefulness of a screening test **when applied to a particular population** is the **predictive value.** This measure depends on the frequency of the disease in the population to which the test is applied [2]. The predictive value of a test tells us how much the screening test results reduce our uncertainty about the presence or absence of disease in a particular patient. The **positive predictive value** of a test is the probability that the disease is present when the test is positive.

$$\text{Positive predictive value} = \frac{TP}{TP + FP}$$

The **negative predictive value** of a test is the probability that the disease is absent when the test is negative.

$$\text{Negative predictive value} = \frac{TN}{FN + TN}$$

For example, suppose we wish to screen a population of 1000 men for duodenal ulcer. The prevalence of this disease is known to be about 10% in the general population [3]. Therefore, **before screening** a sample of 1000 men we would expect 100 to have the disease and 900 to be nondiseased. In the present example we have selected a screening test with 90% sensitivity and 80% specificity demonstrated from previous validity studies. We can thus fill in the cells of the table as follows:

	Disease		
	Present	**Absent**	
Test	**+**	**−**	
+	TP 90	FP 180	270
−	FN 10	TN 720	730
	100	900	1000

From previous studies:
Prevalence of disease: 10%
Sensitivity of test: 90%
Specificity of test: 80%

From present population:
Positive predictive value:
$TP/(TP + FP) = 90/270 = 33\%$
Negative predictive value:
$TN/(FN + TN) = 720/730 = 99\%$

The positive predictive value of the test in this sample is 33%. This means that our estimate of the probability of duodenal ulcer in a patient with a positive test has increased from 10% **before** screening to 33% after screening. Although our certainty about the disease's presence in patients with a positive test is improved, it is not high. The negative predictive value of this test is 99%. Our estimate of the probability that the disease is absent in a person **with a negative test** increases from 90% before screening to near certainty after screening (99%). In this example, the test is more useful in patients with negative results than in those with positive results.

This example demonstrates the general principle that **when the prevalence of disease is low, screening tests are more useful in ruling out the possibility of disease than in establishing its presence** (i.e., negative test results are more useful than positive ones). Conversely, **when the prevalence of disease is high, positive test results are more useful than negative ones.** For this reason, screening is usually directed toward populations where the prevalence of disease is high. To illustrate this principle, let us consider the following example:

Suppose we again apply the screening test used in the previous example to a sample of 100 first-degree relatives of duodenal ulcer patients. In this group, the prevalence of ulcer is expected to be about 30% [3]. Because we already know the sensitivity and specificity of the test, we can complete the table below as follows:

	Disease		
	Present	**Absent**	
Test	**+**	**−**	
+	TP 27	FP 14	41
−	FN 3	TN 56	59
	30	70	100

From previous studies:
Prevalence of disease: 30%
Sensitivity of test: 90%
Specificity of test: 80%

From present population:
Positive predictive value:
TP/(TP + FP) = 27/41 = 66%
Negative predictive value:
TN/FN + TN = 56/59 = 95%

In this sample, the estimated prevalence of ulcer disease is 30% before screening and 66% after a positive test result has been obtained. Thus, a positive result in a sample of relatives of patients with ulcer disease is much more useful in increasing our certainty that ulcer is present than in a sample from the general population. A negative result is also very useful in this sample because it increases our certainty that the patient is ulcerfree from 70% to 95%.

III. Summary

Sensitivity and specificity are measures of the accuracy or validity of a test when compared to an established standard. They remain constant regardless of population. Predictive value, either positive or negative, is a measure of the usefulness of a test in a particular population and depends on the prevalence of disease in that population. A positive test result will be more useful than a negative result in a population in which the prevalence of the disease is high. A negative test result will be more useful than a positive one in a population where the prevalence is low [2]. See Chap. 10 for a detailed example of a screening test and Chap. 11 for questions for evaluating screening tests.

IV. References

Griner et al [2] and the *Mayo Clinic Proceedings* series "Statistics for Clinicians" [4] give further discussion on evaluating diagnostic tests.

1. Gumaste VV, et al. Serum lipase levels in nonpancreatic abdominal pain versus acute pancreatitis. *Am J Gastroenterology* 88(12):2051–2055, 1993.
2. Griner PJ, et al. Selection and interpretation of diagnostic tests and procedures. Principles and applications. *Ann Intern Med* 94 (4, part 2):555–600, 1981.
3. Braunwald E, et al. *Harrison's Principles of Internal Medicine.* New York: McGraw-Hill, 1991. P 1233.
4. O'Brien PC, Shampo MA. Statistics for clinicians 9. Evaluating a new diagnostic procedure. *Mayo Clin Proc* 56:573–575, 1981.

PRINCIPLES OF HYPOTHESIS TESTING

3

Approach to the Study of a Risk Factor and an Outcome

The second and more frequent purpose of research studies found in the medical literature is to answer questions about the disease process or clinical practice. These questions are usually posed in terms of a hypothesis about the presence of a causal association between a risk factor and an outcome.* This chapter introduces a framework with which we can view these studies. This framework should be a useful tool for critically evaluating the literature and conducting original research.

*Statisticians generally refer to hypothesis testing as conducting tests of significance, which will be covered in Chap. 3. However, in the context of this book, the term is used in a broader sense to refer to the entire process of establishing a causal association between a risk factor and an outcome. This distinction will become clear to the reader when the issues of statistical significance and establishing the "effect size" of a risk factor are discussed.

I. The Risk Factor and Outcome

The following are examples of hypotheses that might be found in medical studies:

1. Smoking causes lung cancer.
2. Drug A is better than Drug B in curing Disease X.
3. Gender is linked to arteriosclerotic heart disease (ASHD).

In each hypothesis we can identify a risk factor and an outcome. The **risk factor** is the cause, and the **outcome** is the result. In the preceding hypotheses,

1. Smoking is the risk factor, and lung cancer is the outcome.
2. The drug (A or B) is the risk factor, and cure of Disease X is the outcome.
3. Gender is the risk factor, and development of ASHD is the outcome.

Risk factors can be either positive or negative. A **positive** risk factor, when present or high, **increases** the chances that the outcome will occur or increases the level of the outcome. Consider the following examples:

Smoking is a **positive** risk factor in lung cancer because it **increases** the chances that lung cancer will occur.
Obesity is a **positive** risk factor for hypertension because it **increases** the chances that hypertension will occur.
High cholesterol is a **positive** risk factor for heart disease because it **increases** the chances of heart disease.
Salt intake is a **positive** risk factor for high blood pressure because, when high, it causes an **increase** in blood pressure.

A **negative,** or protective, risk factor, when present or high, **decreases** the chances that the outcome will occur or decreases the level of the outcome.

A low-cholesterol diet is a **negative** risk factor for heart disease, because, when present, it **decreases** the chances of heart disease.
Bupivacaine hydrochloride is a **negative** risk factor for postoperative pain, because, when given, it **decreases** the level of pain.
The Salk vaccine is a **negative** risk factor for polio, because, when given, it decreases the chances of getting polio.

II. Comparing Two or More Groups

To test hypotheses about the relationship between a risk factor and an outcome, one must always compare two or more groups. Statements about a single group of subjects are meaningless in the absence of a control or comparison group.

> For example, we might read the following statement in an advertisement for Drug X: "Drug X relieved headaches in 50% of the subjects tested." To be able to assess the effectiveness of Drug X, we need to know what percentage of headaches were relieved in subjects given placebo ("sham") treatment or no treatment at all.

Groups can be defined on the basis of the risk factor and compared on outcome, or vice versa. How the groups are defined and compared determines the study design.

> Let us refer to the previous hypothesis that smoking (the risk factor) causes lung cancer (the outcome). To test this hypothesis, we identify two **risk factor** groups: smokers and nonsmokers. We then compare the two groups on outcome: the percentage of subjects who develop lung cancer.
>
> As another example, we may wish to test the hypothesis that gestational age is a risk factor in the development of hypertrophic pyloric stenosis (HPS) in infants. We identify two **outcome** groups, HPS infants and normal infants, and compare them on the risk factor: gestational age at birth.

When we find a difference between the groups, we must consider the possible explanations for this difference:

A spurious association: The difference in the groups is due to non-comparability—that is, a difference in the composition of the groups. This association is the subject of bias and confounding.
A chance association: The difference in the groups is due to chance. This association is the basis of statistical analysis.
A causal association: The difference in the groups is due to a true causal association between the risk factor and the outcome.

In order to prove our hypothesis and conclude that the last explanation is correct—that is, that the risk factor led to or caused the outcome—we must first rule out the other two explanations. This process is fully described in succeeding chapters in this part.

Most of the examples in this book will for simplicity refer to comparison of only two groups of subjects. Usually the groups are those with disease present or absent or, alternatively, those with the risk factor present or absent. However, most of the principles given can be extended to comparing more than two groups, such as those with different levels of a risk factor or outcome.

III. Summary

In this chapter we established a framework for looking at the majority of medical research studies: testing hypotheses about a causal relationship between a risk factor and an outcome.

1. A risk factor is a cause, and an outcome is a result.

    a. A positive risk factor, when present or high, increases the chances that the outcome will occur or increases the level of the outcome.
    b. A negative risk factor, when present or high, decreases the chances that the outcome will occur or decreases the level of the outcome.

2. To test hypotheses concerning the relationship between a risk factor and an outcome, one must always compare at least two groups. If a difference is found between these groups, three possible reasons must be considered:

    a. A spurious association
    b. A chance association
    c. A causal association

Chapter 12 gives examples of studies that test hypotheses and lists questions for evaluating these studies.

Study Design

As stated in Chap. 3, the purpose of most medical research studies is to assess the presence and magnitude of a causal association between a risk factor and an outcome. This involves comparing two or more groups. How these groups are defined and compared determines the kind of study design used.

I. Cohort Study

If the groups are defined on the basis of the risk factor and compared with respect to the outcome, the study is a **cohort** study. The design of a cohort study is depicted in Fig. 4-1, where $RF+$ and $RF-$ refer to presence of the risk factor and $D+$ and $D-$ refer to development of the disease.

A sample of subjects is drawn from a larger population and divided into two groups: those with the risk factor present ($RF+$) and those with the risk factor absent ($RF-$). For risk factors with more than two levels (e.g., absent, low, medium, high), there will be more than two groups. Subjects in each risk factor group are then followed over time to determine the outcome—whether or not the disease or condition under study occurs. Finally, the groups are compared on the proportion of subjects who develop the disease ($D+$).

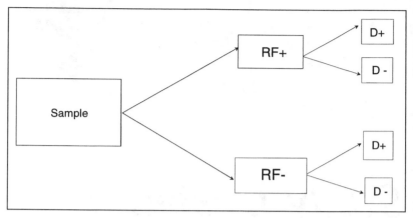

Fig. 4-1.   A cohort study

The Framingham study is an example of a cohort study [1]. As one aspect of this study, a sample of subjects free of heart disease was initially chosen from the U.S. population and its members classified as hypertensive (risk factor present) or normotensive (risk factor absent). Subjects were then followed over time to determine newly occurring cases of myocardial infarction (outcome). The hypertensive and normotensive groups were compared on the incidence of myocardial infarction.

Cohort studies can be **prospective,** when the risk factor groups are identified at the start of the study and followed into the **future** to determine the outcome status of each subject. They can also be **retrospective,** using past records or interviews to determine the **past** risk factor status of subjects and searching the records over time to determine the subsequent outcome status of each subject. In both the prospective and retrospective cohort studies, all subjects must be free of the disease at the start of the study period, when their risk factor status is determined. The risk factor groups thus identified will then be followed, either retrospectively or prospectively, for some period and compared on their **incidence** rates during this period. Risk factor and outcome status are thus determined **at two different points in time.**

Cohort studies can also be **cross-sectional,** when the risk factor and outcome status of a subject are determined **at the same time.** In this case they estimate the **prevalence** rates in the groups.

For example, two researchers wish to study the relationship of blood group and astigmatism. They select a sample of subjects and, for each subject, determine the blood group (risk factor) and whether the subject **currently** has astigmatism (outcome). The researchers then divide the subjects into four groups according to blood group (A, B, AB, O) and compare the prevalence of astigmatism in the four groups. This is a cohort study because subjects are classified on the basis of the risk factor (blood group) and compared on the basis of outcome (presence of astigmatism). This is also a cross-sectional study because the presence of astigmatism (outcome) is determined **at the same time** as a subject's blood group (risk factor).

Risk factors that can be studied with a cross-sectional cohort design do not change over time and cannot be altered by disease status. This constraint exists because a characteristic to be evaluated as a risk factor in any study must have been present before the outcome developed.

> For example, we could not use a cross-sectional design to study the relationship of blood glucose level (risk factor) and hypertension (outcome) because the presence of hypertension may alter blood glucose level. If we find that the prevalence of hypertension is higher in subjects with high glucose levels than in those with low or moderate levels, we do not know whether hypertension is the cause of high blood glucose, whether high blood glucose is the cause of hypertension, or whether both conditions are the result of some other risk factor. On the other hand, in a study of sex and hypertension, if we find that the prevalence of hypertension is greater in men than in women, we can infer that sex is a risk factor for hypertension. This inference is reasonable because sex is an unchanging attribute that cannot be altered by disease.

Cohort studies are useful in several instances:

1. When the investigator wants control over follow-up and diagnosis of outcome. The procedures for determining risk factor status and outcome can be more consistent and reliable if they are defined by the investigator in advance and carried out by a limited number of carefully trained study personnel.
2. When the investigator wants to estimate the incidence of disease in a population.*
3. When the investigator wants to study many outcomes.

---

*Only prospective or retrospective cohort studies, not cross-sectional cohort studies, can estimate incidence rates. Cross-sectional studies only estimate prevalence rates.

II. Clinical Trial

A **clinical trial** is a special type of prospective cohort study in which the investigators **assign** subjects to risk factor groups—(called treatment groups because they are based on a particular treatment or procedure)—rather than simply **observing** the risk factor status of subjects. The design of a clinical trial is represented in Fig. 4-2. The researchers randomly assign a sample of subjects to treatment groups (RXA, RXB). They then follow subjects in each group over time to determine outcome (disease) status (D+, D−).

> For example, in order to test the effectiveness of the Salk vaccine in preventing poliomyelitis, school children in the sample group were randomly assigned to receive the vaccine (risk factor or treatment present) or placebo (risk factor or treatment absent). Both sets of children were then followed over time and compared on the incidence of polio (outcome).

A special type of clinical trial called a **crossover clinical trial** is used when each subject serves as his or her own control. Instead of assigning different treatments to two (or more) groups of subjects, the investigator assigns the same subject two (or more) different treatments in different time periods and compares the subject's responses in the different periods. This type of clinical trial has certain advantages in that it requires fewer subjects than a clinical trial and is better able to control individual subject differences than a standard clinical trial can.

Fig. 4-2. A clinical trial

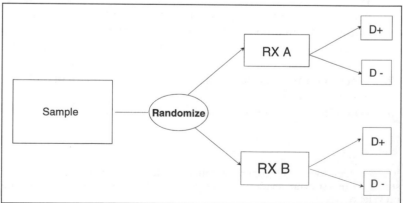

For example, to determine whether Drug X is effective in lowering blood pressure, we could compare the blood pressure of a group of subjects before taking Drug X with their blood pressure after taking Drug X. To compare two drugs and a placebo, we could administer the placebo, Drug X, and Drug Y to subjects at different time periods and compare their blood pressure readings during the different time periods. We would have to allow for a "washout" period between blood pressure readings to allow the effects of one drug to disappear before we gave the next drug.

A clinical trial is used when the investigator wants control over how the treatment is administered to ensure consistency and maximum treatment effectiveness. Most clinical trials are **randomized clinical trials.** Randomization avoids the bias in choice of subjects that might occur if treatment were decided by the patient's physician. It also maximizes the possibility that the treatment groups will be comparable on other nontreatment factors. Additionally, it allows the calculation of the probability that the results occurred by chance by satisfying the sampling assumptions of statistical testing and estimation concerning random selection of subjects.

Prospective cohort studies and clinical trials have two major drawbacks: They are costly in terms of personnel and resources, and they usually require a long time to complete. A long follow-up period is often needed to determine outcome. During this time subjects may drop out and study personnel may lose interest, with a subsequent breakdown of study procedures. Furthermore, changes in the methods of diagnosis or treatment over time may affect outcome classification. Additionally, the risk factor status of subjects may change over time. For example, subjects classified as nonsmokers at the start of a study may become smokers during the study period. Consequently, investigators must maintain rigorous follow-up procedures to keep patients in the study and provide incentives to maintain morale among study personnel.

III. Case Control Study

If the groups are defined on the basis of outcome and compared with respect to risk factor status, the study is a **case control** study. The design of a case control study is represented in Fig. 4-3. Subjects are classified on the basis of outcome—that is, whether the disease or condition under study is present or absent. The outcome groups

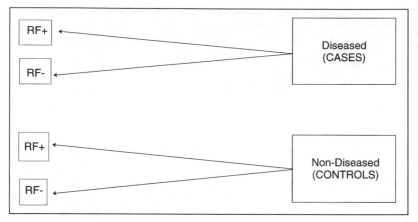

Fig. 4-3.   A case control study

are then compared on the proportion of subjects with the risk factor present.

For example, in a study to assess the relationship of smoking to lung cancer, a researcher identifies all patients with lung cancer (cases) who are diagnosed at a certain hospital in a certain time period. The researcher also identifies a second group of patients with other diseases (controls) from the same hospital who are diagnosed during the same time period. The prevalence of smokers (risk factor) in each outcome group is compared.

A case control study is **retrospective** if cases and controls are identified in the present and risk factors are ascertained from the subject's history (past records or interviews about past events).

For example, to conduct a retrospective study on the relationship of childhood rubella (risk factor) to development of adult Guillain-Barré syndrome (outcome), we could identify all Guillain-Barré patients in a given population (cases) and compare them with a sample of nondiseased subjects (controls). If the proportion of subjects with a history of rubella is different in the two groups, we would conclude that rubella is related to adult Guillain-Barré syndrome.

Case control studies can also be **cross-sectional,** if both outcome and risk factor status are ascertained at the same time.

An example of a cross-sectional case control study is provided by Mac Mahon et al [2]. In order to study the relationship of coffee-drinking (risk factor) and cancer of the pancreas (outcome), the researchers compared the coffee-drinking habits of pancreatic cancer patients in 11 large hospitals (cases) to patients in the same hospitals with other diseases not associated with the pancreas or hepatobiliary tract and not known to be associated with smoking or alcohol (controls).

Case control studies are useful in several instances:

1. When a rare disease with a low incidence would require a huge number of nondiseased subjects to be studied prospectively to obtain a sufficient number of cases. In such situations it is more efficient and less costly to identify all cases and a sample of controls for study.
2. When a long lag period between risk factor exposure and development of outcome makes a cohort study unfeasible.
3. When a prospective study cannot be done because of limited resources or because results are needed quickly.
4. When the risk factor is unknown.

> In the preceding example of Guillain-Barré syndrome, the case control study was an appropriate choice of study design because Guillain-Barré syndrome is rare. If we wanted to study hypertension, a cohort study design might be more appropriate, with adequate resources and time, because hypertension is relatively common.

A major drawback of case control studies is the fact that the proportion of cases in the study does not represent the proportion of people with the disease in the population. Therefore, researchers cannot make estimates of disease incidence.

Chapter 12 provides illustrative examples and guidelines for reading and evaluating cohort and case control studies.

IV. Meta-Analysis

Because the medical literature contains so many studies, we need an objective, scientific means of interpreting the results of multiple studies. The discipline of meta-analysis has been steadily developing in the last 20 years to answer this need. Meta-analysis is a systematic, objective way to assemble data from many studies and arrive at a pooled estimate of treatment effect.

Meta-analysis should not be confused with reviews of the literature. In literature reviews, the choice of studies for review is generally driven by some theoretical framework envisioned by the reviewer in a subjective attempt to make sense of the multitude of studies in a subject area. The reviewer is not necessarily attempting to combine evidence for the efficacy of a given treatment, but is often trying to elucidate some theoretical connection between the studies that he or she has reviewed. In contrast, a meta-analysis is more akin to a retrospective cohort study in which the subjects are clinical studies. The data from these studies are pooled according to objective statistical methods.

The quality and accuracy of meta-analyses vary depending on the methods used in the selection of studies for analysis and the pooling of their results. Chapter 12 gives an illustrative example and questions to consider when reading and evaluating a meta-analysis. For those interested in a more detailed description of meta-analysis, L'Abbé et al [3] give an excellent discussion.

V. Summary

To test hypotheses about the causal association between a risk factor and an outcome, two or more groups of subjects must be compared. The basis on which these groups are defined and compared determines the kind of study design:

1. Cohort studies define groups on the basis of the risk factor and compare them on outcome.
2. Clinical trials are a special type of cohort study in which the investigator assigns subjects to risk factor groups based on some treatment or procedure.
3. Case control studies define groups on the basis of outcome and compare them on the risk factor.
4. Meta-analysis is a special type of study design in which the researcher analyzes the results of many separate studies, usually randomized clinical trials, to derive a pooled estimate of treatment effectiveness and statistical significance.

Cohort studies can be prospective, retrospective, or cross-sectional, depending on the time at which the risk factor and outcome are determined. Case control studies can be retrospective or cross-sectional. Each type of study design has its own advantages and disadvantages.

VI. References

1. Dawber TR, Meadors GF, Moore FE Jr. Epidemiological approaches to heart disease. The Framingham study. *Am J Public Health* 41:279–286, 1951.
2. MacMahon B, et al. Coffee and cancer of the pancreas. *N Engl J Med* 304:630–633, 1981.
3. L'Abbé KA, Detsky AS, O'Rourke K. Meta-analysis in clinical research. *Ann Intern Med* 107:224–233, 1987.

Spurious
Association

I. Bias

As stated in Chap. 3, when researchers find a difference between the
groups under study, they must consider three possible explanations
for this difference:

1. Spurious association
2. Chance association
3. Causal association

In order to conclude that the groups differ because of a causal association, they must first rule out the other two types of association.

   The first type of association is a spurious or artifactual association
caused by noncomparability or inequality of the groups. When comparing two or more groups, we assume that the groups are alike in
every respect except the defining characteristic (i.e., risk factor status
in cohort studies or outcome status in case control studies). We assume
that the groups are treated alike in all study procedures and that their
makeup is similar with respect to other risk factors not under study.

For example, in a randomized clinical trial comparing surgical and medical treatment for gallstones, we assume the exact same makeup of the two treatment groups with respect to other risk factors (e.g., age, sex, type of gallstones) and assume identical treatment (e.g., ancillary, supportive care) except that one group is medically treated with diet and one group is surgically treated with cholecystectomy.

As another example, to study the relationship of blood group and leukemia in a case control study, we assume that leukemia cases and normal controls are alike with respect to the presence of other diseases and risk factors such as age, sex, and exposure to toxic drugs or x-rays.

Noncomparability of the study groups in the selection of subjects or loss to follow-up (selection bias), measurement of the study characteristic (misclassification bias), or makeup of the study groups (confounding bias) can lead to a biased estimate of the difference between the groups in the characteristic of interest: outcome in cohort studies and risk factor status in case control studies.

For example, suppose that a case control study is conducted to determine the relationship of prior maternal oral contraceptive use and congenital defects. Cases are selected from a pediatric clinic at a city hospital, and controls are selected from a pediatric private practice. A higher rate of prior oral contraceptive use is found in controls.

We cannot conclude from this study that oral contraceptive use protects against congenital defects because of the existence of selection bias. Cases were selected from a population of clinic patients, and controls were selected from a population of private practice patients. It is possible that these two groups will have different patterns of contraceptive use because of the differing socioeconomic status of the patients' mothers or because the mothers' own physicians have different patterns of prescribing oral contraceptives for these groups. If so, cases and controls would have differing rates of maternal contraceptive use irrespective of their disease status. Thus, selection bias among cases and controls would result in a spurious association of contraceptive use and congenital defects.

As another example, a study is conducted to determine whether laparoscopic hernia repair is superior to traditional (open) hernia repair with respect to hospital length of stay. A series of **historical controls** (treated in a prior time period) receiving open hernia repair are compared with a current series of patients receiving laparoscopic hernia repair.

The potential for bias exists because there may be temporal changes in supportive or ancillary care or reimbursement policy that affect length of stay. Thus, study groups chosen from two different time periods can be considered to have received different treatment. Furthermore, criteria for selection of patients for treatment may change over time, resulting in a different makeup of the two groups with respect to other clinical characteristics that may affect length of stay. This is referred to as **confounding bias,** or simply confounding, and will be further discussed in the next section.

Selection bias may also be introduced by the differential attrition of subjects when a long-term outcome is under study.

> For example, **drop-out rates** (the rate at which subjects leave a study) may differ for two treatment groups. If treatment toxicity is a reason for dropping out and drop-outs are not counted in the final analysis, one treatment group will appear less toxic than the other simply because more subjects with toxic reactions from this group have left the study.

Misclassification bias can occur in cohort or case control studies when group differences exist in the measurement of the study characteristic.

> For example, consider a case control study to determine if an association exists between x-ray exposure of mothers during pregnancy and the presence of congenital defects in their children. A group of mothers of children with birth defects is questioned about prior x-ray exposure during pregnancy. A group of mothers of normal children is also questioned. The frequency of reported prior x-ray exposure is compared in the two groups. The potential for misclassification bias exists on the part of the **subject**—the mother—because mothers of defective children may be more likely than mothers of normal children to remember events in pregnancy because of the unfortunate outcome. The potential for bias also exists on the part of the **interviewer** or observer if he or she knows to which group the subject belongs. The interviewer may consciously or unconsciously try harder to elicit a history of x-ray exposure in mothers of children with birth defects.

> As another example, suppose a clinical trial is performed to determine the effect of bupivacaine hydrochloride injection on postoperative pain. Nursing personnel administer a five-point pain scale to each subject at 6 and 24 hours after surgery. The patient's subjective perception of pain may be biased by his or her own knowledge of the treatment received. Likewise, the nurses' knowledge of the patient's treatment may influence the way in which they administer the pain scale, again introducing measurement bias.

Several measures can be taken to avoid bias in the design of a study. For cohort studies, selection bias may be prevented in the following ways:

1. **Choose all subjects** from the same population. They should differ only in their exposure to the risk factor.
2. **Use randomization** in clinical trials so that the choice of treatment group is not based on physician or patient preference.
3. **Complete follow-up** on outcome for subjects who withdraw from the study, to prevent differential attrition rates in the study groups.

Misclassification bias may be prevented in these ways:

1. **Blind the observers.** Make them unaware of the risk factor status of subjects to ensure comparability in the assessment of outcome.

   For example, use of a placebo in a randomized clinical trial makes both the subject and observer blind to the treatment that the subject is receiving (risk factor). This practice eliminates the possibility of misclassification bias in the determination of outcome.

2. Carefully **define the criteria** for outcome assessment to ensure consistency throughout the study and comparability of risk factor groups on assessment of outcome.

For case control studies, selection bias may be avoided or reduced as follows:

1. **Choose several control groups** (e.g., from several disease categories or several institutions), including one from the general population. This technique will allow several comparisons with cases and several estimates of the difference between cases and controls. These estimates can be compared to determine whether bias is present. If all estimates are similar, bias in the selection of control groups likely does not exist.
2. **Determine risk factor status** of deceased cases, and include them in the study.

Misclassification bias may be minimized as well.

1. **Blind the subject and observer** to the disease status of the subject. If blinding is not possible, use information recorded before
   risk factor exposure and use comparable methods of assessing
   risk factor status of cases and controls.

   For example, in the aforementioned study on x-ray exposure and
   birth defects, x-ray exposure could be determined from prenatal
   clinic records rather than interviews and would thus be free of misclassification bias.

It is usually difficult to prove or disprove the presence of bias in
any study on hypothesis testing. The investigators must therefore
demonstrate that they took the preceding measures to avoid bias. If
not, bias cannot be ruled out as an explanation for group differences.

II. Confounding

Confounding is a type of bias that can result from differences in the
makeup of the study groups. **Confounding is present when a third
factor (confounder) is related to both the risk factor and the outcome and thereby biases the degree or direction of the association
between the risk factor and outcome.**
   Confounding can work in two ways: to create an apparent difference between the groups when none actually exists, or to mask a real
difference. Consider the following example of confounding:

   Suppose we are conducting a clinical trial comparing two antibiotics,
   A and B (risk factor) for prophylaxis of surgical site infection (outcome) in patients with upper abdominal surgery. Suppose that patients randomized to antibiotic A (Group A) happen, by chance, to be
   older (mean age 74 years) than those randomized to antibiotic B
   (Group B, mean age 52 years). Suppose also that older patients are
   more likely to develop surgical site infection (SSI) than younger patients. We now have two ways in which the study groups are known
   to differ: antibiotic usage and age. If we find a greater incidence of SSI
   in Group A, we won't know if this difference is due to the fact that
   Group A used antibiotic A and Group B used antibiotic B, or that
   Group A is older than Group B, or both. If, on the other hand, we find
   no significant difference in SSI rates between the groups, we cannot
   be sure that the older age of Group A patients is not offsetting any

beneficial effects of Drug A. In this example, if the treatment groups differ on age but if age has no effect on the development of SSI (outcome), then confounding will **not** be present. Likewise, confounding by age will not be present if age has an effect on SSI rate, but the ages of the study groups are similar.

As another example, consider a case control study to determine the relationship between occupation (risk factor) and chronic obstructive pulmonary disease, or COPD (outcome). A group of patients with COPD (cases) is compared to a group of nondiseased subjects (controls) on occupational status. It is found that a higher proportion of cases are coal miners than are controls. Can we assume that working in a coal mine is a cause of COPD? Because smoking is a known risk factor for COPD, we should first assess the smoking status of our two comparison groups. It is possible that smoking is related to occupation (risk factor) as well as to COPD (outcome) and that coal miners tend to have a higher proportion of smokers than other professions. If this were the case, then the apparent association of coal mining and COPD might be due instead to the association of coal mining and smoking.

Confounding has two possible sources. The first source is bias in the selection of subjects for study: Differences in the selection of the study groups can result in the presence of confounding. The second source is chance. Even with an unbiased study design like a blinded, randomized clinical trial, substantial imbalance among the study groups in baseline characteristics may lead to confounding.

Confounding can be eliminated or controlled for in the design of the study, in the analysis, or both. Control of confounding **in the study design** can be accomplished by using the following:

1. **Restriction,** or limiting the characteristics of subjects eligible for study.

   For example, the clinical trial on antibiotic prophylaxis for SSI could have been restricted to patients between 30 and 50 years of age. This would have minimized differences between the groups on age.

   As another example, the case control study on COPD and occupation could have been restricted to nonsmokers.

Although the use of restriction controls confounding, it limits the generalizability of the study results to other patient populations that are not similar to the study subjects. This diminishes the utility of this method.

2. **Matching** subject characteristics. For each subject in one group, choose another subject for the other group who matches the first subject on one or more characteristics. Matching can be used for cohort studies or case control studies. If there are three or four groups in a study, three-way or four-way matching is possible. It is difficult to match on more than one or two factors in a study.
3. **Randomization** of subjects in clinical trials. Randomly assign subjects to treatments. This maximizes the possibility that treatment groups will be comparable on all characteristics. This is one of the major advantages of clinical trials.
4. **Stratification** of subjects in clinical trials. Divide patients into strata, or levels, of a particular characteristic, then randomize patients into treatment groups within each stratum.

> For example, consider the clinical trial on antibiotic prophylaxis for SSI. To control for confounding by age, patients could have been divided into separate age strata (younger than age 45, age 45 or older) and then randomized within each stratum. Other appropriate age strata could have been chosen.

Stratification ensures equal numbers in each treatment group within each stratum of a characteristic, avoiding confounding by that characteristic.

Even if investigators attempt to control confounding in the study design, an imbalance may still exist among the study groups on one or more characteristics after completion of the study. In other cases, it is impossible or impractical to control for confounding in the design. Furthermore, unpredicted group differences may occur in some characteristic. In these cases, there are several ways to control for confounding in the **data analysis phase** of the study:

1. **Stratification** of subjects. Even if not used in the design, stratification can be used **after** the study is complete. A weighted average of the difference in study groups across all strata gives an estimate, with confidence limits, of the overall difference between the groups. Estimates of the magnitude of difference between groups within individual strata indicate whether differences in the direction or size of the relationship between the risk factor and outcome exist within various subgroups of patients, and whether these differences are statistically significant.

For example, consider a study of two different treatments for high blood pressure, Treatment A and Treatment B. Researchers can stratify subjects into sex and age groups and then compare treatments on mean drop in blood pressure within sex-age strata. The results of stratification might look like Table 5-1.

As the table shows, Treatment B had a greater mean drop in blood pressure than Treatment A for men in both age groups, but not for women.

If stratification results in too many strata with too few patients in each stratum, results can be misleading or unreliable. Therefore, it is best to limit stratification to a few strata based on one or two important confounding characteristics.

2. **Use regression analysis or mathematical modeling** to control for the effects of many confounding variables at once, to give an adjusted estimate of the difference between study groups, and to test whether this difference is statistically significant. Such regression techniques include **analysis of covariance, multiple regression, Cox regression, multiple logistic regression, and discriminant analysis.**

    In the case control study on occupation and COPD, multiple logistic regression could have been used to control for the presence of smoking, family history, stress level, and other potential confounding factors.

Bias, including confounding bias, is the major pitfall of clinical studies and should be carefully examined and controlled for in any

Table 5-I. Mean drop in blood pressure (mm) according to treatment, age, and sex

	Age			
	< 65		≥ 65	
Men	A*	B	A	B
	5.5	10.5	4.2	12.2
Women	A	B	A	B
	4.3	4.1	4.0	4.2

*A, Treatment A; B, Treatment B.

study. The investigator should take great care to demonstrate that he or she controlled for all potential forms of bias in the design of the study and, if necessary, in the statistical analysis.

III. Summary

When differences occur among the study groups, the possibility of a spurious association from bias must be ruled out before the researcher can infer a causal association between the risk factor and outcome. Different treatment or experience of the study groups in selection of subjects for study, measuring and recording of information, or attrition can lead to a biased estimate of the difference between the groups in the characteristic of interest (outcome in cohort studies and risk factor status in case control studies).

Confounding, a special type of bias, is present when a third factor (confounder) is related to both the risk factor and the outcome under study and thereby biases or distorts the apparent association of the risk factor and outcome. Control of confounding can be achieved in the design or analysis of the study. Control of other types of bias can be achieved only in the design. See Part III, Chap. 12 for questions to determine if bias or confounding is present in a particular study.

IV. References

Three editorials give a further discussion of bias and confounding as they occur in the medical literature [1–3].

1. Bailer JC. When research results are in conflict. *N Engl J Med* 313:1080–1081, 1985.
2. Moore GF. How to achieve surgical results by really trying. *Surg Gynecol Obstet* 497–498, 1963.
3. Angell M. The interpretation of epidemiologic studies. *N Engl J Med* 323:823–825, 1990.

Chance Association

As we stated in the preceding chapters, there are three possible explanations for finding a difference between groups.

1. Spurious association
2. Chance association
3. Causal association

Chapter 5 explained spurious association, and Chap. 7 describes causal association. This chapter focuses on chance association, which may be ruled out by statistical tests.

I. Computing a Test Statistic

A **test statistic** is a number computed from the sample data using an appropriate formula.

For example, Fig. 6-1 shows the formula for the **unpaired t-statistic,** used to test the difference between means of two independent groups.

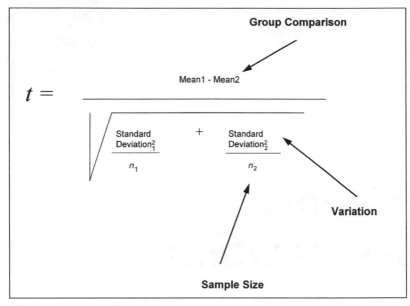

Fig. 6-1. Anatomy of a test statistic

There are three components of a test statistic:

1. The **group comparison** component is the magnitude of the difference (in this case, means) **between** groups.
2. The **variation** component is the variability, or spread, among subjects **within** each group (standard deviation).
3. The **sample size** component is the number of subjects in each group (n).

Each of these components will affect the magnitude of the statistic.

II. Statistical Significance

Using the value of a test statistic and its **degrees of freedom** (also a function of sample size), we can find a *p*-value (also called α, significance level, or probability of Type I error) by consulting a table of values for that statistic. This table is a listing or *frequency distribution* of all possible values for that statistic and the probability of obtaining each value by chance. The majority of test statistics you will encounter have frequency distributions of one of four types: the normal distribution (z), the t distribution (t), the chi-square distribution (χ^2), and the F-distribution (F). These statistics are therefore reported as z, t, χ^2, or F. For example, the Pearson Chi-square test, the logrank test, and the Mantel-Haenszel test all result in statistics that follow a chi-square (χ^2) distribution, and their test statistics are reported as "$\chi^2 = ...$"). On the other hand, the results of the analysis of variance test follow an F-distribution, and its results are therefore reported as "F = ...".

The table of values or frequency distribution for a statistic is usually set up so that we can determine the probability of obtaining some value or greater for a given sample size. **The *p*-value is the probability that a test statistic as large as the one obtained from the data could have occurred by chance when no real difference between the groups exists.**

> For example, if a statistic is known to follow the chi-square distribution, the probability of obtaining a value of 3.84 or greater for that statistic is 0.05.

A *p*-value of 0.05 means there is a probability of 5%, or 1 in 20, that a test statistic could have resulted from chance when no true difference between the groups actually existed. With a *p*-value of 0.01, the probability is 1 in 100.

A low *p*-value shows that the statistic is unlikely to have been obtained by chance and that the statistic is more likely to reflect a true difference between the groups being compared. The point at which we can rule out chance is arbitrary, but it is conventionally 0.05. **If *p* is 0.05 or less, we call the results "statistically significant" and rule out chance as an explanation for group differences found.**

Because the size of a statistic is a function not only of the size of the difference between groups but also of the size and variability of each group, the same magnitude of difference can be either highly significant or nonsignificant in different situations. For example, an extremely large sample size will render trivial differences between groups significant. On the other hand, large group differences of potentially great clinical relevance may be statistically nonsignificant when the sample size is small. This issue is addressed more fully in the context of "clinical significance" in Chap. 7 and confidence intervals in Chap. 9.

III. Statistical Power

When a study reports negative (nonsignificant) results, the issue of statistical power becomes important. **Statistical power** is the likelihood that differences of a given magnitude will be found statistically significant in a study. In other words, power is the ability of a study to detect clinically relevant differences between study groups. Power is expressed as a probability, or percent, between zero and 100%. Generally, statisticians consider power of 80% or higher adequate for a study.*

Power is an important consideration in the design of a study. Ideally, the magnitude of difference between groups that would hold clinical interest should be defined before conducting the study. Researchers should select a sample size that provides an adequate chance of detecting such a difference and report this as part of the study methods.

Once a study is complete, power becomes relevant only when the results are negative (i.e., when no significant difference is found between the groups). Under these conditions, one must question whether the size of the study was adequate to detect a clinically relevant difference. Because small studies have limited power to achieve statistical significance even when relatively large differences exist between groups, the results of such studies **cannot** prove a lack of a causal association between a risk factor and an outcome. In such cases, we might instead conclude that a potentially relevant difference exists between the groups and requires further investigation in a larger study. Such caution is especially important in "equivalence studies," which are designed to demonstrate that a new treatment is "as good as" a standard treatment and should be substituted for the standard because it has an advantage such as decreased cost or lower toxicity. As Richard Simon put it, "The best way to ensure that a nonsignificant difference will be obtained is to use an inadequate sample size" [1]. In such studies the researchers should demonstrate that power was adequate to detect a clinically relevant difference between the comparison groups.

---

*You may have heard the terms "Type II error" or "beta error" used in connection with power. They are the inverse of power, or the chances of failing to detect true differences between the study groups. Therefore, when power is 80%, the chance of Type II error is 20%.

IV. Multiple Comparisons

The p-value is the probability that a **single** statistical test result has occurred by chance when there is no real difference between the groups. If we conduct multiple statistical tests in the same study, our probability of finding significant results by chance alone increases.

> For example, if we compute 20 statistical tests on the same set of data we are likely, by definition, to get one test with a p-value of 0.05 by chance alone, even when no true differences exist among the comparison groups.

Researchers performing multiple tests should use some method to control for this likelihood. The simplest method is to divide the p-value of 0.05 by the number of tests performed and to set this number as the level to rule out chance. This is referred to as a **Bonferroni correction.**

> For example, if we perform five statistical tests, we should insist that any single test attain a p-value of less than 0.01 to be considered statistically significant. The required p-value for significance if we perform 10 tests should be 0.005.

There are many other ways to address the problem of multiple testing or multiple comparisons, and the appropriateness of each method depends on the nature of the multiplicity. For instance, special procedures are available to compare risk factor groups on multiple **outcomes.** In contrast, multivariate procedures can be used to evaluate the effect of multiple **risk factors** on a single outcome. Pairwise comparison procedures such as Tukey's or Scheffe's procedures can be used to compare the means of multiple **groups,** two at a time. As an alternative to multiple comparison procedures, some authors prefer to apply statistical analyses to one primary outcome and to treat descriptively other secondary comparisons [2–4]. The important consideration for the critical reader is that the problem of multiple comparisons, if it exists in a study, must be addressed and controlled for in some way. If not, one can only assume that the stated p-values are invalid. The article by Smith and colleagues further discusses this issue [4].

The preceding discussion applies as well to the calculation of multiple confidence intervals in a study. To control for this situation, we could restrict the calculation of confidence intervals to the one or two major comparisons of the study or calculate a higher-level confidence interval (e.g., 99% instead of 95%) that would be equivalent to using a p-value of 0.01 instead of 0.05.

V. Summary

Statistical testing rules out the possibility of a chance association between a risk factor and an outcome. A test statistic is a number computed from the data using an appropriate formula. The p-value is the probability that a test statistic of a given magnitude obtained from the data could have occurred by chance in the absence of a true difference between groups. In order to rule out chance as an explanation for group differences found in a study, the p-value should be 0.05 or less.

The larger a test statistic, the smaller the p-value. The size of a test statistic and the corresponding p-value are a function of three factors:

1. The size of the difference between the study groups
2. The variability within the groups
3. The sample size of the groups

The power of a study is its ability to detect clinically relevant differences among comparison groups when such differences truly exist. The level of power of a study should generally be at least 80%. The larger the power, the better.

If we apply multiple statistical tests to the same set of data, the probability of finding statistically significant results increases. This chapter describes various ways to adjust for multiple comparisons of the data.

The concepts covered in this chapter are applied to evaluating the literature in Part III, Chap. 12.

VI. References

1. Simon R. Confidence intervals for reporting results of clinical trials. *Ann Intern Med* 105:429–435, 1986.
2. Johnson AF. The need for triage on questions related to efficacy: multiple comparisons and Type II errors. *J Clin Epidemiol* 41:303–305, 1988.
3. Pocock SJ, Hughes MD, Lee RJ. Statistical problems in the reporting of clinical trials. *New Engl J Med* 317:426–432, 1987.
4. Smith DG, et al. Impact of multiple comparisons in randomized clinical trials. *Am J Med* 83:545–550, 1987.

Causal Association

I. Evidence for a Causal Association

Once spurious association (bias and confounding) and chance have been ruled out as explanations for an association between a risk factor and an outcome in a study, several criteria should be considered in order to establish that the association is causal (i.e., that the risk factor caused the outcome). The presence of strength, consistency, biological plausibility, temporal correctness, or specificity gives evidence of a causal association. Although it is not necessary that all five elements exist to establish causality, the more that are present, the greater the likelihood that an association is causal.

A. Strength. The strength of relationship between a risk factor and an outcome is measured by the magnitude of difference between the study groups, sometimes called the "effect size." The greater the effect size, the greater the strength of the relationship between the risk factor and the outcome. The effect size can be expressed as a **difference** between groups in proportions or means, or as a **ratio** of one group over another.

For example, in a cohort study of birth control pill use and breast cancer, the incidence of breast cancer in pill users is 5 per 100,000. The incidence in nonusers is 1 per 100,000. The effect size could be expressed by saying that the incidence of breast cancer in pill users is 4 per 100,000 greater than that in nonusers (difference), or alternatively that the incidence is 5 times that of pill users (ratio).

As another example, consider a clinical trial to compare Diets A and B on weight loss. The mean weight loss of subjects on Diet A (Group A) is 20 pounds; that for subjects on Diet B (Group B) is 10 pounds. The effect size could be expressed by saying that Group A had a mean weight loss 10 pounds greater than that of Group B (difference) or that the mean weight loss of Group A was twice that of Group B (ratio).

Effect size expressed as a difference is a function of the strength of relationship between the risk factor and the outcome and also of the frequency or magnitude of the outcome in the population. Expressed as a ratio, however, it is solely a function of the strength of relationship and indicates the likelihood of a causal association. In other words, effect size expressed as a difference between groups conveys the **magnitude** of the comparison; expressed as a ratio, it conveys the causal **importance** of the comparison.

For example, a difference of 2% among groups is much more important from a causal perspective if the rates are 1% and 3% than if they are 31% and 33%. Likewise, a difference of 10 pounds is more important if the group means are 2 pounds and 12 pounds than if they are 900 pounds and 910 pounds.

In assessing a causal relationship, therefore, we shall focus on the difference between groups expressed as a ratio. For dichotomous risk factors that can be classified as either present or absent (e.g., maleness, normal blood pressure, coffee-drinking, toxic exposure, new treatment received) the strength of the relationship between the risk factor and the outcome can be directly measured by the relative risk.* The **relative risk** is the incidence of disease in people who have the risk factor compared with the incidence in people who do not have the risk factor. The higher the relative risk, the stronger the relationship between the risk factor and the outcome.

*Note that in case control studies, the odds ratio is used instead of the relative risk. The odds ratio is explained in App. A, with an example of computing the relative risk and odds ratio.

Consider the following statements a rule of thumb.

A relative risk of **1** indicates no relationship.
A relative risk of **2** indicates a weak relationship.
A relative risk of **4** indicates a fairly strong relationship.
A relative risk of greater than **4** indicates a strong relationship.

Computation of adjusted relative risks using multivariate analysis or other adjustment procedures gives a truer estimate of the strength of an association when confounding is present.

As Chap. 9 explains, when assessing the strength of a relationship, researchers should consider not only the point estimate of relative risk but also its 95% confidence interval.

B. Consistency. Consistent findings in more than one study showing an association between a risk factor and an outcome make it more likely that the association is causal. If several studies conducted by different investigators in different populations show similar results, we can be more certain that any association found between the risk factor and outcome is real and causal, not an artifact of one study.

Examples of associations that have shown consistency across different populations with different study designs are smoking and lung cancer, cholesterol and arteriosclerotic heart disease, smoking and cardiovascular disease, family history and breast cancer, and salt intake and hypertension.

C. Biological Plausibility. The results of a study must fit into the framework of existing biological knowledge. One way in which data can demonstrate biological plausibility is the existence of a *dose-response relationship*—an association between the degree of exposure to the risk factor and the size of the change in the outcome. This association can be either **positive** (an increasing change in outcome with increasing degree of exposure) or **negative** (a decreasing change with increasing degree of exposure).

For example, an experimental study was conducted to study the effect of different concentrations of a growth hormone (bFGF) on neovascularization of the limb in rabbits. Investigators gave bFGF in 1 μg and 3 μg doses to two groups of rabbits and gave only saline to a control group. They used various measures of neovascularization, including

$TCPO_2$ concentration in the blood after two weeks of treatment. The mean $TCPO_2$ concentration for the three groups was as follows:

Group	Mean $TCPO_2$
0 μg	42
1 μg	66
3 μg	72

There was an increasing $TCPO_2$ level with increasing dose. This finding is evidence of a positive dose response relationship and gives biological credence to the possibility that BFGF enhances limb neovascularization.

D. Temporal Correctness. The risk factor must precede the outcome for an association to be causal.

For example, the association of a low-fiber diet and colon cancer found in a case control study could not be considered causal unless it could be established that the cancer patients were on low-fiber diets before the onset of their cancer. Otherwise, it might be postulated that the presence of cancer precipitated a change in diet for the cases.

E. Specificity. The risk factor is related to only one outcome. Conversely, only one risk factor is found related to the outcome.

For example, if everyone who ate the tuna salad at a corporate picnic developed gastroenteritis and none of the people who avoided the tuna got gastroenteritis, we could conclude that the tuna was the cause of the gastroenteritis.

As another example, several case control studies of rheumatic fever identify a preponderance of strep throat by history in the cases compared with controls. No other diseases by history have been implicated in rheumatic fever. This is good evidence of a causal association between strep throat and rheumatic fever.

Although the presence of specificity is evidence for a causal association, its absence does not bar causality. It is possible that one disease has several causes or that one risk factor causes several different diseases.

For example, smoking has been implicated as a cause of several types of cancer as well as cardiovascular disease.

II. Establishing Clinical Significance

Once we have ruled out bias, confounding, and chance and established causality, we must address a final consideration: Is the relationship between the risk factor and outcome clinically relevant? In assessing clinical significance, we shall again examine the strength of the relationship. This time, however, we shall focus on group **differences** rather than **ratios** to determine whether the results are clinically significant. As previously stated, a difference is a function of the strength of relationship and also of the frequency or magnitude of the outcome in the population. The clinician should focus on the difference between groups in assessing clinical significance. When dealing with discrete outcomes expressed as rates, such as disease, we refer to this difference as attributable risk. **Attributable risk** is the difference in the rate of disease (usually incidence) in people who have the risk factor and those who do not have the risk factor.

Whether clinicians will conclude that a particular difference from a study is clinically significant will depend on how they intend to use the results of the study.

For example, suppose a study of 5000 patients shows that the incidence of surgical site infections from laparoscopic colectomy is 5% compared with 5.5% for open colectomy. Because of the large sample size, the results are statistically significant. Are they clinically significant?

If a large hospital that does 1000 colectomies a year were considering replacing open colectomy with laparoscopic colectomy as the standard, the results of this study might be considered clinically significant. Reducing the surgical site infection rate from 55 per 1000 to 50 per 1000 per year, or by 5 infections per year, would result in considerable cost savings over a period of 10 years. On the other hand, the cost savings for a hospital that does only 100 colectomies per year would be only 1 infection every 2 years and may not hold great clinical significance.

Likewise, if the primary consideration is the effect on an individual patient, the small increased risk of infection from 5 per 100 to 5.5 per 100 may not be a clinically significant consideration when weighed against the increased cost of laparoscopic colectomy to the patient.

As another example, consider a new drug that proves to be statistically significantly better than the standard treatment for high blood pressure in a large-scale clinical trial. In a trial of 10,000 patients this benefit may represent a lowering of systolic blood pressure by only 2 mm (95% confidence interval of 1–3 mm) compared with the standard drug. Whether clinicians should get excited about such a difference depends on whether they are considering these results from a global or individual patient point of view. If a modest lowering of systolic blood pressure by the new drug results in a cost savings of 50 cents per patient, the head of the inpatient pharmacy at a large hospital might consider the results clinically significant, whereas a private physician considering recommending the new drug for her patients may not.

As mentioned earlier, the 95% confidence interval for the difference should also be considered when assessing clinical significance.

As we have seen, ruling out bias, confounding, and chance will tell us that an association between a risk factor and an outcome is real. Satisfying the criteria in the previous section tells us that the relationship is causal. Establishing clinical significance tells us that the relationship is relevant or useful.

III. Summary

Once we have ruled out the possibility of a spurious or chance association, we must establish a causal association. The following attributes in a study give evidence of a causal relationship between a risk factor and an outcome:

1. Strength of the relationship, indicated by the relative risk
2. Consistency of the relationship
3. Biological plausibility of the relationship, indicated by the presence of a dose-response relationship, among other things
4. Temporal correctness (when the risk factor precedes the outcome)
5. Specificity of the relationship (a one-to-one relationship between the risk factor and outcome)

Once we have established causality, we must then decide whether the results of the study are clinically useful or relevant.

More about Statistical Tests

The statistic or formula used to rule out chance as an explanation for group differences depends on the kind of outcome being analyzed and the type of comparison being made. Statistics can be classified into two major categories—univariate and multivariate—depending on the number of risk factors being analyzed.

I. Univariate Statistics

Univariate statistics measure the relationship of **one** risk factor to a given outcome.

> For example, if an investigator wishes to examine the relationship between sex (risk factor) and systolic blood pressure (outcome), she could compare the mean blood pressure for a group of women with that for a group of men using the t-test.
>
> As another example, if an investigator wishes to determine if there is an association between blood group (risk factor) and leukemia (outcome),

he may compare the prevalence rate of the disease in a sample of subjects from each of the four blood groups using chi-square analysis.

Univariate statistics are more commonly used and easier to compute than multivariate statistics. They usually involve comparing the mean or median value of two or more groups or comparing the proportion of subjects who possess a given attribute or who fall into various categories. The most common forms of univariate tests are the Pearson chi-square test, t-test, analysis of variance, correlation, and logrank test. Their statistics are reported as, respectively, χ^2, t, F, r, and χ^2.

Univariate statistics can further be classified into **parametric** and **nonparametric** statistics. Parametric statistics are used when the outcome of interest is continuous. These statistics make certain assumptions about the distribution of the data. The most common parametric statistics are the t-test, analysis of variance (or F-test), and the correlation coefficient. All three assume that the data are normally distributed, or bell-shaped, when graphed.

Nonparametric statistics make no assumptions about how the data are distributed and are therefore often used when the assumptions of a parametric test cannot be satisfied. This is often the case when the sample size is small or the outcome of interest is discrete or ordinal. The most common examples of nonparametric statistics are the Pearson chi-square test, the Kruskal-Wallis analysis of variance, and the rank sum test.

Survival analysis is a form of univariate nonparametric analysis used when the outcome of interest is the length of time to some event. To conduct survival analysis, we need for each subject both a **beginning point** (e.g., date of birth, diagnosis, surgery) and an **end point** (e.g., date of death, recurrence, stroke). If a subject fails to undergo the event (e.g., death, recurrence, or stroke) by the time the study is completed, his or her end point will be the end of the study period or the date of the last follow-up for subjects not followed to the end of the study, i.e., those "lost to follow up." These subjects are called **censored** subjects.

> For example, in a study of cancer patients' survival, the beginning point is the diagnosis of cancer, and the endpoint is the date of death or last follow-up.

With this information, a "survival interval" can then be calculated for each subject. This interval is the time elapsing (days, months, years) between the subject's beginning point and end point.

For example, a patient is diagnosed with cancer on June 15, 1980, and dies on June 15, 1981. His survival interval is one year.

As another example, a subject is diagnosed on February 10, 1981, and followed until February 10, 1982, at which time she is lost to follow-up. Her survival interval is also one year, but she is treated as censored.

Also, a randomized clinical trial is begun on January 1, 1985, for a period of 3 years. Patients enter into the study at various times. A patient who enters on March 31, 1987, and is still alive at the end of the study period (December 31, 1987) has a survival interval of 9 months and is treated as censored. Another patient who enters the study on June 1, 1985, and dies on December 1, 1985, has a survival interval of six months but will be treated as a death rather than as a censored subject.

Survival interval is a generic term indicating the length of time to some event and does not necessarily refer to remaining alive.

Examples of commonly used survival intervals are disease-free survival from cancer, referring to the time to recurrence in cancer studies, and stroke-free interval for patients with carotid artery disease.

As previously mentioned, the outcome of interest in survival studies is not the number of events (e.g., deaths) but the length of time a subject "survives" from the starting point. Results of survival analysis are usually presented as a graph or curve depicting the percent of patients surviving, or event-free, at various times from the starting point. Percent of patients surviving is plotted on the y-axis, and time elapsed from the beginning point is plotted on the x-axis.

For example, Fig. 8-1 shows the results of a retrospective study of survival for two groups: those with liver metastases present at the time of a diagnosis of colon cancer, and those without liver metastases at diagnosis.

If all patients "die," or undergo the event under study, calculation of the graph is straightforward. If some subjects are censored, either from loss to follow-up or termination of the study, calculations are more complex, but the interpretation of the graph remains the same. Two methods used to calculate survival when some subjects are censored are the **actuarial** or **life table** method and the **Kaplan-Meier** or **product limit** method. These methods differ in the way censored observations are treated and the way survival times are graphed. The actuarial method uses a survival interval (weeks, months, years)

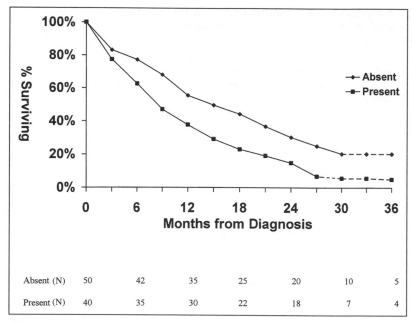

Fig. 8-1. Example of a survival curve: cumulative percent survival by presence of liver metastases

for each subject and is displayed as a line graph, like the one in Fig. 8-1. Survival times for patients are calculated in intervals (i.e., the number who die in the first month, the second month, etc). This method is most appropriate with large samples (greater than 30 patients) where it is meaningful to group survival times for subjects into intervals.

The Kaplan Meier method uses exact survival times for each subject and is displayed as a stepgraph like the one in Fig. 8-2. The steps on the graph represent exact times of death for patients. The graph steps down each time a patient dies. As with the actuarial method, the y-axis represents the proportion of subjects surviving and the x-axis represents time from the starting point. Unlike the actuarial method in which the x-axis is marked in equal intervals, in a Kaplan-Meier graph the x-axis is marked at points at which subjects die. This method can be used with small or large samples.

In both the actuarial and Kaplan-Meier methods, censored observations are counted in the survival curve for as long as they are fol-

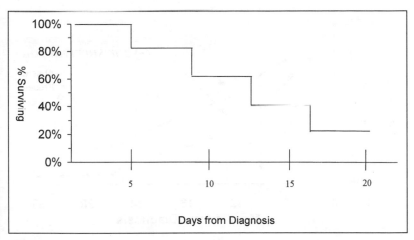

Fig. 8-2. Kaplan Meier survival curve

lowed, and then dropped from the calculations. Therefore the survival curve is based on decreasing numbers of patients over time. The number of patients on which the curve is based (the number at risk who are followed for each period of time or longer) is often reported along the horizontal axis, as in Fig. 8-1. As a rule of thumb, the portion of a survival curve based on less than 10 patients is not valid. This portion of the curve should be represented as a dotted line. For example, in Fig. 8-1, the lower curve is not valid after 27 months and the upper curve is not valid after 30 months.

There are several statistics that can be used to describe either type of survival curve.

- The *x*-**year survival rate** is the percent of patients still "alive," or event-free, *x* years from diagnosis.
- The **median survival** is the point at which 50% of the patients have "died," or undergone the event in question.

These statistics can also be used to compare two survival curves.

For example, the median survival in Fig. 8-3 is approximately 12 months for patients with liver metastases absent and 9 months for patients with liver metastases present. The one-year survival rates are 55% and 38%, respectively.

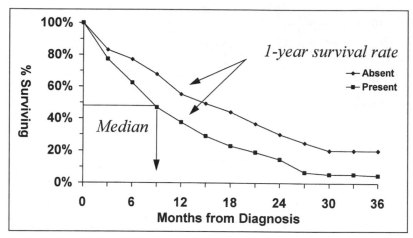

Fig. 8-3. Comparison of survival curves

The statistical test most commonly used to compare the survival experience of two or more groups is the logrank test. The logrank test is further described in App. A.

A brief description of the most common univariate tests is given in Table 8-1. More complete descriptions and examples of these and other less frequently used tests and measures are given in App. A. A step-by-step explanation of how to choose an appropriate univariate statistical test is given in Chap. 5.

Table 8-1. Summary of common univariate tests

For normally distributed continuous data (parametric)

Paired, or matched *t:* to compare paired measurements on each subject or on matched subjects

Unpaired, or student's t: to compare means of two groups of subjects

Analysis of variance (ANOVA): to compare means of two or more groups of subjects

Pearson correlation coefficient: to assess the direction and strength of linear (straight-line) relationship between two different measures taken on one set of subjects

For ordinal or non-normal data (nonparametric)

Median test, or rank sum test: to compare medians or ranks of two or more groups

Continued

Table 8-1.   (continued)

Kruskal-Wallis one-way ANOVA: to compare ranks of more than two
groups

Sign test, or Wilcoxon signed rank: to compare paired or matched measurements

Spearman/Kendall rank correlation: to assess the strength of a relationship
between two different measures on one set of subjects

For discrete data (nonparametric)

Pearson chi-square: to compare the classification of two or more groups

Fisher's exact test: to replace the Pearson chi-square when sample size is
small

McNemar's test of symmetry: to compare the classification of matched
subjects or paired measurements taken on each subject

For time-to-event data

Logrank test: to compare the survival times of two or more groups

II. Multivariate Statistics

Multivariate statistics measure the relationship of a combination of
several risk factors to one outcome.

For example, a researcher is interested in identifying the clinical findings on admission (risk factors) that are related to the development of
sepsis (outcome) in patients with pneumonia. He conducts a case control study comparing patients with and without sepsis on the presence of various risk factors on admission. Multiple logistic regression
compares the two groups on age, sex, WBC, admission blood pressure, temperature, serum albumin, and type of organism identifed in
sputum culture.

As another example, researchers wish to study the effect of several
different growth factor hormones (risk factors) on weight gain in im-
mature rabbits (outcome). They use multiple regression to identify the
growth hormones that significantly affect weight gain.

Also, a physician wishes to compare two treatments for lung cancer
(risk factor) on length of survival from diagnosis (outcome). To control for differences between the study groups in other factors such as
age, gender, stage at diagnosis, and histologic grade, she includes all
of these variables along with treatment group in a Cox regression

analysis. This analysis allows her to determine if treatment group is significant in the presence of these other risk factors.

With the advent of computers, multivariate statistics are being used and reported more and more often in the medical literature. Interpreting them, however, is not as straightforward as interpreting univariate statistics and requires some further explanation of the concepts involved. In regression, the most common type of multivariate analysis, a mathematical model or formula relates the risk factors to the outcome.

For example, after gathering data on height, age, and weight for a large sample of subjects, we could derive the following model to express the relationship of weight in kilograms to height in centimeters and age in years:

$$\text{weight} = 0.32 \times \text{height} + 0.1 \times \text{age} + 5$$

Then, knowing a person's height and age, we could predict his or her weight by substituting the actual height and age in this formula. According to the formula, a person 163 cm tall and 60 years old should, on average, weigh 63 kg:

$$\text{weight} = (0.32 \times 163) + (0.1 \times 60) + 5 = 52 + 6 + 5 = 63$$

The number 5 in the preceding formula is known as a **constant** and is not associated with a particular risk factor. The numbers 0.32 and 0.1 are known as **regression coefficients** and are the numbers, or weights, by which we multiply the risk factors (height and age) to obtain the predicted value of the outcome (weight). Each risk factor has a coefficient associated with it. The coefficient indicates the mathematical relationship of the risk factor to the outcome. The sign of the coefficient shows the direction of this relationship. Risk factors with positive coefficients are directly related to the outcome; those with negative coefficients are inversely related.

In the preceding example, the coefficients for height and weight are both positive, indicating that as height or age increase, weight also increases.

The coefficients and constants in the formula do not change, but the value of the risk factors (height and age) vary for each individual. The absolute value of the coefficient depends on the scale of measurement of the risk factor as well as the strength of the relationship of the risk factor to the outcome. If all risk factors were measured on the same scale, the absolute value of the coefficient would indicate only the strength of the relationship between the risk factor and the outcome: More important factors would be those with larger coefficients because they would have greater weight in the regression formula for predicting outcome. Because risk factors are usually measured on different scales (e.g., years, pounds, degrees) the size of the coefficients cannot be directly compared. **Standardized coefficients** adjust for the scale of measurement. They are computed by dividing the coefficient by its standard error. This allow direct comparison of coefficients for risk factors in a regression model. The standardized coefficients indicate the relative importance of the risk factors.

> For example, in a model of clinical and operative factors in the development of postoperative complications, suppose age had a standardized coefficient of 4.0 and estimated blood loss had a standardized coefficient of 2.0. In this model, age would be twice as important as blood loss in the development of postoperative complications.

Standardized coefficients cannot be used in a regression formula to calculate an individual's predicted outcome. The original coefficients must be used instead.

The risk factors used in multivariate regression can be measured on any type of scale: a **continuous** scale (e.g., age, duration of disease, preoperative blood pressure), an **ordinal** scale (e.g., level of education, APACHE score, performance status), or a **dichotomous** scale (e.g., presence or absence of some characteristic such as maleness, preoperative bleeding, obesity). The measurement of the outcome also affects the type of multivariate regression used.

- **Multiple regression** is used to assess the relationship of several risk factors to a *continuous* outcome such as length of surgery, length of hospital stay, or postoperative creatinine level.
- **Multiple logistic regression** is used to assess the relationship of various risk factors to the *occurrence of an event,* such as recurrence of cancer, development of intraoperative bleeding, or death.
- **Cox regression** is used to assess the relationship of various risk factors to outcomes involving *time to the occurrence of an event,* also known as survival time. Examples are survival time from diagnosis, time to recovery, or time to recurrence of cancer. In Cox regression, when survival time is the outcome, a coefficient with a positive sign

indicates an increase in the likelihood of the event occurring when the risk factor is present and therefore a decrease in survival time. A negative coefficient indicates a decrease in the likelihood of the event occurring and therefore an increase in survival time.

- **Discriminant analysis** is used to classify individuals into one of *two or more outcome groups* on the basis of several risk factors. A formula or set of formulas is constructed to predict the group to which an individual belongs. It can be used as an alternative to logistic regression but is most appropriate when all risk factors are continuous.

For example, information on various growth hormones is obtained on normal-height and growth-retarded patients. Discriminant analysis is used to determine if the two groups can be "discriminated" on the basis of growth hormone levels.

The second portion of App. A gives a description of commonly used multivariate statistics. The beginning of App. A gives a summary table of their usage.

Regression analysis has two major purposes: screening and prediction. **Screening** involves the evaluation of several risk factors to determine which are significantly related to outcome. If the purpose of a study is the identification of important risk factors for a given outcome, analysis will focus on hypothesis testing, or the statistical significance (p-value) of each factor in the model and the relative importance of each factor to the outcome. In effect, a separate hypothesis is tested for each risk factor in this model. If a risk factor is significant in multivariate regression, it is related to the outcome of interest **after controlling for** the effects of other significant risk factors in the regression model. In this way, regression can be used to control for confounding in a study. It shows whether the risk factor of interest is significantly related to the outcome after controlling for confounding risk factors.

Prediction uses the model to predict outcome in a given individual or group whose outcome is unknown. The fit of the model to the data (i.e., how well the model actually predicts the outcome) is critical, and some nonsignificant variables may be included in the model because they improve prediction. Regression may be used in this context to develop a screening test for disease. For example, when the outcome is the presence of some disease, a cutoff point for the predicted probability of disease derived from the regression model may be used as a screening test to classify individuals as positive or negative for that disease. Alternatively, the presence of **any** significant factors identified in the regression model can be classified as positive on the screening test, and the absence of **all** factors can be considered negative. Chapter 10, example 1, illustrates how multiple logistic regression may be used to develop a screening test for the presence of a positive CT scan.

Researchers can use a regression model to control for confounding in estimating effect size by comparing the predicted outcomes of the study groups. This gives an "adjusted" estimate of effect size for the risk factor of interest after removing or controlling for the effects of confounding factors.

> For example, a study is conducted to determine the protective effect of using helmets on head injury in bicycle accidents. Researchers can use a logistic model to calculate an adjusted relative risk of head injury for victims with vs. without helmets after controlling for age, traveling speed, and involvement of a motor vehicle.

> As another example, researchers can use Cox regression to compare adjusted five-year survival rates for stroke patients with surgical vs. medical treatment after controlling for age, sex, and severity of stroke.

> Regression can also be used in case control studies, to compare adjusted risk factor status in cases and controls. For example, to study the effect of age at menarche on breast cancer, a group of women with breast cancer (cases) was compared to women without breast cancer (controls). Multiple regression was used to compute an adjusted difference between the two groups in age at menarche after controlling for race and socioeconomic status.

III. Summary

The two major types of statistics—univariate and multivariate— differ on the number of factors being tested. Univariate statistics measure the relationship of one risk factor to an outcome. Univariate statistics can be parametric, when researchers make certain assumptions about the data. Parametric statistics are generally used with continuous variables and include assumptions about the distribution of the data. Nonparametric statistics include no assumptions about the distribution and are therefore useful when sample size is small or the outcome is discrete or ordinal. Survival analysis is a type of nonparametric analysis used when the outcome of interest is the length of time to some event. It determines the percent of patients still alive or event-free at different points in time (i.e., the survival rate).

Multivariate statistics measure the relationship of several risk factors to one outcome. Regression is a form of multivariate statistics in which a mathematical model or formula relates the risk factors to the outcome. Multiple regression, multiple logistic regression, Cox regression, and discriminant analysis are all types of multivariate analysis used with types of different outcome. Regression analysis has two purposes. The first is screening, to select or identify risk factors that are significantly related to an outcome. Here regression can be used to control for the presence of confounding factors in assessing the significance of a particular risk factor. The second purpose is prediction of the outcome in an individual when his or her risk factor status is known. Here regression can be used to control for the confounding factors when assessing effect size.

Appendix A gives descriptions of the usage and computation of specific univariate and multivariate tests along with examples.

IV. References

The *Mayo Clinic Proceedings* series "Statistics for Clinicians" [1–6] and an excellent summary by J. Worcester [7] give further descriptions of particular statistical tests and measures. See ref. 8 for additional detail on survival analysis.

1. O'Brien PC, Shampo MA. Statistics for Clinicians 1. Descriptive statistics. *Mayo Clin Proc* 56:47–49, 1981.
2. O'Brien PC, Shampo MA. Statistics for Clinicians 5. One sample of paired observations (paired *t* test). *Mayo Clin Proc* 56:324–326, 1981.
3. O'Brien PC, Shampo MA. Statistics for Clinicians 6. Comparing two samples (the two-sample *t* test). *Mayo Clin Proc* 56:393–394, 1981.
4. O'Brien PC, Shampo MA. Statistics for Clinicians 7. Regression. *Mayo Clin Proc* 56:452–454, 1981.
5. O'Brien PC, Shampo MA. Statistics for Clinicians 8. Comparing two proportions: the relative deviate test and chi-square equivalent. *Mayo Clin Proc* 56:513–515, 1981.
6. C'Brien PC, Shampo MA. Statistics for Clinicians 12. Sequential methods. *Mayo Clin Proc* 56:753–754, 1981.
7. Worcester J. The statistical method. *New Engl J Med* 274:27–36, 1966.
8. O'Brien PC, Shampo MA. Statistics for Clinicians 11. Survivorship studies. *Mayo Clin Proc* 56:709–711, 1981.

Using Confidence Intervals in Hypothesis Testing

A direct parallel exists between test statistics and confidence intervals for a difference between groups. This parallel rests on the fact that both the test statistic and the confidence interval are based on the same three components: magnitude of the difference, sample size, and variability. As a result, confidence intervals can be used instead of test statistics to compare means or proportions in two groups.

I. Confidence Interval for the Difference in Means

If the 95% confidence intervals for the means of two groups do not overlap, there is a significant difference between the groups at $p < 0.05$.

An even more direct and preferable method of comparison is to compute the 95% confidence interval for the **difference** in means.

If the 95% confidence interval for the difference in means or proportions between two groups does not include 0, then the groups are significantly different at p < 0.05.

The formula for calculating the confidence interval for the difference in means is as follows [1]:

$$\text{mean}_1 - \text{mean}_2 \pm 2 \times \sqrt{\frac{s_1^2}{n_1} + \frac{s_2^2}{n_2}}$$

where s_1 and s_2 are the standard deviations from groups 1 and 2 and n_1 and n_2 are the sample sizes.*

For example, researchers conduct a study comparing two diets (Diet A and Diet B) on their effectiveness in weight reduction. They randomly assign 40 subjects to one of the two diets and weigh each subject at the beginning of the study (before the diet is begun) and after three months. They calculate the mean weight loss for each diet group along with the standard deviation (amount of variability) of the group. The mean weight loss for Group A is 20 pounds. The mean weight loss for Group B is 10 pounds. Therefore, a difference of 10 pounds exists between the groups. The standard deviation of Group A is 6.5, and that of Group B is 4.3.

Substituting these values in the preceding formula, we can obtain a 95% confidence interval for the difference between means:

$$20 - 10 \pm 2 \times \sqrt{\frac{6.5^2}{20} + \frac{4.3^2}{20}}$$

$$= 10 \pm 2 \times \sqrt{\frac{42.25}{20} + \frac{18.49}{20}}$$

$$= 10 \pm 2 \times \sqrt{2.11 + .93}$$

$$= 10 \pm 2 \times \sqrt{3}$$

$$= 10 \pm 2 \times 1.74$$

*This formula, which uses the individual standard deviations from each group, can be used when the standard deviations of the two groups are unequal. When the standard deviations are equal, a more complicated formula using the pooled standard deviation for the two groups can be calculated. This more complicated formula is omitted here because in practice the two formulas give similar results, and the simpler formula is more appropriate when the standard deviations for the two groups differ.

$$= 10 \pm 3.5$$

$$= 6.5 \text{ to } 13.5$$

Because this 95% confidence interval does not include 0, we conclude that there is a significant difference between the two diet groups in mean weight loss.

II. Confidence Interval for the Difference in Proportions

Although the correspondence between confidence intervals and tests of significance is not as direct for proportions, it is close enough to give the same interpretation for the difference in proportions between two groups [2]. The formula for the 95% confidence interval for the difference in proportions follows:

$$p_1 - p_2 \pm 2 \sqrt{\frac{p_1 (1 - p_1)}{n_1} + \frac{p_2 (1 - p_2)}{n_2}}$$

where p_1 and p_2 are the respective proportions in groups 1 and 2 and n_1 and n_2 are the sample sizes.

For example, suppose a public health worker wanted to compare the prevalence of measles in two classrooms in an elementary school. The first class had 3 cases out of 25 children and the second class had 5 cases out of 20 children. The proportions and sample sizes in the 2 classes would be:

$$p_1 = 0.12, n_1 = 25$$

$$p_2 = 0.25, n_2 = 20$$

We can substitute these values in the above formula to obtain a 95% confidence interval for the difference in proportions in the two classes:

$$(0.12 - 0.25) \pm 2 \sqrt{\frac{0.12 \times (1 - 0.12)}{25} + \frac{0.25 \times (1 - 0.25)}{20}}$$

$$= -0.13 \pm 2 \sqrt{\frac{0.12 \times (0.88)}{25} + \frac{0.25 \times (0.75)}{20}}$$

$$= -0.13 \pm 2 \sqrt{\frac{0.11}{25} + \frac{0.19}{20}}$$

$$= -0.13 \pm 2 \sqrt{0.0044 + 0.0095}$$

$$= -0.13 \pm 2 \sqrt{0.0139}$$

$$= -0.13 \pm 2 \times 0.12$$

$$= -0.13 \pm 0.24$$

$$= -0.37 \text{ to } 0.11$$

or a difference in prevalence which ranges from 37 per hundred less in the first class to 11 per hundred more. Since this confidence interval includes 0, we conclude there is no significant difference in the prevalence of measles in the two classes.

Suppose now the above-mentioned proportions, 0.12 and 0.25, were obtained from two schools, each with 100 students. Substituting these numbers in the preceding formula, we obtain a 95% confidence interval for the difference in proportions of -0.24 to -0.02, or a prevalence between 2 and 24 per hundred less in the first school. Since both the lower and upper limits of this confidence interval are on the same side of 0, i.e., the confidence interval does **not** include 0, we conclude there **is** a significant difference in the prevalence of measles in the two schools at $p < 0.05$.

III. Confidence Interval for the Relative Risk

When expressing the difference between groups as a ratio of proportions (relative risk), we test whether the relative risk is different from 1. **If the 95% confidence interval does not include 1, we conclude that the relative risk is significant at $p < 0.05$. If the 99% confidence interval does not include 1, the relative risk is significant at $p < 0.01$.** As detailed in App. A, the relative risk can be computed by setting up a table like the following:

TABLE 9-1.   Relative risk

Risk Factor	Disease		Total
	Present	Absent	
Present	a	b	$a + b$
Absent	c	d	$c + d$

$$\text{The relative risk (RR)} = \frac{a}{a+b} \div \frac{c}{c+d}$$

The simplest way to calculate the confidence interval for the relative risk is to obtain the confidence limits for the natural log of the relative risk (logRR) and then convert these to limits for the original RR. Note that all computations in steps 1-4 below can be done with a scientific calculator.

1. Take the natural log of RR (use the LN or ln key on a scientific calculator).
2. Calculate the standard error (SE) for logRR, using entries from the above table:

$$SE = \sqrt{\frac{1}{a} - \frac{1}{(a+b)} + \frac{1}{c} - \frac{1}{(c+d)}}$$

3. As with any confidence interval, add and substract twice the standard error to logRR to get its 95% confidence limits.
4. Take each of these confidence limits to the power of e (e is approximately 2.71). To do this you can use the antilog key(e^x) on a scientific calculator. The result is the confidence limits of the original relative risk.

For example, the director of employee health at a large medical center wishes to estimate the risk of back injury from lifting patients. He conducts a cohort study comparing back injury in health care workers who lift patients and those who don't. To calculate the relative risk and its 95% confidence interval, the researcher sets up a table as follows:

TABLE 9-2.   An example of relative risk

Lifting	Back Injury Present	Absent	Total
Present	20	80	100
Absent	5	95	100

$$RR = \frac{20}{100} \div \frac{5}{100} = 4$$

The risk of back injury is 4 times greater for health care workers who lift patients than those who don't.

The 95% confidence interval is calculated as follows:

1. $LogRR = \log_e 4 = 1.4$
2. SE of $logRR = \sqrt{\dfrac{1}{20} - \dfrac{1}{100} + \dfrac{1}{5} - \dfrac{1}{100}} = 0.5$
3. The 95% confidence limits of $logRR = 1.4 \pm 2 \times 0.5 = 1.4 \pm 1.0 = 0.4$ to 2.4
4. The antilogs of these limits $= e^{0.4}$ to $e^{2.4} = 1.5$ to 10.9

which is the 95% confidence interval for the relative risk.

Other worked examples for computing the 95% confidence interval for the relative risk are given in Section III, Examples 2 and 4.

IV. Confidence Interval for the Odds Ratio

As explained in App. A, in case control studies or when the proportion of disease is small in cohort studies, the relative risk cannot be directly calculated. Instead we use the **odds ratio** to estimate the relative risk from the data. We can calculate the odds ratio with the same table used to calculate the relative risk (Table 9-1 above).

The odds ratio is

$$(a \times d) \div (b \times c)$$

The easiest way to compute the confidence limits for the odds ratio is a method derived by Haldane [3] and is similar to that for the relative risk.

1. First take the natural log of the odds ratio (logOR). (This is the *LN* or *ln* key on a scientific calculator.)
2. Apply the following formula to Table 9-1 to compute the standard error for logOR

$$SE = \sqrt{\dfrac{1}{a} + \dfrac{1}{b} + \dfrac{1}{c} + \dfrac{1}{d}}$$

3. Add and subtract twice the standard error to logOR to get its 95% confidence limits.
4. Take these limits to the power of e (2.71) using the antilog key (e^x) on a scientific calculator. The result is the confidence limits of the original odds ratio.

When n is small (< 100), add 0.5 to each number in the formula for the standard error.

In the previous example of back injury and lifting, we could compute the odds ratio from Table 9-2 as follows:

$$\text{The odds ratio} = (20.5 \times 95.5) \div (5.5 \times 80.5) = 4.42$$

$$\text{The log of the odds ratio} = \log_e 4.42 = 1.49$$

$$\text{The standard error of the log odds ratio} =$$

$$\sqrt{\frac{1}{20.5} + \frac{1}{80.5} + \frac{1}{5.5} + \frac{1}{95.5}} = \sqrt{0.25} = 0.50$$

$$\text{The 95\% confidence limits of the log odds ratio} =$$
$$1.49 \pm 2 \times 0.5 = 1.49 \pm 1 = 0.49 \text{ to } 2.49$$

The antilog of these limits is 1.6 to 12.0, which is the 95% confidence interval for the odds of having lifted for health care workers with and without back injury.

Examples 2, 3, and 4 in Part III, Chap. 12, provide other worked examples for computing the 95% confidence interval for the difference in two proportions and the odds ratio respectively.

IV. Using Confidence Intervals to Describe Effect Size

Using confidence intervals to compare groups gives more meaning to estimates of the magnitude of difference between groups (effect size). A narrow confidence interval will tell us more about the true effect size. A wide confidence interval, on the other hand, can include both small and large effect sizes, and we will be less certain about the strength or direction of the relationship between the risk factor and outcome. Although not detailed here, computer programs give confidence intervals for the correlation coefficient, median survival, survival rates, and coefficients in multivariate analysis. The confidence interval approach can be used to evaluate effect sizes measured by these estimates as well.

Simon suggests that confidence intervals become especially important when results are marginally significant [4]. Examination of the confidence interval to determine whether it is predominantly positive or negative indicates that it is compatible with positive or negative differences between groups. Determining how large an effect size is compatible with the confidence interval identifies whether results have potential clinical importance.

To illustrate the value of confidence intervals in interpreting effect sizes, we shall use the aforementioned study of diet and weight loss.

Consider three scenarios in the example of the study on diet and weight loss. Each has a difference in mean weight loss of 10 pounds between the two diet groups but differing sample sizes or standard deviations. These three scenarios are depicted in parts 1, 2, and 3 of Fig. 9-1. Each diamond or cross represents the number of pounds lost for an individual subject. The diamonds represent the weight loss for subjects in Group A. The crosses represent the weight loss for subjects in Group B. The dotted lines represent the mean weight loss for each group.

Part 1 depicts our previous example with 20 people in each group. We calculated the 95% confidence interval as lying between 6.5 and 13.5, which is compatible with a moderate to large difference in weight loss between the groups. The 99% confidence interval for the difference between groups is 5.5 to 14.5, indicating that this difference is statistically significant at $p < 0.01$ level. We can thus rule out chance as an explanation for the difference in weight loss between the study groups.

Part 2 depicts data with the same mean weight loss of 10 pounds and sample size of 20 in each group, but with greater variability, as shown by the greater spread of points about the mean and the higher standard deviations (21.8 and 20.1, respectively). This example results in a 95% confidence interval of −3.3 to 23.3, which is compatible with either a slight superiority of Group B, but more likely with a superiority of Group A, anywhere from small to quite large in magnitude. Because the 95% confidence interval includes 0, we cannot rule out chance as an explanation for the difference of 10 pounds that we observed between our groups.

Part 3 again depicts data with the same group difference of 10 pounds and the same degree of variability as in Part 1 (i.e., 6.5 for Group A and 4.3 for Group B). However, the sample size for each group is only 3. The 95% confidence interval is now 1 to 19, which indicates a statistically significant difference between the groups but gives us little certainty as to whether this difference is very small or quite large.

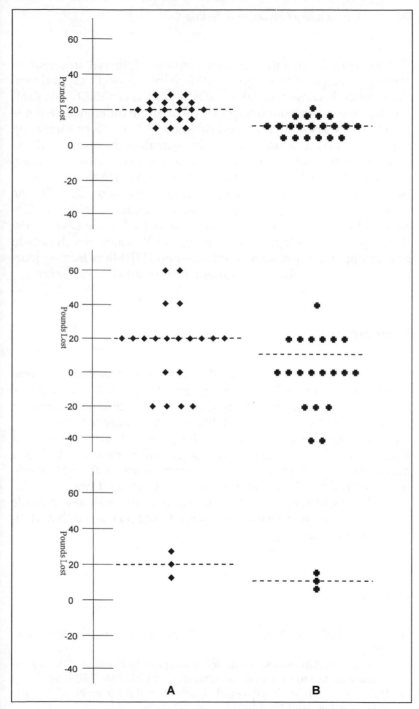

Fig. 9-1. Three situations of a study on diet and weight loss, showing effect of magnitude, variability, and sample size on confidence intervals

Thus, confidence intervals can convey additional information about the magnitude of group differences as well as statistical significance, because they take into account the variability and sample size, which affect our interpretation of group differences. For this reason, in the last ten years medical journals have given increasing importance to confidence intervals in estimating the size of a difference between groups and have put less focus on statistical testing, which merely dichotomizes this difference as significant or non-significant. Several authors have discussed this issue [2, 4–7]. The current "Uniform Requirements for Manuscripts Submitted to Biomedical Journals" instructs authors to "avoid sole reliance on statistical hypothesis testing, such as the use of P values, which fails to convey important quantitative information" [8]. Many leading journals use these guidelines as requirements for article submission.

V. Summary

Confidence intervals can be used instead of test statistics to compare means or proportions in two groups. Like statistics, confidence intervals are a function of the magnitude of the difference between groups, sample size, and variability. A 95% confidence interval for the difference in means or proportions between two groups that does not include 0 indicates a significant difference at $p < 0.05$. For differences expressed as a ratio of proportions, if the 95% confidence interval for the relative risk does not include 1, then the relative risk is significant at $p < 0.05$. Confidence intervals also provide valuable information about effect sizes, based on the width and direction of the interval.

References

1. Pocock SJ. *Clinical Trials. A Practical Approach.* Chichester, NY: Wiley, 1983.
2. Gardner MJ, Altman DG. Confidence intervals rather than P values: estimation rather than hypothesis testing. *B M J* 292:746–750, 1986.
3. Haldane JBS. The estimation and significance of the logarithm of a ratio of frequencies. *Ann Hum Genet* 2:309–311, 1956.

4. Simon R. Confidence intervals for reporting results of clinical trials. *Ann Intern Med* 105:429–435, 1986.
5. Rothman KJ. A show of confidence. *N Engl J Med* 299(24):1362–1363, 1976.
6. Altman DG, et al. Statistical guidelines for contributors to medical journals. *B M J* 286:1489–1493, 1983.
7. Pocock SJ. Current issues in design and interpretation of clinical trials. *Stat Med* 290:39–42, 1985.
8. Uniform requirements for manuscripts submitted to biomedical journals. *N Engl J Med* 324(6):424–428, 1991.

APPLICATION TO EVALUATING THE LITERATURE

The chapters that follow give examples of each major type of study design found in the medical literature, for both hypothesis testing and estimation. The beginning of each chapter lists questions appropriate for evaluating the studies that follow. After each example is an evaluation of that example using the preceding questions. Each example has been written to illustrate one or two major problems that may be encountered with each type of study design.

With the exception of Example 6 on meta-analysis in Chap. 12, all examples are fictitious and have never been published. However, all are similar to those found in medical journals. Unlike the examples, the references cited in them refer to real studies that have been published.

Estimation

The following questions can be used to evaluate studies whose purpose is to describe the characteristics of a population. Example 1 describes a screening test. General questions for estimation studies are given first in this chapter. Specific questions to evaluate screening tests are given in the following chapter.

I. Questions for Estimation

1. To what types of people should the results of this study be generalized (i.e., what are the characteristics of the population from which this sample was chosen)?
2. Was there bias in the selection of subjects for the sample so that resulting estimates are not valid?
3. Were confidence intervals reported for the estimates given?

   If the study gives standard deviations or standard errors for means, we can calculate the confidence intervals for means ourselves. We can also calculate the confidence intervals for proportions according to the formulas on pages 12 and 13.

4. Does the size and variability of the sample chosen result in precise or imprecise estimates, i.e., narrow or wide confidence intervals?

    As a rough guide, we can consider the precision of an estimate

    - good if the standard error is less than 10% of the estimate
    - fair if the standard error is 10% to 15% of the estimate
    - poor (imprecise) if the standard error is greater than 15% of the estimate.

Imprecise estimates limit the usefulness of the study for estimation.

EXAMPLE 1

A Screening Test

Prediction of Positive CT Testing for Adult Patients
with Head Trauma
Jerome H. Jones, Michael T. Farber, and Frederick S. Smith

Abstract

This study evaluated 200 consecutive adult patients with acute head trauma referred for computed tomography (CT) of the head. The purpose was to develop a screening test for prediction of positive CT results. Information was collected on all patients on type of injury and selected clinical factors assessed on admission to the trauma center. A multiple logistic regression was performed to identify those factors predictive of a positive CT scan. Four significant factors were identified: injury severity score (ISS) greater than 10, Glasgow coma score (GCS) less than 15, presence of seizure, and presence of a focal neurologic deficit on physical examination. Of 105 patients with a positive CT scan, 100 had one or more significant factors present on admission (sensitivity, 95%). Eighty of 95 patients with a negative scan had none of the four factors present (specificity, 84%). Of 115 patients with one or more factors present, 100 had a positive CT scan (positive predictive value, 87%). Of 85 patients with no factors present, 80 had a negative CT scan (negative predictive value, 94%).

We conclude that in patients with acute head trauma, these four factors provide a useful, valid, and safe screening tool to determine the necessity of CT scanning.

Introduction

Since its introduction in 1972, CT has quickly become established as a definitive diagnostic tool [1]. Because of its noninvasive nature, coupled with ever-increasing refinements in accuracy and diagnostic detail, the use of CT scanning for all types of diseases and conditions has continued to increase.

One result of the advances in CT technology is an increase in cost to patients owing to the high costs of CT hardware and software and the time commitment it requires from technicians and physicians. In an age of scarce health care resources and cost-containment demands from legislators, hospital administrators, and managed care providers, use of technology such as CT scanning is under increasing scrutiny. In this climate, stricter criteria for use of such high-technology tools and an assessment of their yield for diagnosis is needed.

A recent study of 1,551 CT scans of the head estimated a positive yield of 30% for initial scans in patients with acute head trauma [2]. Increasing this yield by eliminating patients unlikely to have a positive scan would increase the efficiency of this test as a diagnostic tool and result in sizeable cost savings.

We designed the present study to develop an effective screening mechanism for predicting positive CT scan results. Our aim was to significantly reduce unnecessary CT scanning by identifying a subgroup of patients unlikely to benefit from CT scan while maintaining the quality of care of our patients.

Methods

All consecutive patients age 18 or older with acute head injury seen by the Trauma Service at Belmont Medical Center (BMC) between January 1, 1993, and June 30, 1993, and referred for CT scanning of the head were identified from the hospital's trauma registry. BMC is a large tertiary care hospital located in Belmont, Rhode Island, that serves the western half of the state. It is a Level I trauma center and receives approximately 1,200 trauma patients per year, mostly by Emergency Medical Service (EMS) transport under the triage guidelines of the American College of Surgeons Committee on Trauma [3]. It is the only CT scanning facility within a radius of 100 miles.

The CT scans at BMC were performed without contrast on a Technicare Quantum 2060 (Technicare, Cleveland, Ohio) scanner. All CT scans were read by a neuroradiologist.

For all patients referred for CT scans of the head during the study period, information was recorded on details of injury and selected clinical factors assessed on admission to the BMC Trauma Service. The clinical factors included two measures of injury severity: the GCS [4], measured on a 15-point scale, and the ISS [5], measured on a 75-point scale. Also recorded were delay from injury to admission, mechanism of injury, type of injury (blunt or penetrating), patient age and sex, vital signs on admission (heart rate, blood pressure, respiratory rate), and neurologic signs including loss of consciousness, focal neurologic deficit, and seizure.

Multiple logistic regression (MLR) was used to identify factors predictive of a positive CT [6]. A forward stepwise procedure was used, with a maximum likelihood method to calculate the regression coefficients. The likelihood ratio criterion was used to determine the significance of individual factors in the regression model. Cutpoints were chosen for continuous variables entered into the MLR so as to optimize the difference in the proportion of positive scans for patients above and below the cutoff.

We developed a screening test using the presence or absence of significant factors identified in the MLR. Patients with one or more of the significant factors present were classified as positive; patients with no significant factors present were classified as negative. We then calculated the proportion of patients with positive CT scans who had one or more factors present (sensitivity). We also calculated the proportion of patients with negative scans who had none of the predictive factors present (specificity), the probability of a positive CT scan in patients with one or more factors present (positive predictive value), and the probability of a negative scan when no factors were present (negative predictive value).

Results

A total of 235 patients received CT scans of the head during the study period. Complete information was available on 200 patients, so these 200 made up the sample group for all subsequent analyses.

Mean age of all patients was 32 (SE 6.7). Ninety-eight patients (49%) were male. Vital signs for all patients on admission included a mean systolic blood pressure of 115 (SE 6.7), mean heart rate of 140 (SE 7.9), and mean respiratory rate of 64 (SE 7.1). Patients had a mean delay from time of injury to admission of 60 minutes (SE 4.6); ten patients (10%) had a delay greater than 60 minutes.

Of the 200 patients, 40% had a GCS less than 15 on admission and 60% had a GCS = 15, with a range of 3 to 15. ISS on admission ranged from 3 to 53; 20% of patients had an ISS greater than 10.

Table 10-1 lists signs and symptoms present on admission. The most frequent symptoms were headache and vomiting. Seizure and focal neurologic deficits were infrequent. Blunt trauma was the major type of injury, present in 160 patients (80%); the other 40 patients suffered penetrating injuries (20%). Motor vehicle accidents were the most frequent mechanism of injury, present in 120 patients (60%). Falls were responsible for injuries in 60 patients (30%), and assault was the least frequent mechanism, present in 20 patients (10%).

One hundred five patients (53%) had positive CT scan results. In these patients, the primary finding was hematoma in 51 (49%), contusion in 23 (22%), concussion in 18 (17%), and diffuse injury in 13 (12%). Fifty-six (59%) of the 95 patients with normal scans were admitted to the hospital for observation or treatment of other injuries. None underwent surgery. There were no deaths in this group. Of the 105 patients with positive scans, 96 (91%) were admitted to the hospital. Twenty-six patients with positive scans (25%) were sent for emergency surgery as the result of the positive scan findings. Two patients with positive scans (2%) died.

The results of the MLR are shown in Table 10-2. Four factors were significantly related to the finding of a positive scan: ISS greater than 10, GCS less than 15, presence of seizure, and presence of focal neurologic deficit. One hundred of 105 patients with a positive CT scan had one or more significant factors present, for a sensitivity of 95%. Of 95 patients with a negative scan, 80 had no factors present, resulting in a specificity of 84%. Of 115 patients with one or more factors present, 100 had positive CT results for a positive predictive value of

Table 10-1. Symptoms on admission

Characteristic	Number present	Percent of total*
Vomiting	85	43
Headache	90	45
Amnesia	12	6
Loss of consciousness	41	21
Seizure	6	3
Focal neurologic deficit	8	4

*$n = 200$

TABLE 10-2.   Significant factors in positive CT scans

Factor	Coefficient (β)	Standard error of β	Significance
ISS > 10	0.288	0.041	< 0.0001
GCS < 15	0.035	0.009	0.0047
Seizure	1.115	0.549	0.0226
Focal neurologic deficit	0.888	0.032	0.0369

87%. Of 85 patients with no factors present, 80 had negative CT results, for a negative predictive value of 94%.

Discussion

We found four factors to be significantly predictive of a positive result for CT: ISS greater than 10, GCS less than 15, presence of seizure, and presence of a focal neurologic deficit. When these factors were absent, the likelihood of a positive result was only 6%, compared with 87% when present. By avoiding scans in those patients with none of the predictive factors, we would have saved 85 tests in a 6 month period, which, at an average cost of $600 per test, would result in yearly savings of more than $100,000.

We believe these cost savings would have occurred without causing any treatment disadvantage to patients not receiving scans. There were five false negatives in our study—that is, patients who had no significant factors present but who had a positive CT scan. Of these patients, one had minimal cerebral contusion, two had mild concussion, one had a mild diffuse cerebral edema, and one had a minimal right subdural hematoma. None of these conditions required surgery, and none of the patients had deterioration of their status after hospitalization or experienced any clinical sequelae. If these patients had not had a CT scan, they would probably have been sent home with instructions to return to BMC if they had any change in condition. In these cases, failure to perform a CT scan would have had little effect on the outcome or treatment, because no special treatment was administered during their hospitalization.

Use of these clinical criteria to reduce the population of head-injured patients who receive CT scans will increase the efficiency of this test in detecting clinically significant abnormalities and result in extensive cost savings. In the current health care climate, such cost savings are no longer optional but mandatory. We have shown that this savings can be achieved without compromising the quality of care for the acute head-injured patient.

II. Questions for Estimation Applied to Example 1

The description of patients at the beginning of the results section in Example 1 gives the characteristics of patients referred for CT scans of the head. We will apply the questions below to see if the estimates from this example are accurate for this population.

1. To what types of people should the results of this study be generalized (i.e., what are the characteristics of the population from which this sample was chosen)?

   The patients in this study come from a large referral hospital and the only CT scanning facility for a large area. For these reasons we can assume that they represent a cross-section of patients from the western part of the state referred for CT scans of the head. However, since a description of the geographic area is not given in the study, we cannot determine whether the population is primarily urban, suburban, rural, or mixed. This type of information would help us determine the type of patient population to which the estimates of the present study can be generalized.

2. Was there bias in the selection of subjects for the sample so that resulting estimates are not valid?

   A high proportion of the total number of patients scanned (200 of 235) were evaluated, so it appears that there is no significant bias in the estimates from this study. There may be minimal bias present from the 35 patients not included because of incomplete information. The authors do not explain why these patients had incomplete information, but it seems unlikely that their exclusion caused significant bias.

3. Were confidence intervals reported for the estimates given?

   According to the methods described on pages 12 and 13, we can estimate the 95% confidence intervals for the means and proportions given. The results should look like those in Tables 10-3 and 10-4 allowing for rounding of decimals.

Table 10-3.   Confidence intervals for means in Example 1

Characteristic	Mean	Standard error	95% Confidence interval
Age	32	6.7[3]	19–45
Blood pressure	115	6.7[1]	102–128
Heart rate	140	7.9[1]	124–156
Respiration rate	64	7.1[2]	50–78
Delay from injury to admission (min)	60	4.6[1]	51–69

[1] Good precision of estimate
[2] Fair precision of estimate
[3] Poor precision of estimate

TABLE 10-4.   Confidence intervals for proportions in Example 1

Characteristic	Proportion Present	n	Standard error	95% Confidence interval
GCS < 15	0.40	200	0.03[1]	0.33–0.47
ISS > 10	0.20	200	0.03[2]	0.15–0.26
Vomiting	0.43	200	0.03[1]	0.36–0.50
Headache	0.45	200	0.03[1]	0.38–0.52
Amnesia	0.06	200	0.015[3]	0.03–0.09
Loss of consciousness	0.21	200	0.03[2]	0.15–0.27
Seizure	0.03	200	0.01[3]	0.01–0.05
Focal neurologic deficit	0.04	200	0.01[3]	0.01–0.07
Blunt injury	0.75	200	0.03[1]	0.69–0.81
Penetrating injury	0.25	200	0.03[2]	0.19–0.31
Motor vehicle accident	0.60	200	0.03[1]	0.53–0.67
Fall	0.30	200	0.03[2]	0.24–0.36
Assault	0.10	200	0.02[3]	0.06–0.14

[1] Good precision of estimate
[2] Fair precision of estimate
[3] Poor precision of estimate

4. Does the size and variability of the sample chosen result in precise or imprecise estimates, i.e., narrow or wide confidence intervals?

Judging the precision of an estimate (mean or proportion) depends on the size of the standard error *relative to* the estimate. For example, Table 10-3 shows age and blood pressure both have a standard error of 6.7. However, this represents 20% of the mean for age and only 6% of the mean for blood pressure. By the criteria given in Question 4, page 86, the precision of the mean would be considered poor for age but good for blood pressure. Estimates in Tables 10-3 and 10-4 are predominantly of good or fair precision: the majority have standard errors less than 15% of the mean or proportion.

A. Summary of Analysis.   The patients in the study described in Example 1 represent a wide cross-section of patients referred for CT and can be considered a representative sample of adult patients with acute head injury. Because most estimates have good to fair precision, this study provides a good description of characteristics of all patients referred for CT scans. Results may differ for smaller facilities with more select populations.

III. References

1. Hounsfield GN. Computerized transaxial scanning (tomography). *Radiology* 46:1016–1022, 1973.
2. Macpherson P, Jennett B, Anderson E. CT scanning and surgical treatment of 1551 head injured patients admitted to a regional neurosurgical unit. *Clin Radiol* 42(2):85–87, 1990.
3. American College of Surgeons: Committee on trauma field categorization of trauma patients. *Bull Am Coll Surg* 71:17, 1986.
4. Teasdale G, Jennett B. Assessment of coma and impaired consciousness. *Lancet* 2:81–84, 1974.
5. Baker SP, et al. The Injury Severity Score: a method for describing patients with multiple injuries and evaluating emergency care. *J Trauma* 27:602–606, 1987.
6. Cox DR. *Analysis of Binary Data*. London: Methuen, 1970.
7. Lee ET. Identification of Prognostic Factors Related to Survival Time. In *Statistical Methods for Survival Data Analysis*. Belmont, CA. Lifetime Learning, 1992:256–257.

Screening Tests

The following questions can be used to evaluate screening tests, a special type of estimation.

I. Questions for Screening Tests

1. What is the primary purpose of the test?

   a) Is it early detection of people with the disease?

       (1) What will be gained by early detection?
       (2) Are facilities available for referral and definitive testing of people who screen positive?

   b) Is it to rule out people with the disease?

       (1) What are the risks for false negatives?
       (2) What are the costs of false positives?

2. How was the presence of disease established? Was it definitive?
3. Are the operating characteristics good enough to satisfy the primary purpose of the screening test?

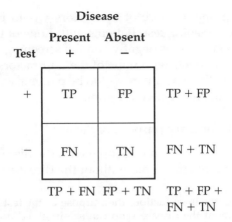

a) What is the sensitivity? *Calculate TP/(TP + FN)*
b) What is the specificity? *Calculate TN/(FP+ TN)*

The primary purpose of the test will determine which is more important: high sensitivity or high specificity. Whether the sensitivity or specificity of a test is considered acceptable or not depends on the cost of false negatives or false positives, respectively.

4. On what population was the test based? Was it broad enough that the test's operating characteristics will apply to other populations? Is the sample unbiased? Is the sample size large enough to give precise estimates?
5. Is the test fast and easy to apply? Is it reproducible?
6. Is it relatively inexpensive?
7. Could a different cutoff have been used to improve sensitivity or specificity?
8. With estimates of the positive or negative predictive value and the aim of the test specified in Question 1, was the screening test useful for its major purpose **in this population?**

II. Questions for Screening Tests Applied to Example 1

The screening test in Example 1 is based on the four factors significantly related to a positive CT scan. According to the authors, patients having one or more of the factors would be classified as positive on the screening test. Patients with none of the factors present would be classified as negative on the screening test. False negatives would be patients with none of the four factors present and a positive CT scan. False positives would be patients with one or more factors present and a negative CT scan.

1. What is the primary purpose of the test?

    a) Is it early detection of people with the disease?
    b) Is it to rule out people without the disease?

    As stated in the introduction, the purpose of the test is to rule out people without the disease who can safely avoid undergoing CT scan.

    (1) What are the risks for false negatives?

    In the case of acute head injury, the risks for false negatives could be delayed diagnosis or treatment. The authors concluded, however, that there would be no risks for false negatives, because no delay in diagnosis or treatment was seen in the present study. They maintained that the treatment would have been no different for these patients if they had not had a CT scan, except that they may not have been admitted to the hospital for observation. The patients in this study did not require surgery and did not develop any clinical sequelae to their abnormal scan.

    (2) What are the costs of false positives?

    The cost of false positives would be the cost of a scan, roughly $600. The patient would also experience increased discomfort and anxiety, although this would be minimal in the case of CT scanning.

2. How was the presence of disease established? Was it definitive?

    The presence of disease was established by CT scan of the head, which is a well-established diagnostic criterion for head injuries. The presence of abnormal findings, however, is not always definitive on CT, and this fact was not discussed by the authors. There was no category for "uncertain" findings in this study, and it is unclear whether this category was absent in the study or whether the authors reclassified these findings into positive or negative tests. This issue could affect the estimates of sensitivity and specificity from the present study.

3. Are the operating characteristics good enough to satisfy the primary purpose of the screening test?

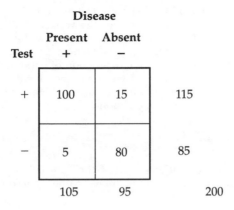

	Disease		
	Present	Absent	
Test	+	−	
+	100	15	115
−	5	80	85
	105	95	200

a) What is the sensitivity?

$$\frac{TP}{TP + FN} = \frac{100}{105} = 95\%$$

b) What is the specificity?

$$\frac{TN}{(TN + FP)} = \frac{80}{95} = 84\%$$

Since the aim of the present study was to achieve cost savings by identifying patients who are unlikely to benefit from CT while not missing clinically significant injury, the most important characteristics to consider are its negative predictive value and sensitivity. With regard to the latter, a sensitivity of 95% is considered good, but whether it is good enough for the purposes of the present study depends on the cost of false negatives. As discussed in the answer to question 1-1, the authors contend that the present study demonstrates no increased risk of delayed diagnosis or treatment for false negatives. Thus the second aim of the study, not compromising the quality of care of patients, has been achieved. Negative predictive values with regard to the first aim of the study will be discussed in the answer to Question 8.

4. On what population was the test based? Was it broad enough that the test's operating characteristics will apply to other populations?

    The authors state that BMC is a large tertiary care hospital with a Level I trauma center, that it serves the western half of Rhode Island, and that it is the only CT scanning facility within a 100-mile radius. Because it is a referral hospital serving a large portion of the state, it presumably represents a cross-section of patients from this area. However, more information about whether the area is metropolitan or rural or mixed would help confirm whether these results may be generalized to other populations.

Is the sample unbiased?

A high proportion of patients (200 of the 235 patients scanned) were evaluated, so there does not appear to be significant bias in the estimates from this study.

Is the sample size large enough to give precise estimates?

From Table 11-1, we can evaluate the precision of estimates of the operating characteristics of the test.

According to our criteria for precision given in the last chapter, the sample size of the current study gives good precision for estimating

Table 11-1.   Confidence intervals for screening characteristics from Example 1

	Rate	n	Standard error	95% Confidence interval
Sensitivity	0.95	105	0.02[1]	0.91–0.99
Specificity	0.84	95	0.04[1]	0.76–0.88
Positive predictive value	0.87	115	0.03[1]	0.81–0.93
Negative predictive value	0.94	85	0.03[1]	0.88–1.00
% False negatives with hematoma	0.20	5	0.18[2]	0.45–1.15
% False negatives with surgery	0.00	5	—	0.0–0.6

[1] Good precision of estimate
[2] Poor precision of estimate

the operating characteristics of the test. On the other hand, estimates regarding false negatives are imprecise, being based on only five patients. Therefore, the authors' conclusions about the absence of risks for false negatives should be interpreted with caution and have not been adequately proven from this study.

One further issue regards the validity of estimates of the screening test's operating characteristics. A major criticism of the present study is the fact that the accuracy of the screening test was determined on the same population from which the test was derived. Ideally, one should derive a test on one sample and test it for accuracy on a different sample. Testing for accuracy on the same sample may artificially inflate estimates of the accuracy of the test.

5. Is the test fast and easy to apply? Is it reproducible?

Establishing the presence of the four factors that comprise the screening test is part of the initial admission procedure for any acute head-injured patients, so no special measurements specific to this screening test are needed. It is therefore easy to apply. The criteria are clear and objective (e.g., loss of consciousness) and therefore reproducible.

6. Is it relatively inexpensive?

Yes, the screening test is inexpensive because the criteria are already assessed as part of the general admission procedure. Therefore, there is no extra cost to apply the screening test.

7. Could a different cutoff have been used to improve sensitivity and specificity?

In the present study, the "cutoff," or criterion for a positive screening test, would be the number of significant factors necessary to be classified as "positive" on the screening test. Altering this cutoff would alter the sensitivity and specificity of the test. For example, requiring that at least two significant factors be present to screen positive would in effect make the criterion for administering a CT scan more stringent and reduce the number of false positives, thereby increasing the specificity of the test. This would correspondingly not only decrease the sensitivity (increase the number of false negatives) but would also increase the cost of false negatives. People with one of the factors present would be more likely to have clinically significant injuries and the cost of missing these injuries would be higher than with the present cutoff, possibly compromising the quality of care of these patients. In the present study, this would not be desirable in one of its aims was not to compromise quality of care.

As an alternative to choosing any one, two, three, or four significant factors as a criterion for the screening test, we could make use of the stepwise nature of multiple logistic regression (MLR) and use presence of the factors included in either steps 1, 2, 3, or 4 of the MLR. This would, in effect, give us the most **significant** one, two, three, or four factors instead of **any** one, two, three, or four factors as possible cutpoints.

As explained in Chap. 8, MLR can be used to predict the probability of an event for an individual based on his or her status on significant factors. In Example 1, the coefficients for the factors given in Table 10-2 could have been used in a formula to predict an individual patient's likelihood of a positive scan. Instead of the presence of significant factors as a criterion for CT scanning, the **predicted probability** of a positive scan could have been chosen as the criterion for the screening test. For example, if 0.50 were chosen as the cutoff, patients with a predicted probability greater than 0.50 would be classified as positive on the screening test and considered for CT scanning; patients with a predicted probability below this level would be classified as negative and would not be scanned. The sensitivity and specificity of this screening test could then be calculated. As explained in Chap. 2, altering the cutoff would alter the sensitivity and specificity of the screening test.

Use of the predicted probability of a positive scan rather than the presence or absence of significant factors as a screening criterion has the advantage of giving the investigator greater control over the sensitivity and specificity of the test because of the infinite number of possible cutoffs. It also has the advantage of making full use of continuous variables such as GCS or ISS by including their actual values rather than cutpoints (GCS < 15 or ISS > 10) in determining the probability of a positive scan for an individual patient. It has the disadvantage of being less easy to use, requiring computation of an actual probability for each patient by using a formula instead of simply determining the presence or absence of four risk factors. (Refer to Question 5 on ease of use)

8.   With estimates of the positive or negative predictive value and the aim of the test specified in Question 1, was the screening test useful for its major purpose **in this population?**

Remember that Questions 3 and 4 refer to the inherent accuracy of the screening test regardless of the prevalence of disease, whereas Question 8 refers to the test's usefulness in a given population with a given level of disease prevalence.

The major purpose of the study in Example 1 was to significantly reduce unnecessary CT scanning by ruling out patients unlikely to have positive CT scans. Therefore, the negative predictive value of this test is of interest to us. In this study, the negative predictive value of 94% is high, indicating that this test is useful in its intended purpose. For a patient with none of the four factors present, estimates of his or her chances of having a negative scan go from 48% without screening (the percentage of negative scans in all patients) to 95% when the screening test is negative. According to Chap. 2, the negative predictive value depends on the prevalence of negative scans in the population we are testing and is relatively high in the present study. By contrast, the larger study of 1,551 patients cited in the introduction had only 30% negative scans. The utility would not be as great in this population.

A. Summary of Analysis.   The present study describes a useful screening test for CT scanning of the head, with a high sensitivity and reasonable specificity. The study population is representative of a wide cross-section of patients and can be generalized to many other patient populations. Whether the study achieves its stated aim of developing a test which can substantially reduce unnecessary CT scanning will depend on the population on which the test is used. The benefit cited by the authors applies only to populations with a rate of negative scans similar to that in the present study. Utility in populations with a lower rate of negative scans will not be as great.

The major criticism of the study concerns the accuracy of estimates of sensitivity and specificity. These estimates may be artificially inflated because they were derived from the same population on which the test was developed. More accurate measures would have been obtained if the authors had tested the criteria for screening on a new sample of patients with head injury. For these reasons, further testing of the screening test should be carried out on other populations to obtain truer estimates of sensitivity and specificity.

Hypothesis Testing

The following questions can be used to evaluate studies that test hypotheses about a causal relationship between a risk factor and an outcome. Portions of the questions that apply to specific study designs are indicated. Questions for meta-analytic studies will follow at the end of this chapter.

I. Questions for Hypothesis Testing

A. Identify the Study Design

1. What are the groups to be compared?
2. On what basis are the groups being compared?

    Consider whether the groups are compared on outcome or risk factor.

3. What is the study design?

    Study design is determined by the answers to questions 1 and 2.

B. Rule Out Bias

4. Was bias present in the design of the study?

If the answer to any of the questions under *a*) or *b*) is no, bias could be present.

a)   For cohort studies and clinical trials,

   (1)   Were all subjects taken from the same pool?
   (2)   In assessing outcome, were observers blinded to the risk factor status of the subjects?
   (3)   Was information on outcome obtained in a similar manner for all groups?
   (4)   Was there differential attrition from the study groups?
   (5)   For clinical trials, was randomization used?

b)   For case control studies,

   (1)   Were all subjects taken from the same population?
   (2)   Were controls chosen from an appropriate group?
   (3)   Were multiple control groups chosen?
   (4)   Were deceased cases included?
   (5)   Were observers blinded to the disease status of subjects in assessing risk factor status or did they have information on risk factor status before knowledge of outcome?
   (6)   Was information for risk factor status obtained in a similar manner for cases and controls?

It is the responsibility of the investigator to prove that bias could not exist. If unable to show proof, the investigator must show that bias could not account for the magnitude and direction of the effect size or demonstrate that, if present, bias would actually lessen the effect size rather than increase it.

C. Rule Out Confounding

5.   Were the groups similar at baseline (e.g., by demographics or clinical characteristics)?

Look in tables and text at the beginning of the results section— look for words like "description of subjects."

a)   If the groups were not similar, was the possibility of confounding controlled for in the study design (by restriction, stratification, or matching) or in the analysis (by stratification or regression analysis)?

D. Rule Out Chance

6. Was a statistically significant difference found between the groups?

   The difference is statistically significanct if $p < 0.05$.

   a) If results were not significant,

   (1) Was the sample size adequate to detect a difference of clinical interest?

   Look for some statement of the power of the study or rationale for choosing the sample size. Generally the power of a study should be at least 80%.

   (2) Could bias or confounding be masking real differences between groups?

   Refer to Questions 4 and 5.

   b) If the results were significant, did researchers account for multiple statistical tests in interpreting the *p*-value, and did they perform appropriate multiple comparisons procedures?

   Look for procedures such as Tukey or Scheffe, Bonferroni adjustments of *p*-values when several group comparisons are made, or the use of multivariate techniques when the study includes many risk factors. Likewise, if the study includes multiple confidence intervals for group comparisons, the level of confidence should be correspondingly increased, as discussed at the end of Chap. 6.

E. Establish a Causal Association

7. Was there evidence of a causal association according to the following criteria?

   a) Strength

   Focus on the effect size expressed as a ratio, usually indicated by the size of the relative risk or odds ratio and its 95% confidence interval. Use the following rule of thumb for relative risk:

- A relative risk of 1 indicates no relationship.
- A relative risk of 2 indicates a weak relationship.
- A relative risk of 4 indicates a fairly strong relationship.
- A relative risk greater than 4 indicates a strong relationship.

When determining the strength of the relationship, consider not only the size of the relative risk but also the region where the majority of its 95% confidence interval lies (i.e., what effect size it is mainly compatible with, favoring one group or the other, even if statistical significance has not been achieved).

b)   Consistency

Were the results consistent with other studies cited in the introduction or discussion sections?

c)   Biological plausibility

Was there a dose-response relationship? Do the results fit what is already biologically and clinically known about the outcome? Biological and clinical background should be given in the introduction.

d)   Temporal correctness

Did the risk factor precede the outcome in time?

e)   Specificity

Was there evidence from previous studies or the present one that the association between the risk factor and outcome is specific? Is the risk factor related to other outcomes, or vice versa?

Remember, absence of any of these indicators does not negate a causal association.

F. Establish Clinical Significance

8.   Were the results clinically significant? What is the effect size and its 95% confidence interval?

Focus on the effect size, expressed as an absolute difference between the comparison groups, and the region where its 95%

confidence interval lies. Decide from your own clinical point of view whether an effect size of this magnitude and direction will influence your decisions about treatment or diagnosis. The authors also should give their own interpretation of the clinical significance of the results in the discussion section of the paper.

Even if the results were not statistically significant (see Question 6), determine if most of the 95% confidence interval lies above or below zero (e.g., whether it is compatible primarily with the hypothesis that the mean of Group A is greater than Group B, or vice versa). In this way you can determine if the confidence interval includes an effect size in one direction or the other of potential clinical importance.

EXAMPLE 2

A Randomized Clinical Trial

A Randomized Trial on the Use of Silvadene to Promote Wound Healing and Prevent Surgical Site Infections in Colon Surgery

David J. Wright, MD, John P. Silva, MD, and Thomas C. Posner, MD

Abstract

The present study was designed to assess the effectiveness of silver sulfadiazine (Silvadene) in preventing infection and promoting wound healing in surgery of the colon—a type of surgery at particular risk for surgical site infections.

We prospectively randomized 133 patients undergoing colon surgery to receive either postoperative Silvadene applied topically ($n = 64$) or no treatment ($n = 69$). Patients were followed during hospitalization and seen weekly for 1 month after discharge to determine time to wound healing and presence of postoperative surgical site infection (SSI). The incidence of SSIs for patients in the Silvadene group was 3 of 64, or 4.7%, compared with 12 of 69, or 17.4%, in the control group ($p < .05$). The incidence of other wound-related complications was similar in the two groups (10% in Silvadene patients and 11% in controls). Median time to wound healing was 2 weeks in the Silvadene group and 3 weeks in controls ($p < .001$).

We conclude that Silvadene, when administered prophylactically, promotes wound healing and reduces postoperative SSIs in patients undergoing colon surgery.

Introduction

SSIs are a common cause of postoperative morbidity in patients undergoing surgery of the colon. According to the National Nosocomial Infection Survey (NNIS) [1], the overall rate of SSIs is approximately 8.5%. Risk factors for SSIs are length of surgery greater than the 75th percentile; a preoperative ASA index of 3, 4, or 5; and a surgical wound class of III (contaminated) or IV (dirty). When stratified by risk class NNIS rates for SSIs are 3.18% in patients with no risk factors, 8.47% in patients with one risk factor, 16.11% in patients with two risk factors, and 22% in patients with three risk factors.

The effectiveness of prophylactic systemic antibiotics in reducing SSIs in this type of surgery is well established [2–9]. Silvadene has proved to be an effective antibiotic in the control of infection from second and third degree burns [10–17]. It has broad antimicrobial activity against gram-negative and gram-positive organisms and yeast [11, 14]. It has not, however, been routinely used in the healing of surgically created wounds.

The present study was designed to assess the effectiveness of Silvadene in preventing infection and promoting wound healing in colon surgery.

Methods

All patients undergoing colon surgery by one busy general surgical group (the authors' group) between January 1, 1993, and December 31, 1993, were considered eligible for study. Each patient gave informed consent before enrolling in the study. Randomization was carried out according to the patient's medical record number: patients with record numbers ending in an odd digit were randomized to the Silvadene group, and those ending in an even digit were randomized to the control group.

All patients received an oral bowel cleansing agent the evening before surgery and prophylactic oral cefotetan 1 hour before surgery.

All wounds were left open or loosely approximated for delayed primary closure or secondary closure. For patients in the Silvadene group, the surgeon topically administered 1% Silvadene at the end of surgery, and the nursing staff applied it twice daily to a thickness of $1/16$ in. throughout the patient's hospital stay. Upon discharge from the hospital, the patient received Silvadene and instructions to apply it to the wound, as described, for 1 week. Patients in the control group received no antibiotic treatment at any time following surgery.

Follow-up for surgical wound complications, including SSIs, was performed by the operating surgeon daily during hospitalization and weekly for one month after discharge in the surgeon's office. The surgeons used the Centers for Disease Control (CDC) definition of an SSI [18]. Other wound-related surgical complications recorded were wound dehiscence, erythema, and bleeding.

Healing of the wound was defined as complete closure of the wound with no irregularities. Date of wound healing was considered to be the date of the first follow-up visit at which healing was observed. Time to wound healing was the number of weeks elapsed from date of operation to date of wound healing.

Groups were compared on the incidence of surgical site infections and other wound-related postoperative complications using chi-square analysis, with Yate's correction for continuity. Time to wound healing could only be determined to the nearest week because of the follow-up schedule, so a nonparametric test, the Kruskal Wallis test, was used to compare the two treatment groups on this outcome [19].

Results

Sixty-four patients were randomized to the Silvadene group, and 69 patients were randomized to the control group. Mean age of patients was 37 years for the Silvadene group (SD, 4.2) and 49 years for the control group (SD, 3.5). Patients in the Silvadene group had a mean length of surgery of 1.5 hours (SD, 0.7), and those in the control group had a mean length of 2.3 hours (SD, 0.5). Patients were operated on for acute diverticulitis (20%), inflammatory bowel disease (33%), cancer of the colon (35%), and miscellaneous other conditions (12%). A complete breakdown of indications for surgery and site of surgery for the two treatment groups is presented in Tables 12-1 and 12-2.

The incidence of wound complications in each group is listed in Table 12-3. SSIs were present in 3 of 64 patients (4.7%) in the Silvadene group, compared with 12 of 69 patients (17.4%) in the control group ($\chi^2 = 4.2$, degrees of freedom = 1, $p < 0.05$). There were no significant differences between the groups in the incidence of other types of wound-related complications.

Median time to wound healing was 2 weeks for Silvadene patients compared with 3 weeks for controls ($p < 0.001$).

Discussion

The rate of SSIs in the control group in the present study is comparable to that reported for colon surgery in the NNIS study on postoperative SSIs [1]. Thus, our controls can be considered a representative sample of patients undergoing this procedure, compared with other hospitals across the country. The distribution of our controls according to age, length of operation, and surgical wound class is also comparable to that of other NNIS hospitals, further demonstrating the generalizability of our results to other hospitals.

Table 12-1. Indications for surgery for the two treatment groups

Indication	Silvadene[1]		Controls[2]	
	Number	Percent	Number	Percent
Class II (Clean/Contaminated)				
Resolved diverticular disease	1	2	1	1
Inflammatory bowel disease	22	34	22	32
Cancer	27	42	19	28
Bleeding	1	2	2	3
Class III (Contaminated)				
Acute diverticulitis	10	16	21	30
Perforation	3	5	4	6
Total	64	100	69	100

[1] $n = 64$
[2] $n = 69$

Table 12-2. Site of surgery

Site	Silvadene[1]		Controls[2]	
	Number	Percent	Number	Percent
Sigmoid	36	56	35	51
Cecum	19	30	22	32
Transverse, other	2	3	3	4
Rectum	7	11	9	13
Total	64	100	69	100

[1] $n = 64$
[2] $n = 69$

Table 12-3.   Wound-related complications

Complication	Silvadene[1]		Controls[2]		Total[3]	
	Number	Percent	Number	Percent	Number	Percent
Surgical Site Infection	3	4.7	12	17.4	15	11.3
Erythema	1	1.6	2	2.9	3	2.3
Dehiscence or suture line disruption	3	4.7	4	5.8	7	5.3
Bleeding	7	10.9	6	8.7	13	9.8

[1]$n = 64$
[2]$n = 69$
[3]$n = 133$

The significantly reduced incidence of SSIs found in the Silvadene group—one-fourth that of controls—demonstrates the extreme efficacy of this preparation, when used prophylactically, in reducing the risk of SSIs. The fact that Silvadene was not effective in reducing the risk of other noninfectious wound-related complications indicates the specificity of its effect. The results of our study are entirely consistent with the known bactericidal activity and therapeutic efficacy of Silvadene, which has been previously demonstrated [10-17].

Silvadene is inexpensive and has no documented side effects. In contrast, SSIs raise hospital costs through potentially increased length of stay for initial hospitalization, use of antibiotics to treat infections, additional office visits, and potential readmissions.

In conclusion, prophylactic Silvadene is an effective means of preventing surgical site infections and promoting wound healing and should be routinely used in patients undergoing colon surgery. Based on results of the present study, investigation on the use of this preparation for other surgical procedures seems warranted.

II. Questions for Hypothesis Testing Applied to Example 2

A. Identify the Study Design

1. What are the groups to be compared?

This is a randomized clinical trial, so the groups to be compared are those to which subjects were randomized: Silvadene and control groups.

2. On what basis are the groups being compared?

    Groups are being compared on the basis of outcome. Five major outcomes are compared: development of surgical site infection, development of 3 other wound-related complications, and time to wound healing.

3. What is the study design?

    This is a randomized clinical trial because groups are "randomly" assigned to groups on the basis of the risk factor (treatment) and compared on the basis of outcome. We shall discuss whether treatment assignment was truly random in Question 4a.

B. Rule Out Bias

4. Was bias present in the design of the study?

    a) For cohort studies and clinical trials,

        (1)   Were all subjects taken from the same pool?

    Yes. All subjects were taken from one clinical practice.

        (2)   In assessing outcome, were observers blinded to the risk factor status of the subjects?

    Neither the investigators who assessed outcome nor the subjects were blind to the subjects' assigned treatment group. Because assessment of wound healing and presence of SSI do have subjective components, knowledge of a subject's treatment could have influenced the investigators' assessment of these outcomes.
        Blinding could have been accomplished by giving control subjects a placebo ointment identical in appearance to Silvadene. In this way both subjects and investigators could have been blinded to the assigned treatment.

        (3)   Was information on outcome obtained in a similar manner for all groups?

    Determination of the presence of SSIs, other wound complications, and time to wound healing was the same for all subjects, as described in the methods section.

(4) Was there differential attrition from the study groups?

No losses to follow-up were reported for either group.

(5) For clinical trials, was randomization used?

Treatment assignment was not truly random. Although the investigator did not choose the treatment a subject was to receive, treatment could be predicted based on the patient's medical record number. This allowed for the presence of bias on the part of the investigators enrolling the subject. If the investigators knew that a subject was to receive a treatment that they did not, for some reason, wish the subject to receive, they could choose not to enroll the subject in the study. The number of eligible subjects who did not enroll in the study and the reasons for nonenrollment were not reported, so it is impossible for us to assess whether bias was present in subject enrollment. Because of the method of randomization, we cannot rule out bias as a partial explanation for the study results.

b) Questions for case control studies do not apply.

C. Rule Out Confounding

5. Were the groups similar at baseline (e.g., by demographics or clinical characteristics)?

Although no formal statistical comparison was made, the description of the two groups at the beginning of the results section indicates several baseline differences between them. First, control group patients had a higher mean age than Silvadene patients. It is conceivable that age is a factor in wound healing or development of postoperative complications, and this treatment group imbalance should have been explored. Second, controls had a longer mean length of surgery than did Silvadene patients. Third, Table 12-1 shows that controls had a greater incidence of "contaminated" (Class III) indications for surgery than did the Silvadene group. This was accounted for by the higher incidence of acute diverticulitis in controls versus Silvadene patients (30% versus 16%, respectively). Silvadene patients had a correspondingly higher incidence of clean/contaminated (Class II) procedures, accounted for by the higher incidence of cancer in Silvadene patients compared with controls (42% versus 28%, respectively). We already know from the introduction that wound class and length of surgery are risk factors for SSIs. Therefore, confounding by these factors is a real possibility in this study.

a) If the groups were not similar, was the possibility of confounding controlled for in the study design (by restriction, stratification, or matching) or in the analysis (by stratification or regression analysis)?

Confounding was not controlled for in any of these ways. Therefore, differences in the study groups in outcome **may** be attributable to differences on baseline factors (i.e., confounding cannot be ruled out as an explanation for the group differences in outcome). In this study, the large baseline imbalances between treatment groups in age, length of surgery, and wound class make confounding highly likely.

D. Rule Out Chance

6. Was a statistically significant difference found between the groups?

   A statistically significant difference between the groups was present for two of the five outcomes measured: incidence of surgical site infections ($p < 0.05$) and median time to wound healing ($p < 0.001$).

   a) Questions for nonsignificant results do not apply.
   b) If the results were significant, did researchers account for multiple statistical tests in interpreting the p-value, and did they perform appropriate multiple comparisons procedures?

   Multiple testing was not taken into account in Example 2. A separate statistical test was performed for each of the five outcome measures. To control for this fact, one of two approaches could have been taken:

   • Choose one outcome in advance as the major outcome to submit to statistical testing. Treat group differences in other outcomes descriptively, and not as part of the major study hypothesis to be tested. Because one major outcome was not specified in advance in the present study, this option cannot be applied.
   • Adjust the acceptable p-value for significance. In this case, because five tests were done, including tests for the incidence of SSIs and 3 other complications and median time to wound healing, the p-value for significance would be $0.05/5$, or roughly 0.01. According to this criterion, only time to wound healing would be considered statistically significant in the present study.

Although 95% confidence intervals were not given for the outcome comparisons, the same approach could have been used to control for multiple comparisons. Therefore, instead of using a 95% confidence interval, the researchers should have used a 99% confidence interval.

E. Establish a Causal Association

7. Was there evidence of a causal association according to the following criteria?

   a) Strength

   The relative risk of SSI in controls compared with that in Silvadene patients was 17.4:4.7, or 3.7,[1] a moderate relative risk indicating a moderate negative relationship between the presence of Silvadene and the risk of SSI. Using the data from Table 12-3 and the formula for the 99% confidence limits (considering multiple comparisons) for relative risk given in Chap. 9, page 75 we calculate the 99% confidence interval to lie between −0.8 and 18.2.[2] The confidence interval lies primarily above 1, and is more compatible with a strong than a weak relationship. We can consider this evidence of the strength of the relationship between Silvadene and the incidence of SSIs. Since strength of relationship is generally expressed by degree of relative risk for dichotomous variables, we shall assess the results on time to wound healing in question 8, which deals with clinical significance.

   b) Consistency

   The authors state in the discussion that "the results of our study are entirely consistent with the known bactericidal activity of Silvadene, which h as been previously demonstrated." The results are also consistent with previous studies cited in the introduction, which show that prophylactic systemic antibiotics are effective in reducing SSIs in this type of surgery.

---

[1]We consider controls as the high risk (risk factor present) group and Silvadene as the risk factor absent group, since the risk of SSI for controls is greater. Alternatively we could consider the Silvadene group as having the risk factor present, and consider Silvadene a negative or protective risk factor in which the likelihood of disease is lower when the risk factor is present. In this case the relative risk would be the reciprocal of the one calculated above, or 0.27. This means that the risk of SSI's in the Silvadene group about one-fourth (27%) that of controls.
[2]Using a scientific calculator, we first calculate the natural log of the relative risk (3.7) as 1.31. The standard error is the square root of ($\frac{1}{12} - \frac{1}{69} + \frac{1}{3} - \frac{1}{64}$) or 0.62. The 99% confidence limits of the log of the relative risk are $1.31 \pm 2.58 \times 0.62$ or −0.29 to 2.91. The antilogs of these limits are $e^{0.29}$ to $e^{2.91}$ or −0.8 to 18.2.

c)   Biological plausibility

Bactericidal activity has been previously demonstrated for Silvadene, as stated in the introduction. Reduction of infection at any site would be in keeping with Silvadene's previously demonstrated bactericidal activity. In addition, evidence cited in the introduction that SSIs are susceptible to prophylactic antibiotics also adds biological plausibility to the current results.

d)   Temporal correctness

Treatment was initiated at the end of surgery, so the risk factor (treatment) does precede the outcomes (development of SSIs, other wound complications, or wound healing) in time.

e)   Specificity

The authors state that "the fact that Silvadene was not effective in reducing the risk of other noninfectious wound-related complications indicates the specificity of its effect."

F. Establish Clinical Significance

8.   Were the results clinically significant? What is the effect size and its 95% confidence interval?

There was almost a 13% lower incidence of SSIs in the Silvadene group compared to that in controls. Although no confidence interval was given for this difference, we could compute one by applying the formula for the confidence interval for a difference in proportions (Chap. 9, page 73) to the data in Table 10-3.* The resulting confidence interval is 0.02% to 25.6%. The confidence interval is compatible with both quite small and quite large differences in SSI rates. Thus, with regard to prevention of SSI's, we can only conclude that the clinical significance of Silvadene is uncertain but may be considerable.

The authors also did not report a confidence interval for the other major comparison in the study, difference in median time to wound healing, and this cannot be computed from the data

---

*The difference in proportions is 12.7%.

The standard error of this is $\sqrt{\dfrac{.174 \times .826}{69} + \dfrac{.047 \times .953}{64}}$ or 5%.

The 99% confidence interval is 12.7% $\pm$ 2.58 $\times$ 5% or 12.7% $\pm$ 12.9% or -0.2% to 25.6%.

available. However, a 1-week reduction in this time in the Silvadene group is of potential clinical significance.

The authors further discuss the clinical significance of the study in the discussion section of the paper: "Silvadene is inexpensive and has no documented side effects. In contrast, SSIs raise hospital costs through potentially increased length of stay for initial hospitalization, use of antibiotics to treat infections, additional office visits, and potential readmissions."

G. Summary of Analysis.   Although this study satisfied most of the criteria for a causal association between use of Silvadene and decreased incidence of SSI or improved wound healing, and has potential clinical significance, there are several flaws in the design and the analysis that limit or altogether negate the conclusions. The presence of possible bias in the selection of subjects and the high likelihood of confounding by the more favorable distribution of patients in the treatment group according to known risk factors for SSI most likely exaggerate any effect of Silvadene in reducing SSIs. More carefully designed studies are needed to determine the effectiveness of Silvadene in colon surgery.

EXAMPLE 3

A Cross-Sectional Cohort Study

The Effect of Sex on Resident Performance on the
Surgical Oral Examination
*Joan L. Germain, MD, George P. Silas, PhD, and Pamela T.
Sullivan, PhD*

Abstract

This study was undertaken to determine if extraneous characteristics such as sex influence performance on the structured surgical oral examination. Scores on the oral examination required for licensure in the state of Avalon were reviewed for all examinees during 1991 and 1992 from records of the state Board of Medical Examiners. Exams were graded on a six-point scale from 1 (definite failure) to 6 (superlative pass).

A total of 795 residents took the oral examination during the study period. Information on sex of the residents was unavailable for 39 examinees. Scores were significantly higher for men than for women with a median score of 4.5 for men and 3.5 for women ($p < 0.0001$). There was also a significantly higher proportion of failures among women (26%) compared with men (12%) ($p < 0.05$).

We conclude that sex has a marked effect on performance on the oral surgical examination and that this issue should be explored in future controlled studies.

Introduction

The oral examination is one of the major components of certification in surgery following the completion of residency. The validity and reliability of this test have been subject to criticism, primarily the argument that it does not measure what it purports to measure (i.e., knowledge) [20–23]. In fact, a recent study has shown that nonverbal factors such as style of presentation and mode of dress, in addition to quality of responses, can markedly affect scores of students, even by experienced raters [24].

It is possible that other extraneous factors, particularly the sex of the examinee, may also have an effect on rating of student performance on the oral examination. This study was designed to investigate this hypothesis.

Methods

All applicants for a license to practice medicine in the state of Avalon are required to pass a structured oral examination for licensure. The records of the Avalon Board of Examiners for 1991 and 1992 were reviewed to determine the scores and sex of all oral examinees. Names were not recorded, to preserve the confidentiality of scores. The structured oral examination is graded on a six-point scale defined in Table 12-4. The distribution of test socres for men and women was compared using the Mann-Whitney rank sum test [25]. The proportion of passes in the two groups was compared using the chi-square test, with Yates' correction for continuity [26].

Results

A total of 795 residents took the oral examination during the study period. The examinee's sex could not be determined for 39 examinees, who were eliminated from the study. Of the 756 remaining examinees, 529 were men (70%), and 227 were women (30%).

Table 12-4. Scoring for oral examination

1	Definite failure
2	Marginal failure
3	Weak pass
4	Good pass
5	Strong pass
6	Superlative pass

Distribution of test scores for men and women is given in Table 12-5. The median score for men was 4.5; for women, 3.5. The difference in median scores was statistically significant according to the rank sum test ($p < 0.0001$). There was also a significantly higher proportion of failures among female examinees (59 of 227, or 26%) compared with male examinees (64 of 529, or 12%) ($\chi^2 = 4.35$, degrees of freedom = 1, $p < 0.05$).

Discussion

Our study is among the first to look at the effect of the examinee's sex on oral exam performance. We found that male residents scored significantly higher than female residents did.

Let us postulate the reasons for the large and consistent differences in scoring between men and women. It seems highly unlikely that the

Table 12-5. Distribution of oral exam scores for men and women

		Men		Women	
	Score	Number	Percent	Number	Percent
Fail	1	21	4	39	17
	2	43	8	20	9
Pass	3	32	6	57	25
	4	120	23	68	30
	5	185	35	27	12
	6	128	24	16	7
Total		529	100	227	100

quality of female residents in surgical programs is inferior to that of male residents. Because it has been previously shown that extraneous factors such as presentation style and dress can affect ratings on the oral examination [24], it is entirely possible that examinee sex is also a factor in rating and that examiners are biased against female residents. The results of the present study have confirmed this hypothesis, although the previous study did not.

If sex bias is present on the surgical oral examination, it may be present in all aspects of residents' performance rating during training, as well as in career progress after residency. Further studies are needed to determine to what extent gender bias pervades other aspects of the medical profession during and beyond the training period. At the very least, the oral examination and other forms of resident evaluation should be fully reexamined with respect to fairness. Perhaps we need more objective means of measuring performance in medicine.

We could not examine the effect of other extraneous factors in the present study because only final scores were recorded. No transcripts or videotapes of actual examinations were available to allow study of such factors as dress or presentation style. More controlled studies are needed to determine the extent of the influence of sex on performance and its interaction with these other factors.

III. Questions for Hypothesis Testing Applied to Example 3

A. Identify the Study Design

1. What are the groups to be compared?

   Male and female residents are being compared.

2. On what basis are the groups being compared?

   Scores on the oral examination—the outcome—is the basis.

3. What is the study design?

   Groups were determined on the basis of the risk factor (sex) and compared on the outcome (scores), so the study is a cohort study. It is also cross-sectional, because risk factor and outcome were determined at the same time.

B. Rule Out Bias

4. Was bias present in the design of the study?

    a) For cohort studies and clinical trials,

        (1) Were all subjects taken from the same pool?

Yes. All subjects were identified from records of the Avalon Board of Examiners, as described in the methods section.

        (2) In assessing outcome, were observers blinded to the risk factor status of the subjects?

Sex and oral exam scores were determined at the same time, and there is no indication that observers were blinded to the subject's sex when recording exam scores. Therefore, bias could be present in the recording of data.

        (3) Was information on outcome obtained in a similar manner for all groups?

Oral exam performance (outcome) was determined in a similar manner for both groups by obtaining scores from records of the Avalon Board of Examiners.

        (4) Was there differential attrition from the study groups?

Although this is a cross-sectional study with no follow-up, attrition could be considered for the two groups to have occurred between the time the exam was taken and the time scores were recorded, i.e., nonrecording of scores. In the case of the oral exam, this possibility is extremely unlikely, and so we can discount differential attrition as a source of bias in this study. Failure to take the exam would not be considered attrition in a cross-sectional study as it would in a prospective cohort study. However, it should be kept in mind that the study population represents only surgical residents who complete the oral exam and not all surgical residents.

(5)   For clinical trials, was randomization used?

Not applicable

b)   Questions for case control studies do not apply.

C. Rule Out Confounding

5.   Were the groups similar at baseline (e.g., by demographics or clinical characteristics)?

Similarity of the men and women on other factors was not determined. Because several factors have been cited by the authors as contributing to oral exam scores (quality of content, style of presentation, and dress), failure to examine these factors and determine that the groups were comparable on them leads to the possibility of confounding.

a)   If the groups were not similar, was the possibility of confounding controlled for in the study design (by restriction, stratification, or matching) or in the analysis (by stratification or regression analysis)?

No information was recorded on possible confounding factors, so confounding could not be controlled for in the analysis. Likewise, it was not controlled for in the study design, for example, by choosing only exams of "good quality" (restriction).

D. Rule Out Chance

6.   Was a statistically significant difference found between the groups?

Yes. There was significant difference between the groups in median scores and in the proportion of passes.

a)   Questions for nonsignificant results do not apply.
b)   If the results were significant, did researchers account for multiple statistical tests in interpreting the *p*-value, and did they perform appropriate multiple comparisons procedures?

A statistical test was done for each of the two outcomes compared. The authors did not take this into account. Use of a Bonferroni adjustment would amount to dividing the usual significance criterion 0.05 by the number of tests performed (two) to arrive at a probability of less than 0.025 as a criterion for statistical significance. By this criterion, only differences in median scores were significant.

E. Establish a Causal Association

7. Was there evidence of a causal association according to the following criteria?

   a) Strength

   The relative risk of failure in women versus men is 2.2 (see calculation of the relative risk and its 95% confidence interval in Chapter 9). The 95% confidence interval is 1.6 to 2.9, which is compatible with a weak association between the risk factor and outcome. We cannot consider that the criterion of strength has been met.

   b) Consistency

   The results were inconsistent with the one study [24] that looked at sex and oral exam scores. That previous study had found that examinee sex had no effect on oral exam scores. The reasons for this lack of consistency may be the fact that the extraneous factors controlled for in the former study were not controlled for in the latter study.

   c) Biological plausibility

   The authors acknowledge that the results are not biologically plausible by discounting the explanation that female residents are inferior in performance to men. They postulate instead the social factor of sex bias on the part of the examiner to explain the results.

   d) Temporal correctness

   Because gender is an unchanging characteristic determined at conception, we can conclude that the association between sex and oral exam performance is temporally correct. Sex is an appropriate risk factor for study with a cross-sectional study design because it allows us to make the assumption of temporal correctness.

e) Specificity

The fact that gender is related to a variety of outcomes and that other factors have been shown to be related to oral exam performance indicates a lack of specificity of the association between sex and oral exam performance. As previously stated, however, this lack of specificity should not in itself be considered evidence against a causal association.

F. Establish Clinical Significance

8. Were the results clinically significant? What is the effect size and its 95% confidence interval?

The effect size expressed as a difference in failure rates between male and female residents is 14%. By the methods in Chap. 9, the 95% confidence interval for this difference is approximately 8% to 20%. This would be considered clinically significant to a surgical educator or to a surgical resident. Moreover, even though a confidence interval was not computed, the full point difference in median scores for men and women (4.5 versus 3.5) would also be considered clinically significant because the possible range of scores was only 5 points.

The authors further indicate the clinical significance of their findings in the following statement in the discussion: "If sex-bias is present on the oral examination, it may be present in all aspects of residents' performance rating during training, as well as in career progress after residency. . . . At the very least, the oral examination and other forms of resident evaluation should be fully reexamined with respect to fairness."

G. Summary of Analysis.   Despite the presence of strong, statistically and clinically significant results for median score, there was a large potential for confounding in this study. Cross-sectional cohort studies of this nature clearly cannot adequately control for important confounding of nonverbal factors, which have been shown to strongly influence performance. Furthermore, failure to satisfy most of the criteria for a causal association weakens the results of the present study. Although the study holds potential clinical importance to educators and residents, the reader should be skeptical about the results. The conclusion of the authors that sex bias exists in the oral examination is not warranted.

EXAMPLE 4

A Case Control Study

Job Exposure and Tuberculin Test Reactivity in
Hospital Workers
*Frederick L. Posner, MD, Sarah M. Garber, MD, and David J.
Garber, MD*

Abstract

This study examines the effect of type of service on positive purified
protein derivative (PPD) rates in hospital workers at the Bay Shore
Medical Center (BMC) in Bay Shore, Long Island. Employees who
tested positive on the PPD test for tuberculosis (TB) exposure (cases)
were compared with a group of employees who tested negative (controls). The groups differed in the representation from various clinical
and nonclinical services at the hospital ($\chi^2 = 56.2$, degrees of freedom $= 7$, $p < 0.0001$). As expected, the cases had a higher proportion of employees from both Infectious Disease and Pulmonary Services (34% and 25%, respectively) compared with the controls (15%
and 11%, respectively). However, the increased proportion of employees from Administrative Services in the cases (13%) compared
with controls (3%) and a decreased proportion of employees from the
Surgical Service in cases (4%) compared with controls (21%) was surprising. There were no significant differences between cases and controls in the proportion of employees from other services.

   This study identifies a new, previously unidentified group of hospital workers at risk of TB infection. Environmental and other factors that
contribute to increased risk in this group need to be investigated
through further research.

Introduction

The risk of TB exposure among health care workers has been known
for decades [27–28]. In 1953 Mikol examined the differential risk of
tuberculosis among various types of hospital workers [29]. At highest
risk were nurses; at intermediate risk were physicians, laboratory and
diagnostic technicians, social workers, occupational therapists, phar-
macists, dietary and laundry personnel who had direct patient contact;

and at lowest risk were employees without direct patient contact (office workers, dietary workers without direct patient contact, maintenance personnel).

In recent years, there has been an apparent increase in the incidence of tuberculosis exposure and disease in health care workers [30–32]. Of particular concern are reports of multiple-drug–resistant TB (MDR-TB), which is more difficult to diagnose and carries a higher morbidity and mortality than other forms of TB [27]. However, since the recognition of an upswing in prevalence of TB, few studies have examined the risk among various types of health care workers, particularly hospital workers. Studies that do exist compare the proportions of exposed workers across different hospitals or populations. Most studies report positive PPD rates or postexposure conversion rates rather than actual cases. Annual baseline conversion rate estimates in the last decade range from 0.2% to 44% [27–33]. Postexposure conversion rates range from 4% to 77% [27].

In a decade of increasing incidence of tuberculosis among the patient population, no recent studies have examined the differential risk of tuberculosis exposure among hospital workers in one institution. The aim of the present study is to compare the degree of risk of TB exposure among various types of workers at the same hospital.

Methods

Cases of positive PPD tests, indicating previous exposure to the tuberculin bacillus, were identified from the Employee Health Service of Bay Shore Medical Center (BMC) in Bay Shore, Long Island. All employees who had tested positive at some time in the past were included in this group. In addition, a sample of employees was chosen for interview and PPD testing from the evening shift (11 PM to 7 AM). The evening shift was selected because the slowdown in work schedules during these hours facilitated screening and interviewing. Employees who tested positive as a result of the screening were classified as cases and added to the list with those previously found. All employees who tested negative were classified as controls.

Service of employment and other demographics were determined for cases from Personnel Service records at the time the TB test was first positive, as indicated in the Employee Health records. Current type of service for controls was also determined from Personnel records. Demographic information for controls was likewise obtained from Personnel records.

The chi-square test was used to analyze the difference among cases and controls in the proportion of employees from various hospital services. Adjusted standardized deviates were computed to determine which services were differently distributed among cases and controls [34]. Statistical significance for various services was determined by comparing their standardized deviates to a normal distribution. A significance level of 0.01 was used instead of 0.05, to adjust for the problem of multiple comparisons [35–38].

Results

Table 12-6 compares cases and controls on various demographic characteristics. Cases and controls were similar in all characteristics.

Table 12-7 shows the distribution by service for cases and controls. The column labeled "significance" represents significance of the standardized deviates. There was a significant overall difference among cases and controls in the distribution of employees by service. ($\chi^2 = 56.2$, degrees of freedom $= 7$, $p < 0.0001$). Infectious Disease Service and Pulmonary Service had significantly higher representation among the cases than among controls (34% and 25%, respectively, among cases, compared with 15% and 11%, respectively, among controls) ($p = <0.0001$ and $p < 0.001$, respectively). Administrative Services also had a higher representation among the cases (13%) than among controls (3%) ($p < 0.0005$). The Surgical Service had a significantly lower representation among the cases than controls (4% versus 21%) ($p < 0.0005$). Other services had no significant difference among the cases and controls.

Table 12-6.   Demographic characteristics of cases and controls

	Mean ($\pm$ Standard deviation)	
Variable	Cases[1]	Controls[2]
Years in current service	8.6 (4.3)	7.2 (4.7)
Years at BMC	10.2 (5.5)	8.9 (5.1)
Age	43 (6.3)	41 (5.9)
Percent male	42	45

[1] $n = 76$
[2] $n = 334$

Table 12-7.   Service representation in cases and controls

| Service | TB Test Results | | | | |
| | Cases | | Controls | | |
	Number	Percent	Number	Percent	Significance (p)
Infectious Disease	26	34	50	15	<0.0001
Pulmonary	19	25	35	11	<0.001
Cardiac	7	9	60	18	NS
Surgical	3	4	70	21	<0.0005
Endocrine	4	5	22	7	NS
Administrative	10	13	10	3	<0.0005
Maintenance	3	4	32	10	NS
Dietary	4	5	55	17	NS
Total	76	100	334	100	

Discussion

We expected the predominance of employees from the Infectious Disease Service and Pulmonary Service among the cases. It is well established that employees who come in direct contact with tuberculosis patients are at higher risk of TB exposure [27–32, 39–43].

We cannot explain, however, the surprising findings of a higher proportion of administrative workers among cases compared with controls and the lower proportion of employees on the Surgical Service. Administrative employees have much less frequent contact with patients than do employees on clinical services. Although the difference in representation of administrative workers in cases and controls is not as great as it is for the Infectious Disease Service and Pulmonary Service, it is substantial (13% of cases were from Administrative Services, compared with only 3% of controls).

It is possible that some administrative employees such as nursing supervisors had previous experience on clinical services and previous exposure to TB. The TB test measures only past exposure at some point and does not become negative once exposure is no longer present. However, we feel this could explain only a small proportion of cases and could not account for the significant difference found.

We conclude that hospital administrative employees constitute a potentially high-risk group for TB infection. The particular types of administrative occupations at increased risk and the specific sources of exposure need to be delineated in future studies.

IV. Questions for Hypothesis Testing Applied to Example 4

A. Identify the Study Design

1. What are the groups to be compared?

   Employees who had a positive PPD test (cases) are compared with those who had a negative test (controls).

2. On what basis are the groups being compared?

   Groups are compared on the basis of the risk factor (i.e., type of service).

3. What is the study design?

   This is a case control study, because groups are defined on the basis of the outcome and compared on the basis of risk factor status.

B. Rule Out Bias

4. Was bias present in the design of the study?

   a) Questions for cohort studies and clinical trials do not apply.

   b) For case control studies,

   (1) Were all subjects taken from the same population?

   No. Cases and controls were not taken from the same population. Cases were taken from the population of *all* employees. Workers on the night or day shift could become cases. Controls were chosen from workers on the evening shift only.

   (2) Were controls chosen from an appropriate group?

   The appropriateness of the control group is in question here. Controls may represent a biased sample of all workers. They were chosen from the evening shift, which is likely to have a different distribution of workers by service from the day shift. Specifically, there are likely to be fewer administrative employees on the night shift than on the day shift because they do not generally provide 24-hour services. This bias in the selection of controls could very likely affect the comparison of cases and controls in distribution by service. If the proportion of administrative workers were artificially low in the controls, this would make the proportion of administrative workers in the cases appear artificially high by comparison. Conversely, because nighttime employees would consist mainly of the surgical and medical staff, the proportion of Surgical Service controls would be artificially high, and the proportion of Surgical Service cases would be artificially low by comparison. By the same reasoning, it is entirely possible that the magnitude of difference between cases and controls in the proportion from the Pulmonary Service or Infectious Disease Service is artificially high. One could postulate that fewer consults are done at night and that there would be fewer employees, especially physicians, on largely consultative services like Infectious Disease or Pulmonary. In fact, because of the large potential for bias in this study, no estimate of the difference between cases and controls on any service can be considered valid.

(3)   Were multiple control groups chosen?

No. Selection of additional control groups could have elucidated the bias present in the chosen control group.

(4)   Were deceased cases included?

Yes. Although few deaths would be expected in a population likely to receive good medical treatment, all cases were identified from Employee Health Service records.

(5)   Were observers blinded to the disease status of subjects in assessing risk factor status, or did they have information on risk factor status before knowledge of outcome?

It cannot be determined whether observers were blinded when assessing risk factor status, so bias is possible here.

(6)   Was information on risk factor status obtained in a similar manner for cases and controls?

The service of cases and controls was determined from the same source: Personnel records. However, for cases this represented past service at the time of TB test positivity, and for controls it represented current service. There are two potential sources of misclassification bias here. First, past Personnel records may not be as accurate as current ones, so determination of type of service may be more accurate for controls than for cases. Although it seems unlikely that this is the case, and although it is difficult to imagine how this could affect distribution by service, this possibility cannot be ruled out. Second, because cases represent past service and controls represent current service at the time of the study, any shifts in the distribution of employees by service over time could contribute to the differences in service for cases and controls. An alternative would have been to determine the current service of cases as well. Unfortunately, this could introduce a different source of bias, because the choice of job service may have been guided by the presence of past TB test positivity. Positive cases may not have been allowed to remain in jobs involving direct patient contact and might have been switched to administrative or nonclinical services, which could account for a preponderance of administrative employees in cases compared with controls. With this in mind, the type of determination used in this study (past service at the time of test positivity) seems to carry the lowest potential for bias.

A better alternative for choice of controls would have been matching. This method controls for potential differences in cases and controls that might affect their risk factor status. In the present study, controls could have been matched with cases on year of employment. For each case, one or more controls could have been selected whose service of employment was determined for a time period including the date of TB test positivity.

C. Rule Out Confounding

5. Were the groups similar at baseline (e.g., by demographics or clinical characteristics)?

    Cases and controls were similar on all demographic variables reported. However, because job service was determined historically for cases and currently for controls, the two groups may have been dissimilar on length of time on their current service.

    a) If the groups were not similar, was the possibility of confounding controlled for in the study design (by restriction, stratification, or matching) or in the analysis (by stratification or multivariate analysis)?

    Matching should have been used in this case.

D. Rule Out Chance

6. Was a statistically significant difference found between the groups?

    Yes. There were significant differences between cases and controls.

    a) Questions for nonsignificant results do not apply.

    b) If the results were significant, did researchers account for multiple statistical tests in interpreting the *p*-value, and did they perform appropriate multiple comparisons procedures?

    The authors state in the methods section that "a significance level of 0.01 was used instead of 0.05 to adjust for the problem of multiple comparisons." This is a Bonferroni correction, as described in Chapter 6, page 51.

E. Establish a Causal Association

7. Was there evidence of a causal association according to the following criteria?

    a) Strength

    The odds ratio is the appropriate estimate of effect size for this study because it is a case control study. Odds ratios and 99% confidence intervals allowing for multiple comparisons can be calculated for the different services by applying the methods in Chap. 9 to Table 12-7. For example, we could set up a table like the following to estimate the relative risk of being on an administrative service for cases versus controls:

Administrative Services	Group	
	Cases	Controls
Present	10	10
Absent	66	324

    We calculate the odds ratio as $\dfrac{(10 \times 324)}{(66 \times 10)}$, or 4.9. The log of the odds ratio is 1.59, with a standard error of 0.47 and a 99% confidence interval of 0.38 to 2.80. The confidence interval for the odds ratio is thus 1.5 to 16.3.

Considering that the 99% confidence interval lies completely above 1 and is more consistent with a strong than a weak association between Administrative Services and TB exposure (more of the interval lies above 4 than below 4), we could conclude that the present results for administrative service fulfills the causal criterion of strength. We have shown, however, that because of the potential for large bias in this study, the criterion of strength is in doubt.

Using the same methods, we calculate the odds ratios and 99% confidence intervals for the other services as follows:

Service	Odds Ratio	99% Confidence Interval
Infectious Disease	3.0	1.4 to 6.5
Pulmonary	2.9	1.3 to 6.5
Surgical	0.2	0.03 to 0.7

The confidence intervals for these odds ratios are consistent with a weak-to-strong relationship between Pulmonary Service or Infectious Disease Service and TB exposure and a weak negative association of Surgical Service. We might not consider this sufficient evidence of strength of association for these services, since more of their confidence intervals lie below than above 4.

b) Consistency

According to the authors, the results are not consistent with other studies, which failed to show an excess risk associated with administrative services or a decreased risk with surgical services. The results are consistent with the findings from other studies of an increased risk for pulmonary and infectious disease workers, according to the discussion section.

c) Biological plausibility

The authors do not postulate any reasons why infectious exposure should be increased for Administrative Services, and they recommend further studies to delineate sources of exposure that would make the present results biologically plausible. We therefore cannot consider that the criterion of biological plausibility has been met.

d) Temporal correctness

Because type of service was determined at the same time as disease status for both cases and controls, we can assume that the risk factor (type of service) preceded the outcome. Furthermore, it is unlikely that PPD positivity went undetected for long in a hospital employee population that is presumably regularly screened. Therefore, it is safe to assume that the service on which a case worked at the time of his or her positive PPD test was the service on which his or her exposure occurred. We can conclude that the risk factor preceded the outcome and that the criterion of temporal correctness has been met.

e) Specificity

Specificity was not investigated in the present study and cannot be determined from the literature review the authors provide.

F. Establish Clinical Significance

8.   Were the results clinically significant?

The differences in the proportion of employees on the Infectious Disease Services, Pulmonary Services, and Administrative Services for cases vs. controls range from 10% to 19%. We can calculate the 99% confidence intervals (allowing for multiple comparisons) for these differences according to the methods given in Chap. 9 for the confidence interval of a difference in two proportions.

Service	Difference	99% Confidence Interval
Administrative	0.10	0 to 0.20
Infectious Disease	0.19	0.04 to 0.34
Pulmonary	0.14	0.01 to 0.27
Surgical	−0.17	−0.25 to −0.09

These intervals are compatible with clinically relevant differences from an occupational health viewpoint. The authors allude to the clinical significance of the results in the following statement from the discussion section: "We conclude that hospital administrative employees constitute a potentially high-risk group for TB infection."

G. Summary of Analysis.   Although statistically and clinically significant differences were found in the study, the large potential for bias in the selection of cases and controls invalidates the conclusion that administrative employees are at increased risk for tuberculosis exposure. Although the increased risk of PPD positivity on Pulmonary or Infectious Disease Services has been validated in previous studies, we cannot make estimates from the present study of the magnitude of risk associated with any of the services because of the serious potential for selection bias. It is, in fact, possible that the risk for the Pulmonary or Infectious Disease Services might have been lower had bias been eliminated. It is also possible that the absence of risk found for other services was erroneous. Furthermore, besides the criterion of strength, which is itself in doubt, there is little evidence for a causal association between Administrative Services and TB exposure in this study.

EXAMPLE 5

A Cross-Sectional Cohort Study

The Relationship of Job Stress and Blood Pressure Levels
George T. Caldwell, MD, and Dale C. Farber, PhD

Abstract

This study was designed to investigate the relationship between job stress level and blood pressure. A sample of subjects was chosen from three occupational groups: air traffic controllers (ATCs), physical therapists (PTs), and librarians (LIBs). Subjects were chosen from participants in the annual national meetings of the professional organizations for these occupations. All respondents were administered the Minnesota Stress Measurement Scale (MSMS). In addition, brief clinical examinations were given by trained nurses to measure height, weight, blood pressure, heart rate, and pulse rate. A self-administered questionnaire on demographic characteristics, previous health history, current health problems, and diet was also given.

A total of 159 subjects were surveyed: 42 air traffic controllers, 58 physical therapists, and 59 librarians. The groups were comparable on all demographic characteristics and aspects of medical history except for smoking history. The ATC group had a significantly higher mean systolic blood pressure (154) than either the PT group (133) or the LIB group (129)($p < 0.0001$). There were no differences in diastolic blood pressure. The ATC group also had a significantly higher mean stress level (120), as measured by the MSMS, than either the PT group (110) or the LIB group (105) ($p < 0.05$). Stress level and systolic blood pressure were highly correlated ($r = 0.79$) ($p < 0.0001$).

Introduction

Occupational exposure to environmental hazards and its effect on both chronic and acute disease are the cornerstone of modern epidemiology. But the relationship of illness to occupation is not due solely to the presence of environmental hazards. Several authors have shown occupational differences in the incidence of coronary heart disease (CHD) and mortality from CHD [44–46]. The link between occupation and CHD may be through an altering of physiologic risk factors for disease rather than from environmental exposure. There is a growing body of literature on occupational differences in the prevalence of established risk factors for ischemic heart disease including blood pressure, serum lipid levels, fibrinogen, and plasma viscosity levels [47–55]. Differences have also been found to extend to different work sites within the same occupation [56] and length of service [57]. Factors such as activity level, physical demands, and stress level have been postulated as causes for these differences. Stress has been shown to mediate the relationship of occupation to other health outcomes such as suicide.

In order to better understand the effects of occupation on CHD, this study investigated the relationship between one occupational characteristic—job stress level—and one physiologic risk factor—blood pressure.

Methods

A sample of subjects was chosen from three occupational groups. The groups—air traffic controllers, physical therapists, and librarians—were chosen because they represent professions likely to vary in overall job stress. Subjects were chosen from participants in the annual national meetings of three professional organizations: the Society of Air Traffic Controllers, the American Society of Physical Therapists, and the National Association of Librarians. All respondents were administered the MSMS, a standardized series of questions that measures stress on a scale of 1 to 130. In addition, a brief clinical examination was given to all subjects by trained nurses to measure height, weight, blood pressure, heart rate, and pulse rate. A self-administered questionnaire on demographic characteristics, previous health history, current health problems, and diet was also given.

Differences among the three professional groups in age, height, weight, pulse, blood pressure, and MSMS scores were tested with the analysis of variance [58]. Group differences on all other variables were tested with the Pearson chi-square test. Correlation in MSMS score and blood pressure was determined using the Pearson correlation coefficient (r).

Results

A total of 159 subjects were surveyed: 42 ATCs, 58 PTs, and 59 LIBs. There was no significant difference in mean age for the three occupational groups (32, 38, and 35 years of age, respectively). Other demographic characteristics and medical history of subjects in the three groups are given in Table 12-8. Clinical measurements are given in Table 12-9.

The groups were comparable on demographic characteristics and medical history. The only exception was smoking history. There was a significantly higher proportion of smokers in the ATC group than in the other groups ($\chi^2 = 6.45$, degrees of freedom = 2, $p = 0.039$). As shown in Table 12-9, the three groups were comparable on clinical characteristics other than blood pressure and MSMS scores. However, there were significant differences in the latter two characteristics. The ATC group had a significantly higher mean systolic blood pressure (SBP) (154) than either the PT group (133) or the LIB group

Table 12-8. Characteristics of the three occupational groups

		Occupational group					
		ATC[1]		PT[2]		LIB[3]	
Demographics	Category	Number	Percent	Number	Percent	Number	Percent
Race	White	33	79	50	86	55	93
	Black	8	19	6	10	3	5
	Other	1	2	2	3	1	2
Sex	Male	19	45	22	38	30	51
Chronic disease	Present	5	12	10	17	16	27
Smoking[4]	Present	11	26	7	12	6	10

[1] $n = 42$
[2] $n = 58$
[3] $n = 59$
[4] $p < 0.05$

Table 12-9. Clinical characteristics of the three treatment groups

| | Occupational group | | | | | |
| | ATC[1] | | PT[2] | | LIB[3] | |
Clinical Characteristics	Mean	SD	Mean	SD	Mean	SD
Height	69	29.2	70	39.6	67	24.6
Weight	150	43.4	160	67.0	140	59.1
BP (systolic)[4]	154	28.24	133	27.36	129	26.09
BP (diastolic)	122	55.5	119	76.6	115	88.9
Pulse	77	35.6	72	37.3	74	27.7
MSMS score[5]	120	43.4	110	26.7	105	36.1

[1]$n = 42$
[2]$n = 58$
[3]$n = 59$
[4]$p < 0.0005$
[5]$p < 0.05$

(129) (F = 11.3, degrees of freedom = 2, 156, $p < 0.0001$). There was no significant difference in diastolic blood pressure (DBP).

The ATC group also had a significantly higher mean stress level (120) as measured by the MSMS score than either the PT group (110) or the LIB group (105) (F = 5.92, degrees of freedom = 1,86, $p < 0.05$). MSMS and SBP were highly correlated ($r = 0.79$) ($p < 0.0001$). The correlation with DBP was weaker ($r = 0.5$) and nonsignificant ($p > 0.2$).

Discussion

The three occupational groups in our study were chosen because they were assumed to differ in overall level of occupational stress. The significant difference among the three groups in MSMS scores validated this assumption. The ATC group had the highest stress levels, the LIB group had the lowest, and the PT group had intermediate levels.

There were also strong, statistically significant differences among the three occupational groups in SBP, and a high correlation between stress and SBP. This indicates that the relationship we found between occupation and SBP is likely mediated by the differential stress levels in the three occupational groups.

We have demonstrated a clearly defined relationship between occupation and a risk factor (SBP) for one disease, CHD. Other studies are needed to determine whether occupation is related to other physiologic risk factors for CHD or other chronic diseases.

V. Questions for Hypothesis Testing Applied to Example 5

A. Identify the Study Design

1.   What are the groups to be compared?

     Air traffic controllers, physical therapists, and librarians were compared.

2.   On what basis are the groups being compared?

     The groups are compared on blood pressure and stress score (i.e., on outcome).

3.   What is the study design?

     This is a cohort study because groups are determined on the basis of the risk factor (occupation) and compared on outcome status (blood pressure and stress score). Because risk factor and outcome status are ascertained at the same time, the study is cross-sectional.

B. Rule Out Bias

4.   Was bias present in the design of the study?

     a)   For cohort studies and clinical trials,

            (1)   Were all subjects taken from the same pool?

     Subjects were taken from three different pools—professional society meetings of three groups. In addition, subjects were volunteers. People who attend society meetings and volunteer for a study on blood pressure are likely to be a select group with different characteristics from the general population of ATCs, PTs, and LIBs. Furthermore, factors that predispose ATCs to attend meetings may be different than those that predispose PTs or LIBs, so that these groups may be nonrepresentative of their professions in a different way. In addition, it is possible that screening on clinical characteristics such as blood pressure, height, and weight was performed to determine job eligibility for ATCs and possibly PIs as well. For these reasons, selection bias is highly likely.

(2)   In assessing outcome, were observers blinded to the risk factor status of the subjects?

Observers were not blinded when assessing outcome. Therefore, observer bias may be present in the study.

(3)   Was information on outcome obtained in a similar manner for all groups?

Yes. Information was obtained in a similar manner for all groups, by interview, physical examination, and self-administered questionnaire.

(4)   Was there differential attrition from the study?

Since this was a cross-sectional study, there was no attrition from any group.

(5)   For clinical trials was randomization used? Does not apply.

b)   Questions for case control studies do not apply.

C. Rule Out Confounding

5.   Were the groups similar at baseline (e.g., by demographics or clinical characteristics)?

Table 12-8 showed a significant difference in the groups in the presence of smokers ($p = 0.039$). Therefore, groups were not similar on a factor known to be associated with blood pressure. Because of the potential for selection bias discussed in 4 *a*), it is also likely that groups may differ at baseline on other clinical characteristics that were not recorded.

a)   If the groups were not similar, was the possibility of confounding controlled for in the study design (by restriction, stratification, or matching) or in the analysis (by stratification or regression analysis)?

No effort was made to control for the confounding effects of smoking in this study. Because the percentage of smokers in the

ATC group was more than twice that of the other two groups, and because smoking increases blood pressure, this factor could account in a large part for the increased blood pressure of the ATC group.

D. Rule Out Chance

6. Was a statistically significant difference found between the groups?

There was a statistically significant difference among the groups in SBP and stress levels, as measured by the MSMS score. However, after adjusting for multiple comparisons, differences in stress scores would not be significant.

a) If results were not significant.

(1) Was the sample size adequate to detect a difference of clinical interest?

Some statement of the power of the study to detect clinically significant differences among groups would be helpful in this study, because stress score differences among groups were close to significance after adjusting for multiple comparisons (see 6b) and sample sizes were relatively small, indicating that inadequate power is a potential concern.

(2) Could bias or confounding be masking real differences between groups?

Although bias is possible in the method of selection of study subjects, it is difficult to postulate how this would affect the results. Although observers did know the risk factor (group) status of subjects they were measuring, the clinical characteristics measured—height, weight, blood pressure—are objective ones, not likely to be subject to observer bias. On the other hand, recall bias may be present in the subjects' self-report questionnaire, especially if they were told the purpose of the study.

The proportion of smokers was highest in the ATC group (26% versus 12% and 10% in the other groups) and blood pressure was highest for the ATC group. Therefore, confounding would tend to accentuate rather than mask group differences.

b) If the results were significant, did researchers account for multiple statistical tests in interpreting the *p*-value,

and did they perform appropriate multiple comparisons procedures?

Statistical tests were performed for several comparisons, as reported in Tables 12-8 and 12-9. When the correlation between
stress and blood pressure was added, 11 tests were performed
altogether. Therefore, applying a Bonferroni correction to the p-
value indicates that only p-values of $0.05 \div 11$, or 0.0045, are statistically significant. By this criterion, only group differences in
mean SBP and the correlation between MSMS and SBP were
statistically significant.

An alternative to the Bonferroni adjustment would have been
to perform statistical tests only on the primary outcomes (i.e.,
group differences in mean SBP and mean MSMS scores and the
correlation between SBP and MSMS). Other comparisons
would be treated descriptively because they were not the main
focus of the study but were simply used to assess comparability of groups and the presence of potential confounding. In this
situation, with only three tests performed, a p-value less than
0.017 would be considered significant. With this condition, differences in MSMS scores among the groups would still not be
considered significant.

E. Establish a Causal Association

7. Was there evidence of a causal association according to the
    following criteria?

    a) Strength

Because strength of relationship is generally expressed by degree of relative risk for dichotomous variables, we shall assess
the results for the primary outcome, SBP, a continuous variable,
in question 8 on clinical significance.

    b) Consistency

No other studies have examined the relationship between occupation and blood pressure, so there is no evidence for consistency of the association with other studies.

    c) Biological plausibility

Because it is well established that stress affects blood pressure,
the postulated connection in the present study between occupation and blood pressure mediated by stress does fit with
what is already biologically known about blood pressure.

d)   Temporal correctness

This is a cross-sectional study in which risk factor and outcome status were determined at the same time. Because occupational status is not a constant characteristic and may change over time, we cannot be sure that the risk factor preceded the outcome in time, and the temporal correctness of the association cannot be established.

e)   Specificity

As stated in the introduction, the relationship of other outcomes to occupation has been established by previous studies. Therefore, the condition of specificity is not met.

F. Establish Clinical Significance

8.   Were the results clinically significant? What was the effect size and its 95% confidence interval?

Although the systolic blood pressure of the ATC group was 21 points higher than that of the PT group and 25 points higher than that of the LIB group, the 95% confidence intervals for these differences are 2 to 40 and 7 to 43, respectively.* These are consistent with moderate-to-large differences, which would be important from a clinician's perspective in treating individual patients. The authors interpret the clinical significance of the findings in the following statement from the discussion section: "We have demonstrated a clearly defined relationship between occupation and a risk factor (SBP) for one disease, CHD."

G. Summary of Analysis.   This study shows a strong statistically and clinically significant relationship between occupational group and blood pressure that is also biologically plausible. However, the presence of confounding by smoking status and the strong possibility of selection bias may alter or completely invalidate the results of this study and the conclusions drawn from them. The study may also have had inadequate power to detect potential differences in stress scores among groups, which became insignificant, after adjustment for multiple comparisons. In other words, although chance may be ruled out as an explanation for the

---

*Given the mean and standard deviations from Table 12-9, we can calculate the 95% confidence interval for the difference in two means according to the methods in Chap. 9.

apparent association between occupation and blood pressure, the possibility of confounding or bias has not been adequately ruled out. Furthermore, there was little evidence of a causal association in this study.

VI. Questions for Meta-Analysis

1. What methods were used to locate and include studies?

   An exhaustive search of the published literature as well as sources of unpublished data should be demonstrated; otherwise, the study may be subject to selection bias. Unpublished studies may be weighted toward negative results, and an effort should be made to locate and include such studies.

2. Was the quality of the studies considered?

   Criteria such as blinding, randomization, appropriateness of statistical analysis, and exclusion criteria should be considered when assessing quality of the studies included in the meta-analysis. Some effort should be made to exclude studies below a certain standard or to weight the results according to quality.

3. What were the risk factor and outcome(s) evaluated? Was the same outcome evaluated for all studies?

   If it was not the same outcome, then no overall estimate of treatment effect can be obtained.

4. Were the studies included homogeneous with regard to treatment (e.g., dose), patient population, sample size, and other study characteristics?

   If not, some adjustment for such variation should be included in the analyses.

5. Were the studies homogeneous with regard to outcome (i.e., the magnitude or direction of treatment effect)?

   Different statistical methods are used to estimate a pooled treatment effect when heterogeneity exists, and homogeneity of effect should be examined by graphs or statistical tests. If a lack of homogeneity in treatment outcome exists, determine if this is caused by heterogeneity in patient or treatment characteristics among studies (see Question 3), and find subsets of studies with homogeneous effects to identify a subset of patients who can benefit from the treatment or an optimum dose that provides maximum benefit.

6. Was bias possible in the selection of studies for inclusion?

It should be demonstrated that blinding of treatment results was used in selecting studies or recording data so that no bias is possible from the inclusion of studies with stronger positive results or form the recording of results.

As an illustrative example of meta-analysis, the following abstract from a study by Himel and colleagues [59] is reproduced here. The authors of this study go into great detail in describing their methodology so that it can be used as a model for a meta-analytic approach. Answers to some of the questions below refer to details of the study found in the complete paper, to which the reader may want to refer.

EXAMPLE 6

A Meta-Analysis

Adjuvant Chemotherapy for Breast Cancer. A Pooled Estimate Based on Published Randomized Clinical Trials[59]
Harvey N. Himel, MD, MPH; Alessandro Liberati, MD; Richard D. Gelber, PhD; Thomas C. Chalmers, MD

The use of adjuvant chemotherapy for treating patients with operable breast cancer remains a worldwide controversy. Using the data from published randomized control trials with a minimum two-year follow-up, pooled estimates of relapse-free survival rates and overall survival rates were calculated. Relapse-free survival rates were improved by 12.5% (95% confidence interval [CI] ± 4.5%) at three years and by 8% (CI ± 6%) at five years, with studies using multiple agents showing a greater effect. A significant advantage was also present in overall survival rates at three years, but only for studies involving multiple agents (4% ± 3.5%). Results from combining data for other types of trials were inconclusive. The use of this method is presented to illustrate its value as an explicit and systematic one for combining data from several randomized control trials in assessing a therapeutic controversy.

(*JAMA* 1986;256:1148-1159)

VII. Questions for Meta-Analysis Applied to Example 6

1. What methods were used to locate and include studies?

    The authors reported the results of published data only. Unpublished studies or results reported in abstracts or at annual meetings were not included. They did estimate the number of unpublished studies by contacting the principal investigators for all trials listed in the National Cancer Institute file of closed and active trials. The authors acknowledge that bias may have been introduced by including only the results of published studies. In only one of the six nonpublished trials did the results significantly favor adjuvant chemotherapy. The others showed no significant treatment effect. The authors do not explain why they decided not to include nonpublished studies.

2. Was the quality of the studies considered?

    Quality of the study was considered in the selection of studies. Only randomized clinical trials in which patients were followed for a minimum of 2 years were included. Although not stated in the abstract, quality was also considered by using a quality score based on study design, analysis, patient follow-up, patient selection, and so on.

    Included in the group of studies with low quality were those with poorly reported data in which subgroup analyses were not included or in which no data were available for pooling. In one phase of the meta-analysis, studies with the lowest quality scores were eliminated from the analysis. The authors demonstrated that this practice did not substantially alter the results or conclusions from the analysis that included all studies.

3. What were the risk factors and outcome(s) evaluated? Was the same outcome evaluated for all studies?

    The risk factor was the presence of chemotherapy, and the outcomes were overall survival and relapse-free survival. Differences between treatment and control groups in overall survival and relapse-free survival rates at 3 and 5 years from diagnosis were pooled for all studies combined and for subsets of studies according to type and duration of chemotherapy or patient characteristics.

4. Were the studies included homogeneous with regard to treatment (e.g., dose), patient population, sample size, and other study characteristics?

Studies were homogeneous only with respect to randomization and minimum follow-up—criteria for inclusion in the meta-analysis. They were not homogeneous with respect to sample size, length of follow-up, dose, chemotherapeutic agent used, characteristics of patients such as number of nodes or menopausal status, or quality score. Heterogeneity in sample size was controlled for indirectly by weighting estimates of treatment effect according to variability of results (see Question 5). Variability in treatment regimen, length of follow-up, and patient characteristics were controlled for by stratifying results and deriving separate estimates of treatment effect by type and duration of chemotherapy or by patient characteristics and number of years from diagnosis. The authors found a significant advantage in relapse-free survival for all treatments combined and for multiple-drug regimens at 3 and 5 years after diagnosis. The treatment effect on overall survival was statistically significant only for multiple-agent studies at 5 years. Treatment effects for other subsets of studies were not significant.

5. Were the studies homogeneous with regard to outcome (i.e., the magnitude or direction of treatment effect)?

The estimate of combined treatment effect from all studies was weighted according to the degree of variability of each study's results, which was itself dependent on sample size. Thus, studies with larger sample sizes contributed more to the estimate of overall treatment effect. Homogeneity of treatment effect across studies was tested using the Q-statistic. No significant heterogeneity across studies was found with the Q-statistic. The Q-statistic was also used to derive confidence intervals for the estimated treatment effects on overall survival and relapse-free survival. The width of the confidence intervals reflected the heterogeneity of treatment effects among the studies. Stratification of studies according to treatment and patient characteristics was another means of reducing heterogeneity among the estimates of treatment effect, although, as just stated, such heterogeneity was not a problem in this study. Figures

1-5 in the published paper give an excellent graphical representation of the homogeneity of study results for differences in relapse-free survival rates for various subsets of studies.

6. Was bias possible in the selection of studies for inclusion?

The fact that the criteria for inclusion of studies was clearly stated in the methods section is evidence that bias did not exist on the part of the authors in selecting studies. Although published studies with incomplete or poorly reported data were considered as part of the analysis of study quality, the authors could have attempted to improve the quality of data from these studies by obtaining the requisite data directly from the principal investigators of these studies. Whether the number of such studies made this impractical cannot be determined from the present paper, because the authors did not further address this possibility.

Omission of studies with incomplete data because they were still in progress could not be considered bias in the selection of studies for inclusion because the methods section reports the decision to include only "results that were fully reported in journal articles or monographs." In fact, including preliminary results from a clinical trial could itself be considered a source of bias in overemphasizing early results, and it is therefore legitimate to exclude such preliminary results in estimating treatment effectiveness. There was no bias in the assessment of study quality, because authors were blinded to the identity of the author, institutions, and journal of each study, as explained fully in the companion paper that details the assessment of quality [60].

The authors do acknowledge that some bias may have been introduced by omitting unpublished studies. In general, unpublished studies tend to have negative results, a phenomenon known as publication bias [61–66]. Although they did not include the data in the meta-analysis, the authors did describe the results of six unpublished studies identified from the National Cancer Institute's directory of clinical trials. Most of these studies had insignificant results. However, no systematic attempt was made by the authors to estimate the amount of bias introduced from excluding these studies.

A. Summary of Analysis. The only drawback of this study is some potential for bias in the selection of studies owing to the exclusion of unpublished studies. Otherwise, this is an excellent example of meta-analysis, which, in its entirety, includes a detailed description of methodology and detailed tables and graphs of results. This study provides a model for the conduct and presentation of the results of meta-analysis.

VIII. References

Example 2 References

1. Culver DH, et al. Surgical wound infection rates by wound class, operative procedure and patient risk index. *Am J Med* 91(Suppl 3B): 152–157S, 1991.
2. Single dose prophylaxis in colonic surgery. *Br Med J* 300(6722):464, 1990.
3. Alhan E, et al. Prevention of wound infection in elective colon surgery by the use of systemic ceftriaxone and ornidazole. *Mikrobiyol Bul* 24(1):41–47, 1990.
4. Davey P, et al. Cost-effectiveness of single dose cefotaxime plus metronidazole compared with three doses each of cefuroxime plus metronidazole for the prevention of wound infection after colorectal surgery. *J Antimicrob Chemother* 30(6):855–864, 1992.
5. Gorbach SL. Antimicrobial prophylaxis for appendectomy and colorectal surgery. *Rev Infect Dis* 13(Suppl 10):S815–820, 1991.
6. Hakansson T, et al. Effectiveness of single dose prophylaxis with cefotaxime and metronidazole compared with three doses of cefotaxime alone in elective colorectal surgery. *Eur J Surg* 159(3):177–180, 1993.
7. Korcek J, Palic R. An effective and achievable system of ultrashort antimicrobial prophylaxis in colorectal surgery. *Rozhledy V. Chirurg* 69(11):774–780, 1990.
8. Rohwedder R, et al. Single-dose oral ciprofloxacin plus parenteral metronidazole for perioperative antibiotic prophylaxis in colorectal surgery. *Chemotherapy* 39(3):218–224, 1993.
9. Rowe-Jones DC, et al. Single dose cefotaxime plus metronidazole versus three dose cefuroxime plus metronidazole as prophylaxis against wound infection in colorectal surgery: multicentre prospective randomised study. *Br Med J* 300(6716):18–22, 1990.
10. Fox C. Pharmacology and clinical use of silver sulfadiazine and related topical antimicrobial agents. *Pahlari Med J* 8:45–64, 1977.
11. Munster AM, Helvig E, Rowland S. Cerium nitrate-silver sulfadiazine cream in the treatment of burns: a prospective evaluation. *Surgery* 88(5):658–660, 1980.
12. Salisbury RE, et al. Burn wound sepsis: effect of delayed treatment with topical chemotherapy on survival. *J Trauma* 20(2):120–122, 1980.
13. Hoffmann S. Silver sulfadiazine (Flamazine). An antibacterial agent in the local prevention and therapy of burn wound infections. [Danish]. *Ugeskr Laeger* 146(3):2250–2252, 1984.
14. Hoffmann S. Silver sulfadiazine: an antibacterial agent for topical use in burns. A review of the literature. *Scand J Plast Reconstr Surg* 18(1): 119–126, 1984.
15. Helvig EI, et al. Cerium nitrate–silver sulfadiazine cream in the treatment of burns: a prospective, randomized study. *Am Surg* 45(4):270–272, 1979.

16. Snelling CF, et al. Comparison of silver sulfadiazine and gentamicin for topical prophylaxis against burn wound sepsis. *Can Med Assoc J* 119(5):466–470, 1978.
17. Ugland OM. Silver sulfadiazine in treatment of burns. *Tidsskr Nor Laegeforen* 98(22):1018–1019, 1978.
18. Horan TC, et al. CDC definitions of nosocomial surgical site infections, 1992: a modification of CDC definitions of surgical wound infections. *Am J Infect Control* 20:271–274, 1992.
19. Kruskal W, Wallis W. Use of ranks in one-criterion variance analysis. *J Am Statist Assn* 47:583–621, 1952.

Example 3 References

20. Bull GM. Examinations. *J Med Educ* 34:1154–1158, 1959.
21. Linn BS, Zeppa R. Team testing—one component in evaluating surgical clerks. *J Med Educ* 41:28–40, 1966.
22. Benenson TF, Stimmel B, Aufses A. Concordance of surgical clerkship performance and national board of medical examiners Part II subtest scores: a validation model. *Surgery* 89:692–696, 1981.
23. Newble DI, Elmsle RG. A new approach to the final examinations in medicine and surgery. *Lancet* 2:517–518, 1981.
24. Rowland-Morin PA, et al. Influence of effective communication by surgery students on their oral examination scores. *Acad Med* 66(3): 169–171, 1991.
25. Dixon WJ, Massey FJ. *Introduction to Statistical Analysis,* 4th ed. New York: McGraw-Hill, 1980.
26. Everitt BS. *The Analysis of Contingency Tables.* New York: Wiley, 1977.

Example 4 References

27. Bowden KM, McDiarmid MA. Occupationally acquired tuberculosis: what's known. *J Occup Med* 36(3):320–325, 1994.
28. Sepkowitz KA. Tuberculosis and the health care worker: a historical perspective. *Ann Intern Med* 120:71–79, 1994.
29. Mikol EX, et al. Incidence of pulmonary tuberculosis among employees of tuberculosis hospitals. *Am Rev Tuberc* 66:16–27, 1952.
30. Centers for Disease Control. Nosocomial transmission of multidrug-resistant tuberculosis among HIV-infected persons—Florida and New York, 1988–1991. *MMWR Morb Mortal Wkly Rep* 40:585–591, 1991.
31. Kantor HS, Poblete R, Pusateri SL. Nosocomial transmission of tuberculosis from unsuspected disease. *Am J Med* 84:833–838, 1988.
32. Haley CE, et al. Tuberculosis epidemic among hospital personnel. *Infect Control Hosp Epidemiol* 10:204–210, 1989.
33. Adal KA, et al. The use of high-efficiency particulate air-filter respirators to protect hospital workers from tuberculosis. *N Engl J Med* 331: 169–173, 1994.

34. Everitt BS. *The Analysis of Contingency Tables.* London: Chapman and Hall, 1977.
35. Dixon DO, Divine GW. Multiple comparisons for relative risk regression: extension of the k-ratio method. *Stat Med* 6:591–597, 1987.
36. Johnson AF. The need for triage on questions related to efficacy: multiple comparisons and Type II errors. *J Clin Epidemiol* 41:303–305, 1988.
37. Pocock SJ, Hughes MD, Lee RJ. Statistical problems in reporting of clinical trials. A survey of three medical journals. *N Engl J Med* 317:426–432, 1987.
38. Pocock SJ. Current issues in design and interpretation of clinical trials. *Stat Med* 290:39–42, 1985.
39. Hutton MD, et al. Nosocomial transmission of tuberculosis associated with a draining abscess. *Infect Dis* 161:286–295, 1990.
40. Cantanzaro A. Nosocomial tuberculosis. *Am Rev Respir Dis* 125:559–562, 1982.
41. Centers for Disease Control. Mycobacterium tuberculosis transmission in a health clinic—Florida, 1988. *MMWR Morb Mortal Wkly Rep* 38:256–264, 1989.
42. Centers for Disease Control. Nosocomial transmission of multidrug-resistant tuberculosis to health care workers and HIV-infected patients in an urban hospital—Florida. *MMWR Morb Mortal Wkly Rep* 39:718–722, 1990.
43. Brennen C, Muder RR, Muraca PW. Occult endemic tuberculosis in a chronic care facility. *Infect Control Hosp Epidemiol* 9:548–552, 1988.

Example 5 References

44. Rosengren A, Anderson K, Wilhelmsen L. Risk of coronary heart disease in middle-aged male bus and tram drivers compared to men in other occupations: a prospective study. *Int J Epidemiol* 20(1):82–87, 1991.
45. Weng XZ, He J, Su AM. Prognostic factors in the acute stage of myocardial infarction: analysis of 893 cases. [Chinese]. *Chung Hua Nei Ko Tsa Chih* 29(3):132–134, 1990.
46. Hebert PR, et al. Occupation and risk of nonfatal myocardial infarction. *Arch Intern Med* 152(11):2253–2257, 1992.
47. Facchini F, Gueresi P, Pettener D. Biological age in Italian adults: influence of social and behavioural factors. *Ann Hum Biol* 19(4):403–420, 1992.
48. Ekpo EB, et al. Demographic, life style and anthropometric correlates of blood pressure of Nigerian urban civil servants, factory and plantation workers. *J Hum Hypertens* 6(4):275–280, 1992.
49. Sarker MH, et al. Occupation and blood pressure: a study in rural and urban communities in Dhaka. *Bangladesh Med Res Counc Bull* 19(2):52–57, 1993.
50. Hedberg GE, et al. Risk indicators of ischemic heart disease among male professional drivers in Sweden. *Scand J Work, Environ Health* 19(5):326–333, 1993.

51. Gold MR, Franks P. The social origin of cardiovascular risk: an investigation in a rural community. *Int J Health Serv* 20(3):405–416, 1990.
52. Elwood PC, et al. Exercise, fibrinogen, and other risk factors for ischaemic heart disease. Caerphilly Prospective Heart Disease Study. *Br Heart J* 69(2):183–187, 1993.
53. Hinnen U, et al. Effect of occupation on health behavior and biological cardiovascular risk factors. [German]. *Soz Praventivmed* 38(2): S117–S121, 1993.
54. Niknian M, et al. Use of population-based data to assess risk factor profiles of blue and white collar workers. *J Occup Med* 33(1):29–36, 1991.
55. Nogueira R, et al. Cholesterol and other cardiovascular risk factors among employees of the Universidade Federal do Rio de Janeiro. Prevalence and influence of social variables. [Portuguese] *Arq Bras Cardiol* 55(4):227–232, 1990.
56. Schlussel YR, et al. The effect of work environments on blood pressure: evidence from seven New York organizations. *J Hypertens* 8(7):679–685, 1990.
57. Deyanov C, Hadjiolova I, Mincheva L. Prevalence of arterial hypertension among school teachers in Sofia. *Rev Environ Health* 10(1):47–50, 1994.
58. Tukey JW. Comparing individual means in analysis of variance. *Biometrics* 5:99, 1949.

Example 6 References

59. Himel HN, et al. Adjuvant chemotherapy for breast cancer. A pooled estimate based on published randomized control trials. *JAMA* 256(9): 1148–1159, 1986.
60. Liberati A, Himel HN, Chalmers TC. A quality assessment of randomized clinical trials of primary treatment of breast cancer. *J Clin Oncol* 4(6):942–951, 1986.
61. Begg CB, Berlin JA. Publication bias: a problem in interpreting medical data. *R Statist Soc A* 151(3):419–463, 1988.
62. Chalmers TC. Problems induced by meta-analysis. *Stat Med* 10:971–980, 1991.
63. Green BF, Hall JA. Quantitative methods for literature reviews. *Am Rev Psychol* 35:37–53, 1984.
64. O'Rourke KO, Detsky AS. Meta-analysis in medical research: strong encouragement for higher quality in individual research efforts. *J Clin Epidemiol* 42(10):1021–1024, 1989.
65. Rosenthal R. The "file drawer problem" and tolerance for null results. *Psychol Bull* 86(3):638–641, 1979.
66. Sacks HS, et al. Meta-analysis of randomized clinical trials. *N Engl J Med* 316(8):450–455, 1987.

APPLICATION TO CONDUCTING A STUDY

A Systematic Approach

It is important to use a systematic approach in designing and setting up a research study. A poorly designed study will yield useless results. Use the following approach to ensure that your research efforts will be worthwhile. Although our discussion will be restricted to studies that test hypotheses, this approach can easily be adapted to studies on estimation.

I. Setting Up a Research Study

A. Formulate a Hypothesis
Determine the major question you want to ask. As stated in Chap. 3, this usually comes down to finding an association between a risk factor and an outcome. The following are some general examples of research questions:

- Is a new treatment or technique better than the standard for condition X?
- What factors influence survival or cure from disease Y?

- What factors influence the results of a diagnostic test?
- What factors influence the level of some clinical characteristic?
- Does characteristic X cause disease Y?

B. Do a Literature Review

A literature review is important to determine whether your clinical question or hypothesis is an original one or if it has previously been addressed. If there have been studies done with this hypothesis, use the questions in Part III to evaluate the quality of the studies and whether they effectively tested the hypothesis. Then ask the following questions to decide if your study is worth doing:

1. Is my hypothesis original (i.e., has it been tested before, and how well)?
2. Were the results conclusive? Was the hypothesis satisfactorily tested?
3. Were the results corroborated by many studies, or are more studies needed?
4. If my hypothesis has been tested before, how will my study add to the existing literature?

   a) Is my subject population different from previous ones?

   For example, if the question has already been asked for adults, can I answer it for children? If it has been asked for patients with head trauma, can I answer it for patients with abdominal trauma?

   b) Can I test this hypothesis better than previous studies because of quality or power?

   (1) Were previous studies poor in quality? Did they fail to control for confounding or have sources of bias? Did they use an inappropriate study design, inferior clinical methods, or inappropriate analyses?

   (2) Did previous studies have poor power to detect clinically significant effects because of small sample size or large variability among subjects?

   c) Do I have a new variation on a clinical treatment or technique that has not been tested before?

C. Choose a Study Design

Once you have chosen a hypothesis, you must decide how you will define your comparison groups (i.e., on the basis of the risk factor or the outcome) and whether you will gather information retrospectively or prospectively. Refer to Chap. 4 for the appropriate use of various study designs. Decide what study design is most feasible, considering the resources available to you.

> For example, you may believe that a randomized clinical trial is best to test your hypothesis, but lack of time and personnel make this study design unfeasible. However, you have good records on a large patient base, and you may decide on a retrospective design—either cohort or case control.

D. Decide on Measures to Avoid Bias and Confounding in the Design

These measures depend on the study design you have chosen. For cohort studies, these measures include choosing all subjects from the same population, using randomization in clinical trials, blinding observers, carefully defining the criteria for outcome assessment, and completing follow-up on outcome. For case control studies these measures include blinding the subject and observer to the disease status of the subject, choosing several control groups or nondiseased controls from the general population, and determining risk factor status of deceased cases. Confounding can be eliminated or controlled for in the study design by using restriction or matching in cohort or case control studies; or randomization or stratification in clinical trials.

E. Decide What Information You Need

Decide how you will measure your outcome. Also determine, from your own past experience and from the literature review done in Step 2, if there are other variables that may potentially affect your outcome. In other words, identify other risk factors that may cause confounding in your study. These risk factors are often referred to as "baseline" factors because they are subject characteristics determined at the start of the study period for cohort studies or before the outcome has occurred for a case control study. Data must be collected on these risk factors as well so they can be controlled for in the analysis, if needed.

For example, you may wish to do a study on a new drug for diabetes. You decide that the most appropriate outcome to measure the drug's effect is blood sugar level. You know from past experience and training, as well as from your literature review, that factors such as age, weight, and duration of diabetes all affect blood sugar level. Therefore, you need information on these factors for your study.

No matter what you find, take a tip from a veteran epidemiologist: Age and sex affect **everything,** so always collect this information!

F. Decide How You Will Rule Out Chance

Decide what statistical tests you will use. Sections II and III in Chap. 15 give a detailed approach to choosing the appropriate statistical test. In addition, you must also decide how you will control for confounding, if present, in the analysis (i.e., stratification, regression analysis, or mathematical modeling). Analytic methods for the control of confounding are beyond the scope of this book. It would be wise at this stage to consult a statistician for advice on the best technique to use.

G. Determine the Sample Size You Need for Adequate Power

As discussed in Chap. 6, you must have a sample size large enough to detect a clinically relevant difference between study groups. The sample size depends on the level of the outcome variable you expect to find in your subjects, how large an effect size you want to detect, with what power you wish to detect it, and the level of statistical significance you think meaningful. You will need to prepare the answers to these questions and then consult a statistician or use the methods in App. D to determine the sample size you need.

H. For Clinical Trials, Decide on a Method of Randomization

There are several different methods available for randomly assigning subjects to treatments. Some of the more common techniques are covered in App. E. They serve a major purpose of randomization (i.e., making it impossible to predict the order of treatment assignment). Thus, treatment assignment is not under the control of the investigator.

I. Write a Study Protocol

Once you have decided on the methods for your study, write a formal study protocol. A protocol gives a detailed description of the study methods, to enable anyone to determine the format of your study. It serves as a guide to all those currently involved in the study, or those taking over the direction of the study in the future in the event of a change in personnel. The protocol can also be used as the basis for the manuscript, which will be submitted to a scientific journal upon completion of the study. The protocol describes the "who, what, when, where, and how" of the study.

1. Who

   a) The characteristics of patients to be included or excluded (eligible subjects)
   b) Whether all eligible subjects will be included or a sample will be obtained

2. What

   a) What will be done to the patients (e.g., a description of clinical and surgical procedures, dosages, timing and routes of administration of drugs, equipment used)
   b) What information will be collected

3. When

   a) The expected starting and ending dates of the study. A study begins with accrual of the first patient and ends with the final follow-up on the last patient.

4. Where

   a) Where patients will be found
   b) The institution in which patients will be treated and data gathered

5. How

   a) How potential subjects for the study will be identified and recruited
   b) How many subjects will be included (see Step VII)
   c) How a sample will be chosen if all subjects are not included
   d) How subjects will be entered into the study
   e) How randomization will be performed in randomized clinical trials

   f) How ineligible patients, dropouts, or departures from
       protocol in clinical trials will be recorded
   g) How treatment will be administered and by whom
   h) How information will be obtained

   (1) Who collects the information and at what times
       during the study
   (2) Where information will be obtained (e.g., from
       medical records, laboratory reports, patient inter-
       views)
   (3) A flow diagram of all study activities from patient
       entry to final follow-up
   (4) How results will be analyzed (a description of sta-
       tistical methods to be used). It is advisable to con-
       sult with a statistician to plan the analyses.

An example of a study protocol may be found in App. B.

J. Produce Study Materials; Run a Training Session
The next step is to produce all study materials (including study
forms and randomization materials for clinical trials) and to
train study personnel in all procedures.* This preparation includes procedures for patient accrual and entry into the study,
administration and completion of all study forms, use of instruments, performance of clinical techniques, and administration of
drugs.

K. Conduct a Pilot Study
Run a pilot study to test all forms and procedures to ensure that
the implementation of the study runs smoothly. Results of the
pilot study can be used to determine necessary sample size for
the final study, as described in Step G. Pilot studies generally
consist of 5 to 20 patients, depending on the aims of the pilot
study. If determination of sample size is the major objective and
no information on the expected level or variability of the outcome is available from the literature or experience, a pilot study
of approximately 20 patients is best. If, on the other hand, the

---

*Design of a data collection form is described in Chap. 14.

major objective is to test the study forms and procedures and these are fairly simple and straightforward, 5 to 10 patients should be adequate. If the study methods and data collection procedures do not change dramatically as a result of the pilot study, you can include the subjects in the pilot as study patients.

L. Run the Study
Carry out the study and collect the data.

M. Analyze the Results
Chapter 15 gives a detailed approach to analyzing the results of a study. However, if complex statistical analyses such as multivariate techniques are needed to control for confounding, it would be wise to obtain a statistician to analyze the results.

N. Write the Paper
Chapter 16 gives detailed instructions on writing the paper.

II. Summary

Steps in conducting a study

A. Formulate a hypothesis.
B. Do a literature review.
C. Choose a study design.
D. Decide on measures to avoid bias and confounding in the design.
E. Decide what information you need.
F. Decide how you will rule out chance.
    Choose a statistical test.
G. Determine the sample size you need for adequate power.
    Choose your effect size, significance level, and level of power.
H. For clinical trials, decide on a method of randomization.
I. Write a study protocol.
    Consider who, what, when, where, how.
J. Produce study materials; run a training session.

K. Conduct a pilot study.
L. Run the study.
M. Analyze the results.
N. Write the paper.

III. References

Pocock [1] is an excellent source for further details on the conduct of clinical trials [1].

1. Pocock SJ. *Clinical Trials: A Practical Approach.* Chichester: Wiley, 1983.

Gathering the Data: Designing a Data Form

The data form is the heart of a study. All information essential to the conduct of the study and analysis of the data is contained on this form or series of forms. Proceed with the design of a data form in a systematic manner, as follows.

I. Creating a Data Form

A. List the Items to be Recorded on Each Subject

1. Include subject information: study ID number, name, other identifying information such as medical record number, and the data collector's name or initials. This information is essential in case follow-up on erroneous or missing data is necessary after the study is complete.

2. Cite the grouping variable, which tells us to what comparison group a subject belongs.
3. List one or two outcome variables (the number of outcomes under study should be limited to one or two major outcomes, but the study may contain minor outcomes of interest).
4. Cite other confounding variables that may affect the outcome of interest.

B. Determine Where You Will Obtain the Data

There are two major sources of data.

1. **Primary sources** consist of data generated by the study itself, either through a questionnaire or through use of a measuring instrument (such as a sphygmomanometer, an EKG machine, or an ultrasound. With this source of data the researcher can specify the form and degree of precision to which the data will be recorded and can impose data collection guidelines to ensure consistency in measuring and recording data. However, this type of data is more time-consuming and expensive to collect.
2. **Secondary sources** consist of previously collected data or retrospective data. Examples include hospital records such as laboratory reports, operative reports or other information found in the patient record, and disease registry records. This source of data is readily available and less expensive to collect, but there is no control over the form or precision with which the data has been recorded and no guarantee of consistency or accuracy of recording.

C. Decide How to Measure Each Item

Decide what scale you will use. As stated in Chap. 1, there are three basic scales of measurement: continuous, ordinal, and categorical.

1. **Continuous measurement:** It is best to record continuously measured variables as precisely as possible. For example, record a person's exact age rather than age group; record a person's exact blood pressure reading rather than "high" or "low." These variables can always be grouped later in the analysis if necessary, but they cannot be "ungrouped" if they are not recorded on a continuous scale. The exact degree of precision with which continuous data should be recorded depends on two factors.

a) The level of precision with which the data were origi-
nally recorded, if you are using a secondary source.

b) The purpose of the study. For example, intervals measured in days or hours may be used for diseases with
very short courses, but months are sufficient for diseases of longer duration.

To ensure consistency in recording continuous variables, always
specify on the data form the unit of measurement to be used (e.g.,
ml/hr, μg/dl, cells/μl, days, weeks) and the desired level of precision (e.g., age to nearest whole year; blood pressure to nearest hun-
dredth, weight to nearest tenth of a gram).

2. **Ordinal measurement:** It is best to use ordinal measurement only for variables that do not have a true underlying
continuous scale. This includes generally "subjective" measurements such as symptom severity, degree of pain, and attitudes.

3. **Categorical measurement:** The possible categories of response should be listed on the data form and assigned numeric codes. The respondent should record the number of
the code for each variable.

For example, categories for the variable "underlying disease"
may be listed as follows:

1 = ASHD; 2 = Cancer; 3 = Diabetes; 4 = Other

Categories for sex may be listed similarly:

1 = Male; 2 = Female

The number and precision of categories depends on the purpose of
the study. For example, grouping operations into a few broad categories such as "open" and "closed" may be adequate to answer the
question, "Does the type of procedure affect operating time?" but
more detailed categories may be necessary to answer the question,
"Which surgical procedure produces the least amount of postoperative pain?" If possible, all codes for a variable should be listed on
the data form to ensure accuracy and avoid confusion. In general,

open-ended (noncoded) questions should be avoided. If necessary, first run a small pilot study with open-ended questions to determine what kinds of answers you can expect. Then list the categories of response on the final questionnaire, and ask respondents to choose the category that best matches their response. Use a code for "other" for responses that do not match any of the preselected codes. Leave space for respondents to write in these other responses, which you can code post hoc. This procedure minimizes the amount of text that must be keypunched or read and saves much time and computer disk space.

4. **Dates:** Use dates rather than intervals whenever possible. This practice reduces errors in hand-calculating intervals, which can be done faster and with fewer errors by the computer when two sets of dates are given.

   For example, birth dates, rather than age, should be collected if you need age at diagnosis or age at time of randomization. In this instance, the date of diagnosis or date of randomization must also be recorded.

D. Decide How to Arrange the Items

1. Use boxes (one box for each digit) to record the responses on a data form. This ensures greater legibility and makes it easy for the keypuncher or data entry person to locate responses.
2. Leave enough boxes for the maximum number of digits a response may take. For example, leave three boxes for age measured in years unless the study population consists only of children. Allow enough digits for additional categories of discrete response to be added later, if necessary.
3. Make items well-spaced and easy to read for the data recorder and keypuncher. Ideally, for ease of keypunching, line up all boxes along the left margin of the data form.
4. Leave space for respondents to write in questions or comments when responses are ambiguous or do not fit the choices given.
5. The layout (order) of items on the data form should follow the order in which items appear in the secondary source, or the order in which items are measured with the primary

source. This makes recording of data faster and more accurate because the data recorder does not have to jump back and forth in the secondary source or on the data form. Usually, subject identifying information (name, study number, medical record number) is recorded at the top of the form; subject demographic and baseline information is recorded next; details of treatment are recorded next; and information on follow-up or outcome status is recorded last.

6. Keep data forms to one page (double-sided) whenever possible. Single sheets are easier for keypunching. Second sheets can become detached and lost. If much information is recorded, it may make sense to have two or more separate forms, such as a patient information form and a follow-up form. If you use multiple forms or multiple sheets per form, be sure to repeat subject identifying information on all sheets, in case sheets becomes detached or separated.

7. Put the date the form was created in the upper right or lower left corner to aid in tracking subsequent versions of the form.

8. Avoid using checks as responses. Instead, use "Y" and "N" or "1" and "2" for "yes" and "no" or "present" and "absent."

For examples of various layouts for data forms, see App. C.

E. Write Instructions

Include instructions on finding the information and completing each item on the data form so that recording is as consistent and accurate as possible, especially if you use several data collectors. If necessary, run a training session for data collectors.

F. Run a Pilot Study

A pilot will test whether the data form is unambiguous and easy to use, whether all data collection instructions are understandable, and whether the information for each item is found where expected, if you are using a secondary data source. The pilot study can also help you determine the most frequent responses to open-ended questions.

II. Summary

Designing a data form

A. List the items to be recorded on each subject.
B. Determine where you will obtain the data.
C. Decide how to measure each item.
D. Decide how to arrange the items.
E. Write instructions.
F. Run a pilot study.

Appendix C provides examples of data collection forms.

Entering and Analyzing the Data

Today, computers are used for almost everything, and research is no exception. A computer is helpful for every phase of a research study: conducting a literature review using an on-line computer database and managing references using a reference management program; preparing study materials using a desktop publisher or word-processing program; entering data using a spreadsheet or database program; analyzing data using a statistical analysis program; summarizing results using a graphics program; and writing the final paper using a word-processing program. In this chapter we focus on programs for data entry and statistical analysis, because as a clinician you are likely to have the least familiarity with these types of programs. First we will address how to choose an appropriate program, and then we will describe how to use the program to conduct an analysis of your data.

I. Choosing a Computer Program

Numerous computer programs are available for data entry and statistical analysis. Periodic reviews of statistical packages are given in popular computer magazines such as *PC Magazine* or *PC World* [1]. These reviews list the features of each program and rate them according to various criteria. The following is a list of features to look for when you are choosing a statistics package. These features should be considered the basic requirements of any package you choose.

A. Ease of Use.   The program should be relatively easy to use for the statistics novice or occasional user. Complex programming language should not be required. Instead, menus and help screens should be available to guide the user through the program. Furthermore, a readable, well-organized, and comprehensive manual should accompany the program.

B. Import and Export Functions.   The ability to import and export data files is essential. You may find that data are available from a computerized disease registry or medical record database, and you should be able to be directly transfer (import) this information to your statistics package. Many packages currently available can read text (ASCII) files or spreadsheet files such as Excel or d-Base. Some packages can read files from other common statistics packages such as SPSS or SAS. At the minimum, your package should be able to read ASCII, Excel, or d-Base files, because most any database or statistics package can export files into one of these formats. Data exporting into a variety of formats is also important in case you wish to give your data to a statistician to analyze. Again, most packages can import ASCII, Excel, or d-Base files, so your package should also be able to export files in at least one of these formats.

C. Data Entry, Editing, and Data Management.   About 80 percent of the work in analyzing results involves creating and validating data files through data entry, checking, editing, case subset selection, and variable transformation. Therefore, these functions are essential to any program. The following are specific features you will find useful.

- Error checks for incorrect or invalid values, or the ability to prevent entering invalid values

- A validation feature, allowing duplicate entry of all records to identify and correct keypunching errors
- The ability to skip fields, to allow the key puncher to automatically skip subsequent items that are not applicable following a "no" answer on the data form
- Linked fields, which simultaneously enter category names in an additional field when a number is typed in a linked field
- Repeat fields, which automatically repeat information entered for the previous record (useful when certain answers are common to many subjects; can be overridden when the answer is different)
- A recode feature, which allows recoding of one value to another (useful when you want to combine categories for a categorical variable or to create a categorical variable from a continuous variable, (such as creating 10-year age groups from actual age)
- New variable creation, to create a new variable based on the values of one or more already-existing variables (particularly useful if you need to transform values of your outcome variable in order to satisfy certain assumptions for statistical tests)

  For example, to identify records of patients whose treatment is radiation when many treatments are possible, you can create a new variable called "Radiation," which is coded as 1 if treatment is radiation and 0 if treatment is anything else.

  As another example, you wish to create a new variable, LOGAGE, which is the log of each subject's age, in order to make the data on age normally distributed.

- Subset selection of cases or variables to analyze or save in a new data file

D. Statistics.   A high-powered statistical package with sophisticated statistics routines is neither required nor desired for the clinician. Besides adding significantly to the price and complexity of the program, such advanced statistics should not be used by a nonstatistician. However, the availability of default choices for the various options in these routines allows anyone to run the program and incorrectly use the statistical tests. If you need anything other than the basic statistical tests listed below, you should consult a statistician.

For the clinician, the following statistical and graphic features are adequate.

1. *Descriptive Statistics*
    a) Mean
    b) Median
    c) Mode
    d) Confidence intervals
    e) Test of skewness (useful in testing the assumption of normality on a data set)
    f) Frequencies
    g) Percents
    h) Cumulative frequencies/percents

2. *Analysis of Categorical Data*
    a) Cross-tabulation/contingency tables (chi-square analysis)

3. *Analysis of Continuous Data*
    a) The *t*-test (paired and unpaired)
    b) Analysis of variance
    c) Correlation

4. *Graphics*
    a) Scatterplots
    b) Bar charts
    c) Line charts

E. Programming Features. Although a sophisticated programming language is not desirable, the ability to create and run simple programs or "batch files" is helpful for two reasons. First, a series of commands to transform data or invoke a statistical test can be created and tested for errors without having to retype the commands each time. Second, when the same statistical test is run periodically on new data sets, or for different subsets of the same data, the batch file can be modified to fit the new data and run again, thus saving much time and effort.

F. Recommendations. Many statistics packages on the market contain the features listed in the previous section. Programs cost anywhere from a few hundred to a few thousand dollars, depending on the scope of features and tests available. However, as already stated, it is unnecessary and even undesirable for the clinician conducting occasional research to purchase sophisticated and costly programs. Because much of the cost of these programs is due to inclusion of advanced tests, a clinician who purchases such a program to perform a few simple tests is wasting money. An excellent series of public domain programs developed by the Centers for Disease Control (CDC) contains most of the recommended features. The CDC uses this program, EPI INFO, for its surveillance data, and the program can handle data sets of any size. It can be legally copied from other users for free or purchased directly at the following address:

USD Incorporated
2075-A West Park Place
Stone Mountain, GA 30087 USA
Phone (404) 469-4098
FAX (404) 469-0681

The cost of EPI INFO is approximately $50 for the printed manual and disks.

II. Using the Program

Once you have collected the data, you are ready to start using your statistics program. Use the following approach to proceed through data entry and data analysis.

A. Keypunch the Data.   Recording information and entering data are perhaps the most important steps in conducting a study. If data are inaccurate or incomplete, the statistical analyses and conclusions drawn from them will be invalid. Chapter 14 gave suggestions on form design to facilitate the data entry process and reduce data entry errors by improving readability. In addition, the following suggestions will help ensure accuracy and efficiency in data entry.

1. **Always verify data** by using the verify function on your computer program or by comparing printed output with the original data forms. This is time consuming but worthwhile.
2. If there are many cases, **have one person enter data and another verify it.**
3. If rounding is necessary, **round to the nearest even number** to prevent the bias of always rounding up or down. This bias can occur when a response is given to a greater level of accuracy than requested.

For example, if subjects are asked to record their opinions on certain issues by indicating agreement or disagreement on a scale of 1 to 5, some subjects may respond with 1.5 or 4.5. Because decimal responses were not intended and cannot be entered on the computer, the keypuncher must round the answer. Round 1.5 to 2 and 4.5 to 4.

B. Examine the Data.   Once you have keypunched and verified the data, perform a preliminary examination of the data set. This examination serves three functions:

1. It gives an overview of the study population and helps you familiarize yourself with the data.
2. It helps you identify and correct data entry or recording errors.
3. It allows you to check assumptions of statistical tests and select which tests you will run.

Although the general choice of statistical tests has been made before analysis in the initial planning phase of the study, the ultimate choice of statistical tests depends on characteristics of the final data set. To proceed with a preliminary examination of the data, obtain a set of frequency counts on all variables in the data set, both continuous and discrete. As explained in Chapter 6, a frequency count, or frequency distribution, is a list of all possible values for each variable and how many times each value occurred.

For example, suppose that we collect information about blood type and code that information for each subject as follows:

$$1 = A; 2 = B; 3 = AB; 4 = 0$$

Now suppose we obtain the following frequency distribution for the variable "BLOODTYPE." The first column lists all values for BLOODTYPE that have been keypunched. The second column lists the number of subjects with each value. The third column lists the percent of subjects with each value, and the fourth column lists the percent of subjects with each value or a lower value.

BLOODTYPE	Number	Percent	Cumulative percent
1	14	28	28
2	17	34	62
3	13	26	88
4	5	10	98
6	1	2	100

From column 4 of the table we see that 28% of subjects had blood type 1; 62% had blood type 1 or 2; 88% had blood type 1, 2, or 3; and so on. Notice the value of "6" in the table. Because we have only assigned codes of 1 through 4 for BLOODTYPE, the code of "6" must be an error. We can request the program to select the subset of cases with BLOODTYPE equal to 6 and then list the name or ID number of this subject. We may then refer back to the data form to determine if this was an error in recording or in keypunching the data.

As another example, suppose we record age, a continuous variable, for each subject in a study. The following frequency table was generated by the program EPI INFO:

AGE	Freq	Percent	Cum.
2	1	2.0	2.0%
50	3	6.0	8.0%
52	4	8.0	16.0%
55	7	14.0	30.0%
60	10	20.0	50.0%
62	8	16.0	66.0%
64	6	12.0	78.0%
65	5	10.0	88.0%
67	4	8.0	96.0%
69	2	4.0	100.0%
Total	50	100.0%	100.0%

Mean = 59.1
Std Dev = 9.8
Median = 61.0

By examining the frequency distribution for age, we can see that subjects in the study ranged from age 2 to age 69. From the table we can see that 16% of the subjects were exactly age 62 and that 66% of subjects were age 62 or below. Suppose that the study population had been chosen to be between 50 and 70 years of age. A value of 2 indicates either a recording or keypunching error. Examination of the data form and, if necessary, original patient records, will indicate where the error occurred and what the correct value should be. The error can then be corrected.

For continuous variables, you should also obtain the mean, median, and standard deviation.

The mean age reported in the previous table is 59.1; the median is 61; the standard deviation is 9.8.

If the mean and median are fairly close, the data are likely normally distributed. Lack of normality or a large standard deviation relative to the mean may indicate that a variable does not satisfy the assumptions for parametric tests of means (i.e., the t-test or analysis of variance) and that a nonparametric test should be used. Determining whether continuous data are normally distributed can best be assessed by generating bar graphs of continuous variables. A bar graph is a graphic representation of a frequency distribution, where the height of the bars corresponds to the frequency of a given category or a given value. Figure 15-1 is a bar graph of the previous frequency distribution on age, generated by EPI INFO.

We can use graphs to get an overall picture of how the data are distributed. For continuous data, variables on which our study groups are to be compared (e.g., outcome for cohort studies or risk factor for case control studies) should have an approximately "normal," or bell-shaped, distribution—something like the one in Fig. 15-1. In general, however, for sample sizes of 25 or more, unless the data are highly skewed, lack of normality is not a problem because

Fig. 15-1.   Example of a bar graph

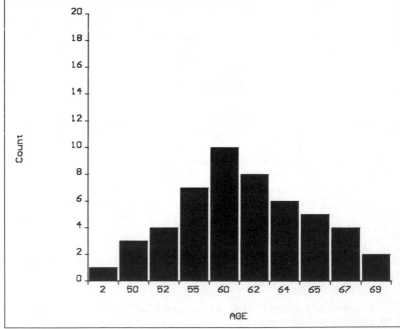

most of the parametric tests discussed here are relatively "robust" to assumptions of normality. With non-normal data in small samples or with highly skewed data in larger samples, try one of the following options.

1. Transform the data so they look normal. Examples of transformation are taking the log of each value, or taking the square root of each value. Statistical programs that allow data transformation can do this easily.
2. Omit extreme values, which are also called **outliers** and are clearly divergent from the rest of the data.

C. Compare the Groups at Baseline. The next step is to generate separate frequency tables or means and standard deviations for each group on potential confounding factors or "baseline" variables. For discrete variables, you can do this more efficiently in many programs by using the contingency tables or cross-tabulation option instead of generating separate frequency tables for each group.

The following is an example of a contingency table generated by EPI INFO. It shows group frequencies for sex for Example 5.

| | Sex | | |
Group	F	M	Total
ATC	19	23	42
PT	22	36	58
LIB	30	29	59
Total	71	88	159

Chi square = 3.93
Degrees of freedom = 4
p value = 0.41512012

Once you have generated information on each variable for each group, it is useful to make your own summary tables, comparing groups at baseline. Take the following steps for each group:

- List the number and percent of subjects in each category for discrete variables.
- List the mean and standard error or 95% confidence interval for continuous variables.

Table 15-1 is an example of a table comparing the three groups in Example 5.

Table 15-1.   Baseline comparison of groups

Variable	Category	ATC[1]		PT[2]		LIB[3]	
		Number	Percent	Number	Percent	Number	Percent
Sex	Male	19	45	22	38	30	51
	Female	23	55	36	62	29	49
Age	Mean	32.2		37.7		35.1	
	SE	2.7		2.5		2.1	

[1]$n = 42$
[2]$n = 58$
[3]$n = 59$

If you find differences among the groups on any of the baseline variables, and if outcome analysis (Step D) shows that the baseline variable on which the groups differ is related to the outcome, the analysis should control for this confounding variable. Discrete confounding variables can be controlled for with a stratified analysis. This entails a separate analysis of the groups for each category of the confounding variable. For example, to control for confounding by sex, a separate analysis could be performed for men and women. Programs such as EPI INFO offer stratified analyses of discrete data. The Mantel-Haenszel procedure, for example, tests whether odds ratios are similar across different strata of a confounding variable when the outcome variable is also discrete. This procedure also gives a pooled estimate and test of significance of the odds ratio for all strata combined. If confounding variables are continuous, or if the groups differ on many variables, you need some sort of multivariate analysis and should consult a statistician.

D. Compare the Groups on the Variable of Interest.   This variable is outcome status for cohort studies and risk factor status for case control studies.

1. Determine the Effect Size.
To do this, compute the difference (in means or proportions) for the variable of interest between comparison groups and the 95% confidence interval for this difference. If your computer program does not compute this, use the methods described in Chap. 9.

2. Choose a Statistical Test on the Difference between Groups.
Use the following questions to make final decisions about which statistical test to use. You should have answered some of these questions in the planning stage of the study, but some cannot be answered until you have examined the actual data.

a) What is the scale of measurement of the variable of interest (nominal, continuous, or discrete?)

Remember that continuous variables are measured on a numeric scale; ordinal variables are measured in categories that have a natural order; and discrete variables are measured in categories or classes with no natural order.

b) If the variable is continuous, is it normally distributed in the study population as a whole?

This was determined by examining a graph of the data in Step B.

c) How many groups are there?

Remember that groups are formed on the basis of the risk factor for cohort studies and outcome for case control studies.

Note that sometimes the purpose of the analysis is not to compare two or more groups but to relate two different measurements taken on one group of subjects. This is called correlation.

For example, suppose we obtain both weight and blood pressure on a group of patients. We want to see if patients' blood pressure varies with their weight—if heavier subjects have higher blood pressure, or vice versa.

A further explanation of correlation is given in App. A.

d) For two or more groups, are subjects from the groups independent (unpaired) or matched (paired)?

For example, suppose subjects are randomized in a clinical trial to one of two treatment groups: Group A and Group B. The two groups would be considered independent because the characteristics of one group do not depend on the characteristics of the other. Subjects from the two groups are not related in any way.

On the other hand, suppose two groups of twins are compared. For every subject in Group A, a twin (a match) is chosen for Group B. The two groups would be expected to be more similar to each other than those in the first example because they are biologically related. The groups can be considered paired, or matched.

Suppose the two groups consist of two sets of blood glucose measurements taken on the same subjects before and after eating. The measurements from the two groups (time periods) should also be more similar than those in the first example because they are taken on the same subjects.

Paired measurements differ from correlation. In paired measurements, the **same variable** is measured on the same subjects at different times or under different conditions. In correlation, **two different variables** are measured on the same subjects at the same time or under similar conditions.

e) For a continuous variable, are group variances equal?
When groups are compared on a continuous variable, equality of group variances should be considered. The variances (which are simply the squared standard deviations) of the groups should be somewhat equal. Practically speaking, if the total sample size is greater than 25, a lack of equal variances is not a problem. As a rule of thumb, the assumption of equal variances is satisfied as follows [2]:

- If the ratio of the largest to the smallest sample size is less than 4:1
- If the ratio of the largest to the smallest variance is less than 20:1

If the ratio of sample sizes is greater than 4:1, the ratio of variances should be correspondingly smaller. As you can see, these guidelines are quite liberal, and the assumption of equal variances is easily satisfied in most cases. With small sample sizes, however, or variances that are not equal by the preceding criteria, try transforming the data or omitting outliers, and then ask the question again.

It should be noted that many computer programs give a formal test of equality of variances such as Levene's test or Bartlett's test as part of the output for t-tests or analysis of variance. These tests tend to be more conservative than the above criteria and need not be followed.

Having answered these questions, we can consult the chart in Fig. 15-2 to determine the appropriate statistical test. Further examples of choosing a test using the decision chart are given at the end of this chapter. Note that only univariate tests are considered here.

3. Run the Chosen Statistical Test.
After running the test, examine the output as follows.

a) Find the test statistic, degrees of freedom, and significance level.

For example, the following output was obtained from the program EPI INFO, which performed an analysis of variance for the data from Example 5. Mean blood pressure was compared for the three occupational groups (ATC, PT, and LIB):

GROUP	Obs	Total	**Mean**	**Variance**	Std Dev
1	42	6469	**154.024**	**797.341**	28.237
2	58	7715	**133.017**	**748.544**	27.360
3	59	7624	**129.220**	**680.864**	26.093

GROUP	Minimum	25%ile	Median	75%ile	Maximum	Mode
1	90.000	154.000	154.500	155.000	234.000	154.000
2	90.000	120.000	133.000	150.000	233.000	100.000
3	90.000	110.000	130.000	140.000	225.000	135.000

15-2. Choosing a test

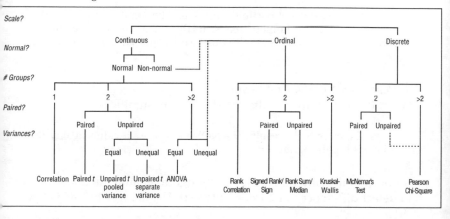

ANOVA
(For normally distributed data only)

Variation	SS	df	MS	F statistic	p-value
Between	16658.975	2	8329.487	**11.314**	**0.000108**
Within	114848.095	156	736.206		
Total	131507.069	158			

Bartlett's test for homogeneity of variance
Bartlett's chi square = 0.304 deg freedom = 2 p-value = 0.859075

The variances are homogeneous with 95% confidence.
If samples are also normally distributed, ANOVA results can be used.

Kruskal-Wallis One Way Analysis of Variance
Kruskal-Wallis H (equivalent to Chi square) =   29.963
Degrees of freedom =   2
p value = 0.000000

Examining the variances for the three groups obtained from the first table, we determine that they are approximately equal. No group variance is more than 20 times that of any other, and the ratio of the largest to the smallest group size is less than 4:1. We should also have examined the graph of the outcome variable (blood pressure) and determined whether it was normal. Results of both parametric (ANOVA) and nonparametric (Kruskal-Wallis) tests are given in EPI INFO in case the assumptions of normality and equal variances are not met. If the graph of blood pressure is not highly skewed, ANOVA is the appropriate test statistic to use, and we only need concern ourselves with these results.

Note that the results of Bartlett's test would be significant ($p < 0.05$) if variances were not homogeneous. In this example, no other test is recommended. This agrees with our assessment that the variances are equal.

4. Reach a Statistical Conclusion.
Is $p < 0.05$? If so, the results are statistically significant.

In our Example 5, the results of ANOVA indicate a p-value <0.000108, which is highly significant.

If not, was the sample size large enough to ensure adequate power to detect differences of clinical interest? The answer to this is "yes" if sample sizes were calculated in advance. (Refer to Chap. 13, Step G, on choosing a sample size.)

E. Summary of the Steps in Statistical Analysis

A. Keypunch the data.
B. Examine the data to get an overview, check for errors, and check assumptions of normality or equal variances for continuous variables.
C. Compare the groups at baseline.
D. Compare the groups on the variable of interest.

    1) Determine the effect size (size of the difference between groups) and its 95% confidence interval.
    2) Choose a statistical test by answering the following questions:

        (a) What is the scale of measurement of the variable of interest?
        (b) If the variable is continuous, is it normally distributed in the study population as a whole?
        (c) How many groups are there?
        (d) For two or more groups, are subjects from the groups independent (unpaired) or matched (paired)?
        (e) For a continuous variable, are group variances equal?

    3) Run the chosen statistical test.
    4) Reach a statistical conclusion. If p is not significant, was power adequate?

III. Examples Using the Decision Chart

In the following examples we shall follow the path of the decision chart as we answer these five questions:

1. What is the scale of measurement of the variable of interest?
2. For a continuous variable, is it normally distributed?
3. How many groups are there?
4. For two or more groups, are subjects from the groups paired?
5. For a continuous variable, are group variances equal?

A. Example 2: A Randomized Trial on the Use of Silvadene to Promote Wound Healing and Prevent Surgical Site Infections in Colon Surgery

This is a randomized clinical trial, so the comparison groups are formed on the basis of the risk factor (treatment) and compared on the basis of the outcome (incidence of SSI or time to wound healing).

To test the first outcome, we follow the path on the decision chart as we answer the following questions:

1. What is the scale of measurement of the variable of interest?

   SSI can be either present or absent. Therefore, it is a discrete variable with two categories.

2. For a continuous variable, is it normally distributed?

   The scale is discrete, so this question is not applicable.

3. How many groups are there?

   There are two groups—Silvadene users and controls.

4. For two or more groups, are subjects from the groups paired?

   Subjects are unpaired; therefore, use the Pearson chi-square as shown in Fig. 15-3.

Fig. 15-3. Choosing a test: Incidence of surgical site infection in Example 2

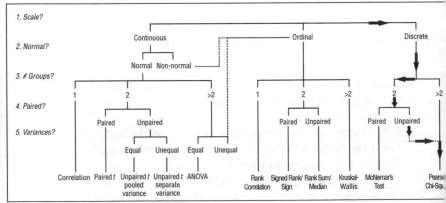

5. For a continuous variable, are group variances equal?

    SSI is a discrete variable, so this question is not applicable.

To test the second outcome, time to wound healing, we again follow the path on the decision chart as we answer the following questions:

1. What is the scale of measurement of the variable of interest?

    Time to wound healing is measured in days—a continuous scale.

2. For a continuous variable, is it normally distributed?

    We can determine if time to wound healing is normal by looking at a bar graph of this variable. The graph in Fig. 15-4 was generated by the program EPI INFO:

    The data on time to wound healing look highly skewed. Furthermore, because patients were followed at only weekly intervals,

Fig. 15-4.   Time to wound healing

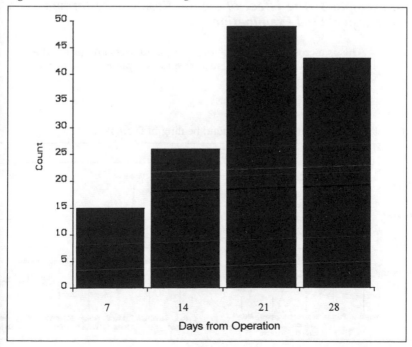

recording of wound healing at times other than 7, 14, 21, or 28 days and so on was not possible. Therefore, the data are not strictly continuous. For both these reasons, we should use a nonparametric test appropriate for ordinal or non-normal data.

3. How many groups are there?

There are two groups to be compared—Silvadene users and controls.

4. For two or more groups, are subjects from the groups paired?

The groups are unpaired. Therefore, the rank sum test is the appropriate test, as shown in Fig. 15-5.

5. For a continuous variable, are group variances equal?

We need not answer Question 5 because, as Fig. 15-4 shows, the data are not strictly continuous.

B. Example 3: The Effect of Sex on Resident Performance on the Surgical Oral Examination

This is a cross-sectional cohort design. Subjects are grouped according to occupation (risk factor) and compared on oral exam scores (outcome).

Fig. 15-5.   Choosing a test: Time to wound healing in Example 2

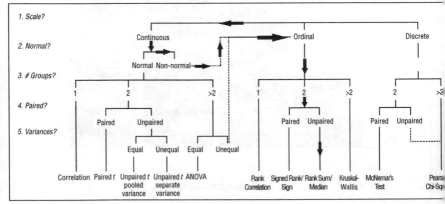

To test this comparison, we again follow the path on the decision chart as we answer the following questions:

1. What is the scale of measurement of the variable of interest?

    Oral exam scores are measured on a scale of 1 through 6 and represent relative degrees of performance. Therefore, the scale is ordinal.

2. For a continuous variable, is it normally distributed?

    The scale is ordinal, so this question is not applicable.

3. How many groups are there?

    There are two groups—men and women.

4. For two or more groups, are subjects from the groups paired?

    The subjects are unpaired; therefore, use the rank sum test, as Fig. 15-6 shows.

5. For a continuous variable, are group variances equal?

    We need not answer Question 5 because, as Fig. 15-6 shows, the scores are ordinal.

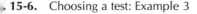

15-6. Choosing a test: Example 3

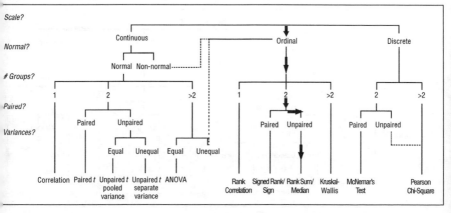

C. Example 4: Job Exposure and Tuberculin Test Reactivity in Hospital Workers

This is a case control study, so the groups are formed on the basis of outcome (PPD test results) and compared on the risk factor (job service).

To test this comparison, we again follow the path on the decision chart as we answer the following questions:

1. What is the scale of measurement of the variable of interest?

    Type of service is a categorical, or discrete, scale.

2. For a continuous variable, is it normally distributed?

    The scale is discrete, so this question is not applicable.

3. How many groups are there?

    There are two groups—cases and controls.

4. For two or more groups, are subjects from the groups paired?

    Subjects are unpaired, so the Pearson chi-square test is appropriate, as shown in Fig. 15-7.

5. For a continuous variable, are group variances equal?

    Because the variable of interest is discrete, Question 5 does not apply.

Fig. 15-7. Choosing a test: Example 4

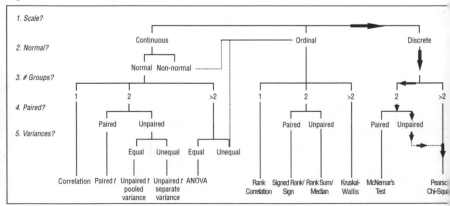

D. Example 5: The Relationship of Job Stress and Blood Pressure

This is a cross-sectional cohort study, so groups are formed on the basis of the risk factor and compared on the outcome. Subjects are grouped according to occupation (risk factor) and compared on blood pressure (outcome).

1. What is the scale of measurement of the variable of interest?

Blood pressure is measured on a continuous scale.

2. For a continuous variable, is it normally distributed?

We can generate the graph of blood pressure for all groups combined using EPI INFO (Fig. 15-8).

The mean is 147, and the median is 140. Considering that the graph is close to bell-shaped, the sample size is greater than 25, and the

Fig. 15-8.   Blood pressure for all groups combined

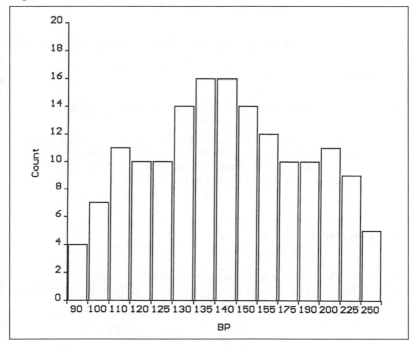

Fig. 15-9.   Choosing a test: Example 5

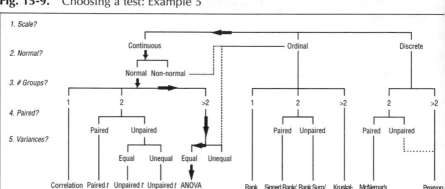

mean and median are close, we can assume the data are normally distributed.

3.   How many groups are there?

There are three groups, ATC, PT, and LIB.

4.   For two or more groups, are subjects from the groups paired?

Subjects are unpaired.

5.   For a continuous variable, are group variances equal?

The variance for each group (797, 749, 681) is given in the computer output on p. 181. The variances are approximately equal according to the criteria on p. 180. Therefore, analysis of variance (ANOVA) is the appropriate test, as shown in Fig. 15-9.

IV. References

1. Canter S. Stat of the art. *PC Magazine* 12(9):227–287, 1993.
2. Tabachnick B. *BMDP Short Course on Analysis of Variance.* BMDP Statistical Software Inc., Philadelphia, PA, October, 1989.

Writing the Paper

The scientific paper not only summarizes the research methodology and findings, but also puts them in a larger context of the prior work that has been done on the subject. Putting your study in a broader context allows you to assess the importance of your work and establish the unique contribution you have made to the question of interest.

The same approach used throughout this book in evaluating studies and conducting your own study can be used to write your paper. Following are some general guidelines for writing a paper and constructing graphs and tables.

I. Format

There are eight major parts to a scientific paper. They are described here in the order they should appear in a paper. Excerpts from the five studies on hypothesis testing from Chap. 12 will be used as examples.

A. Title. The title may state the major subject matter of your paper or may instead focus on a major result or conclusion.

For example, the title from Example 2, "A Randomized Trial on the Use of Silvadene to Promote Wound Healing and Prevent Surgical Site Infections in Colon Surgery," describes only the content of the study.

In contrast, we could rewrite this title to focus on the results and conclusions of the study: "Silvadene Enhances Wound Healing and Prevents Infection in Colon Surgery."

B. Authors.   List the full names and titles of all authors. Cite affiliated institutions as a footnote.

Example 2: David J. Wright, MD, John P. Silva, MD, and Thomas C. Posner, MD

C. Abstract.   Summarize your research hypothesis, study design and methodology, results, and conclusions. The following is the abstract from Example 2:

The present study was designed to assess the effectiveness of silver sulfadiazine (Silvadene) in preventing infection and promoting wound healing in surgery of the colon—a type of surgery at particular risk for surgical site infections **(research hypothesis).**

We prospectively randomized **(study design)** 133 patients undergoing colon surgery **(patient population)** to receive either postoperative Silvadene applied topically ($n = 64$) or no treatment ($n = 69$) **(comparison groups).** Patients were followed during hospitalization and seen weekly for 1 month after discharge **(follow-up methods)** to determine time to wound healing and presence of postoperative surgical site infection (SSI) **(outcomes).** The incidence of SSIs for patients in the Silvadene group was 3 of 64, or 4.7%, compared with 12 of 69, or 17.4%, in the control group ($p < 0.05$). The incidence of other wound-related complications was similar in the two groups (10% in Silvadene patients and 11% in controls). Median time to wound healing was 2 weeks in the Silvadene group and 3 weeks in controls ($p < 0.001$) **(results).**

We conclude that Silvadene, when administered prophylactically, promotes wound healing and reduces postoperative SSIs in patients undergoing colon surgery **(conclusions).**

D. Introduction.   The introduction provides a background for the study and states the purpose and major question or research hypothesis addressed.

After a brief review of the relevant literature to provide a background and rationale for the your clinical question, identify the patient population you are interested in, and state your research hypothesis or purpose of your study. The research hypothesis should be stated in terms of a causal association between the risk factor and outcome. The following introduction is taken from Example 2.

SSIs are a common cause of postoperative morbidity in patients undergoing surgery of the colon **(rationale)**. According to the National Nosocomial Infection Survey (NNIS) . . . the overall rate of SSIs is approximately 8.5%. Risk factors for SSIs are length of surgery greater than the 75th percentile; a preoperative ASA index of 3, 4, or 5; and a surgical wound class of III (contaminated) or IV (dirty) **(background—factors in wound healing)**. When stratified by risk class, the NNIS rates are 3.18% in patients with no risk factors, 8.47% in patients with one risk factor, 16.11% in patients with two risk factors, and 22% in patients with three risk factors present.

The effectiveness of prophylactic systemic antibiotics in reducing SSIs in this type of surgery is well established. . . . Silvadene has proved to be an effective antibiotic in the control of infection from second and third degree burns. . . . It has broad antimicrobial activity against gram-negative and gram-positive organisms and yeast. . . . It has not, however, been routinely used in the healing of surgically created wounds **(rationale)**.

(Statement of purpose or research hypothesis): The present study was designed to assess the effectiveness of Silvadene **(risk factor)** in preventing infection **(outcome)** and promoting wound healing **(outcome)** in colon surgery **(patient population)**.

E. Methods.   This section presents a complete description of the methods used in your study. Describe your study design, comparison groups, and the measures you used to rule out bias, confounding, and chance. Give a description of the subjects included and excluded, the way subjects were accrued, the time period of the study, measures used to avoid bias, randomization procedures if applicable, all treatments and medical procedures administered, methods used in the measurement and collection of data, the type of information collected, and statistical methods used, including sample size determination. The following excerpt comes from the methods section in Example 2.

All patients undergoing colon surgery by one busy general surgical group (the authors' group) **(patient population)** between January 1, 1993, and December 31, 1993 **(period of study)**, were considered eligible for study. Each patient gave informed consent before enrolling in the study. Randomization was carried out according to the patient's medical record number: patients with record numbers ending in an odd digit were randomized to the

Silvadene group, and those ending in an even digit were randomized to the control group **(measures used to avoid bias)**.

All patients received an oral bowel cleansing agent the evening
before surgery and prophylactic oral cefotetan 1 hour before
surgery.

All wounds were left open or loosely approximated for delayed
primary closure or secondary closure. For patients in the Silvadene
group, the surgeon topically administered 1% Silvadene at the end
of surgery, and the nursing staff applied it twice daily to a thickness
of $^1/_{16}$ in. throughout the patient's hospital stay. Upon discharge
from the hospital, the patient received Silvadene and instructions
to apply it to the wound, as described, for 1 week. Patients in the
control group received no antibiotic treatment at any time following surgery **(description of treatment methods)**.

Follow-up for surgical wound complications, including SSIs,
was performed by the operating surgeon daily during hospitalization and weekly for one month after discharge in the surgeon's office. The surgeons used the Centers for Disease Control (CDC) definition of an SSI. . . . Other wound-related surgical complications
recorded were wound dehiscence, erythema, and bleeding.

Healing of the wound was defined as complete closure of the
wound with no irregularities. Date of wound healing was considered to be the date of the first follow-up visit at which healing was
observed. Time to wound healing was the number of weeks
elapsed from date of operation to date of wound healing **(methods
used in measurement and collection of data)**.

Groups were compared on the incidence of surgical site infections and other wound-related postoperative complications using
chi-square analysis, with Yate's correction for continuity. Time to
wound healing could only be determined to the nearest week because of the follow-up schedule, so a nonparametric test, the
Kruskal Wallis test, was used to compare the two treatment groups
on this outcome **(statistical analysis)**. . . .

F. Results.   Present the complete results of your study, focusing on
the major hypothesis tested. Make no interpretation of the meaning of the results and draw no conclusions in this section. Present
only results from your study here.

Establish whether the groups are comparable at baseline by
presenting a table or text comparing the groups on all variables
except the variable of interest. Determine whether the groups are
different on the variable of interest, and establish whether chance
and confounding can be ruled out as explanations if a difference
is found. To do this, report the difference between groups and its
95% confidence interval as well as the results of statistical tests
that control for confounding, if appropriate. If groups are compared on more than one variable, present the results of the major

comparison first, including statistical analyses. Unless you have decided to adjust for multiple comparisons among groups, present the results of minor comparisons last, in a descriptive fashion without statistical analyses. If results are not significant, discuss whether the power of the study was adequate to detect a difference of clinical interest among groups. A statement of the power used to determine sample size should be included in the methods section. Do not give any interpretation of the meaning of the results or conclusions that can be drawn from them in this section. Give only results from the study. Use figures and tables where appropriate to illustrate or summarize results. Instructions on constructing graphs and tables are given in Section II of this chapter.

The results section of Example 5 is excerpted here as an example. Tables 12-8 and 12-9 are omitted to save space.

A total of 159 subjects were surveyed: 42 ATCs, 58 PTs, and 59 LIBs. There was no significant difference in mean age for the three occupational groups (32, 38 and 35 years of age, respectively). Other demographic characteristics and medical history of subjects in the three groups is given in Table 12-8. Clinical measurements are given in Table 12-9.

The groups were comparable on demographic characteristics and medical history. The only exception was smoking history. **(establish whether groups are comparable at baseline).** There was a significantly higher proportion of smokers in the ATC group than in the other groups ($\chi^2 = 6.45$, degrees of freedom $= 2$, $p = 0.039$) **(possible confounding).** As shown in Table 12-9, the three groups were comparable on clinical characteristics other than blood pressure and MSMS scores **(rule out other souces of confounding).** However, there were significant differences in the latter two characteristics. **(establish group differences in outcomes).** The ATC group had a significantly higher mean systolic blood pressure (SBP) (154) than either the PT group (133) or the LIB group (129) ($F = 11.3$; degrees of freedom $= 2,156$; $p = 0.000108$). There was no significant difference in diastolic blood pressure (DBP) **(rule out chance).**

The ATC group also had a significantly higher mean stress level (120) as measured by the MSMS score than either the PT group (110) or the LIB group (105) ($F = 5.92$, degrees of freedom $= 1.86$, $p = 0.025$). MSMS and SBP were highly correlated ($r = 0.79$) ($p = 0.0001$). The correlation with DBP was weaker ($r = 0.5$) and nonsignificant ($p > 0.2$) **(further rule out chance).**

To completely rule out confounding in this study, the authors should have done a stratified analysis for smokers and nonsmokers.

G. Discussion.   This section includes an interpretation of the results, relating them to the relevant literature. Establish evidence for a causal association (strength, consistency, and so on), clinical significance, and the generalizability of your results to other populations. Usually a summary of the major conclusion or conclusions is reserved for the last paragraph. The following is the discussion section from Example 2.

The rate of SSIs in the control group in the present study is comparable to that reported for colon surgery in the NNIS study on postoperative SSIs. . . .Thus, our controls can be considered a representative sample of patients undergoing this procedure, compared with other hospitals across the country. The distribution of our controls according to age, length of operation, and surgical wound class is also comparable to that of other NNIS hospitals, further demonstrating the generalizability of our results to other hospitals **(establish generalizability of results).**

Evidence for a causal association:
   The significantly reduced incidence of SSIs found in the Silvadene group—one-fourth that of controls **(strength)**—demonstrates the extreme efficacy of this preparation, when used prophylactically, in reducing the risk of SSIs. The fact that Silvadene was not effective in reducing the risk of other noninfectious wound-related complications indicates the specificity of its effect **(specificity).** The results of our study are entirely consistent with the known bactericidal activity and therapeutic efficacy of Silvadene which has been previously demonstrated **(consistency/biological plausibility).**
   Silvadene is inexpensive and has no documented side effects. In contrast, SSIs raise hospital costs through potentially increased length of stay for initial hospitalization, use of antibiotics to treat infections, additional office visits, and potential readmissions **(clinical significance).**
   In conclusion, prophylactic Silvadene is an effective means of preventing surgical site infections and promoting wound healing and should be routinely used in patients undergoing colon surgery. Based on results of the present study, investigation on the use of this preparation for other surgical procedures seems warranted **(major conclusion).**

H. References.   This section includes publication information on all articles cited in the paper in the format required by the journal to which you are submitting your paper. Citations should be complete and verified directly from the original papers.

The reference section of Chap. 12 provide examples of reference formats for Examples 2 through 5.

II. Graphs and Tables

Graphs and tables summarize the main results of a study. This section gives guidelines for constructing effective graphs and tables.

A. Graphs.   A graph represents data in pictoral form. In order to construct an accurate graph, consider the following guidelines.

1. Always include a title. The title should be clear and concise and describe what the graph represents:

    a) **Outcome measure** used and the form in which it is reported (e.g., as individual measurements, group means, or proportions)
    b) **Comparison groups** if two groups are being compared, or the population under study if one group is being described
    c) **Time period** under study, if relevant

The following examples show appropriate graph titles:

   Figure 1: Incidence of surgical complications **(outcome)** in appendectomy patients at Community Medical Center **(population)** from June 1993–December 1993 **(time period)**
   Figure 2: Average pain scores **(outcome)** taken in the first 24 hours for the two treatment groups **(groups)**
   Figure 3: The relationship between AB SITE and oral exam scores **(outcomes)** for fourth year residents in U.S. medical schools, **(population)** 1993 **(time period)**

2. Clearly label the axes (vertical and horizontal) and include the scale of measurement of the variables depicted (in., mm, yr). Mark scale divisions with tick marks and number them from 0 to the maximum value included in the data.
3. Clearly label comparison groups. Whether groups are depicted by lines or bars, each should be represented by a separate symbol that is clearly indicated in the legend, as in Fig. 16-1.
4. Keep the graph simple and uncluttered. Do not try to include too much information (such as too many subgroups, more than one set of axes, or multiple graphs on a page).

For more detailed information on constructing graphs, see references 1 and 2.

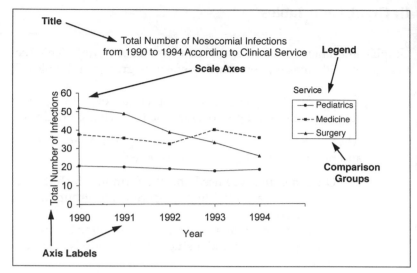

Fig. 16-1. Example of a line graph

B. Tables. For summarizing data in a table, keep in mind the following guidelines:

1. As with graphs, include a title at the top of the table that describes the content, including outcome measure, comparison groups or population, and time period, if relevant.
2. Clearly label columns and rows of the table.
3. If you report means, also report standard errors or standard deviations in parentheses or as a separate column. Label the columns appropriately. Confidence intervals for means are useful to indicate precision. Table 16-1, derived from the data in Example 1, illustrates these points.
4. If you report rates or percentages, also report the numerators and denominators (total sample size) for the rates, along with confidence intervals to indicate precision, as in table 16-2 based on Example 1.
5. When a table represents comparisons between groups (columns) on multiple variables (rows), indicate statistically significant comparisons in the appropriate row with footnotes denoting the level of significance. Table 12-9 on p. 137 from Example 5 is an example of a table of group comparisons.

Table 16-1. Clinical characteristics of patients with CT scans

Characteristic	Mean	Standard error	95% Confidence interval
Age	32	6.7	19–45
Blood pressure	115	6.7	102–128
Heart rate	140	7.9	124–156
Respiratory rate	64	7.1	50–78
Delay from injury to admission (mins)	60	4.6	51–69

Table 16-2. Symptoms on admission for patients with CT scans*

Characteristic	Number present	Percent	Standard error	95% CI
Vomiting	85	0.43	0.035	0.36–0.50
Headache	90	0.45	0.035	0.38–0.52
Amnesia	12	0.06	0.015	0.03–0.09
Loss of consciousness	41	0.21	0.03	0.15–0.27

*$n = 200$

6. As with graphs, avoid giving too much information in a table. As a rule of thumb, tables should be no bigger than 8 columns and 10 rows.

III. References

The papers listed here give additional general guidelines for writing papers, including graphs and tables, and are the uniform requirements for many journals [3–5]. However, individual journals may have slightly different formats and may have their own requirements for items such as photographs, lists of authors, or reference format. Before writing a paper, review the intended journal's instructions for authors. This will save you from spending time later on reformatting or resubmitting an incorrectly formatted paper.

1. O'Brien PC, Shampo MA. Statistics for clinicians 2. Graphic displays—histograms, frequency polygons, and cumulative distribution polygons. *Mayo Clin Proc* 56:126–128, 1981.
2. Statistics for clinicians 3. Graphic displays—scatter diagrams. *Mayo Clin Proc* 56:196–197, 1981.
3. Uniform requirements for manuscripts submitted to biomedical journals. *N Engl J Med* 324:424–428, 1991.
4. Bailar JC, Mosteller F. Guidelines for statistical reporting in articles for medical journals. Amplifications and explanations. *Ann Intern Med* 108:266–273, 1988.
5. Altman DG, et al. Statistical guidelines for contributors to medical journals. *Br Med J* 286:1489–1493, 1983.

Appendix A

A Short Guide to Statistical Tests and Measures

This section describes specific statistical tests and measures, providing details and examples of when and how they are used, what they measure, and what is involved in their computation. The beginning of App. A provides a summary of tests and measures and their use.

Table A-1. Summary of univariate tests

Number of groups	Number of outcomes	Outcome	Standard of comparison	Test
2	1	Continuous, normal	Means	*t*-test, unpaired
2	1	Non-normal or ordinal	Ranks	Median test Rank sum tests: Mann-Whitney or Wilcoxon
2 (paired)	1	Continuous, normal	Means	*t*-test, paired
2 (paired)	1	Non-normal or ordinal	Ranks or sign	Sign test; Wilcoxon signed rank
≥2	1	Continuous, normal	Means	Analysis of variance
>2	1	Non-normal or ordinal	Ranks	Kruskal-Wallis one-way ANOVA
≥1	≥2	Continuous, normal	Means	Repeated measures ANOVA
≥2	1	Discrete	Proportions	Pearson Chi-square test
2 (paired)	1	Discrete	Discordance	McNemar's test
2	1	Time to event	Survival times	Logrank
1	2	Continuous, normal	None	Pearson correlation coefficient
1	2	Non-normal or ordinal	None	Kendall/Spearman rank correlation

Univariate Tests and Measures

Analysis of Variance (*F*): A test used to compare the means for two or more groups. The usual analysis of variance is used when the same measurement is compared on two or more independent groups of subjects. A *repeated measures analysis of variance* is used when two or more measurements are taken on the same subject.

For example, to determine if American Board of Surgery in Training Exam (ABSITE) scores differ by postgraduate (PG) year, investigators compared the year-end ABSITE scores for PG1, PG2, and PG3 residents. They used an analysis of variance to compare the mean score for the three groups.

As another example, to determine if ABSITE scores improve for residents over time, researchers selected a group of residents who entered training in a certain hospital in 1989. They measured test scores on these residents for their PG1 year, PG2 year, and PG3 year and then carried out a repeated measures analysis of variance to look for trends over time.

Also, to determine if there is a difference among training programs in ABSITE scores over time, investigators administered ABSITE tests to residents at four programs for each of their PG years. They used a repeated measures analysis of variance to determine if scores over time were, on average, better for some programs than for others. They also used this analysis of variance to determine if trends over time for the four programs were different (i.e., if in some programs, scores improved and in some, scores declined over time).

Chi-Square Test (Pearson Chi-Square Test)(χ^2): A test used to compare two or more groups of subjects on a discrete variable.

For example, a cross-sectional cohort study is conducted to determine if lung cancer is related to smoking. A group of smokers is compared to a group of non-smokers on the proportion with and without lung cancer in each group. A chi-square test is used to test this comparison.

As another example, a cross-sectional study is carried out to determine if educational level is related to HIV infection. Subjects are divided into three groups by level of education: no high school degree, high school degree, and college degree or above. The three groups are then compared on the results of an HIV screening test. A chi-square test is used to determine if the proportion of positives and negatives is different in the three groups.

Computation: The following general approach can be used to compute the chi-square for two or more proportions:

1. Set up a table of observed frequencies for each category of risk factor and outcome.

Risk factor	Outcome		Row Totals
Present	a	b	$a + b$
Absent	c	d	$c + d$
Column Totals	$a + c$	$b + d$	$a + b + c + d$

2. For each cell in the table, calculate the expected frequency and put it in parentheses next to the observed frequency. The expected frequency for a cell is simply the row total times the column total divided by the grand total. The expected frequency for cell a would be $(a + b) \times (a + c)/(a + b + c + d)$.

   Note that the table can have more than the four cells in this example if there are more than two categories of the risk factor or outcome.

3. For each cell, subtract the expected frequency from the observed frequency and square the result, then divide it by the expected frequency.

$$\frac{(\text{Observed} - \text{Expected})^2}{\text{Expected}}$$

4. Add the results of step 3 for all cells. This is the chi-square (χ^2) value.
5. Calculate the degrees of freedom for the table. This is the number of rows minus 1 times the number of columns minus 1, or $(R - 1) \times (C - 1)$.
6. The significance level of chi-square can be obtained for the appropriate degrees of freedom from Table A-2.

   For example, we might derive the following table from the previous example of level of education and HIV infection. The expected frequency for the first cell (HIV Present/No HS Degree) is $(115 \times 10)/300$, or 3.8. Expected frequencies for all cells are given in parentheses.

Education	HIV Present	HIV Absent	Total
No HS Degree	5 (3.8)	110 (111.2)	115
HS Degree	2 (3.1)	90 (88.9)	92
College Degree/ Above	3 (3.1)	90 (89.9)	93
Total	10	290	300

Table A-2. Percentage points of the χ^2 distribution

D.F.	Probability (P)			
	0.050	0.025	0.010	0.001
1	3.841	5.024	6.635	10.828
2	5.991	7.378	9.210	13.816
3	7.815	9.348	11.345	16.266
4	9.488	11.143	13.277	18.467
5	11.071	12.833	15.086	20.515
6	12.592	14.449	16.812	22.458
7	14.067	16.013	18.475	24.322
8	15.507	17.535	20.090	26.125
9	16.919	19.023	21.666	27.877
10	18.307	20.483	23.209	29.588
11	19.675	21.920	24.725	31.264
12	21.026	23.337	26.217	32.909
13	22.362	24.736	27.688	34.528
14	23.685	26.119	29.141	36.123
15	24.996	27.488	30.578	37.697
16	26.296	28.845	32.000	39.252
17	27.587	30.191	33.409	40.790
18	28.869	31.526	34.805	42.312
19	30.144	32.852	36.191	43.820
20	31.410	34.170	37.566	45.315
21	32.671	35.479	38.932	46.797
22	33.924	36.781	40.289	48.268
23	35.173	38.076	41.638	49.728
24	36.415	39.364	42.980	51.179
25	37.653	40.647	44.314	52.620
26	38.885	41.923	45.642	54.052
27	40.113	43.194	46.963	55.476
28	41.337	44.461	48.278	56.892
29	42.557	45.722	49.588	58.302
30	43.773	46.979	50.892	59.703
40	55.759	59.342	63.691	73.402
50	67.505	71.420	76.154	86.661
60	79.082	83.298	88.379	99.607
80	101.879	106.629	112.329	124.839
100	124.342	129.561	135.807	149.449

From Everett BS. *The Analysis of Contingency Tables.* London: Chapman and Hall, Ltd, 1977, Appendix A.

$$\chi^2 = (5 - 3.8)^2/3.8 + (110 - 111.2)^2/111.2 + (2 - 3.1)^2/3.1$$
$$+ (90 - 88.9)^2/88.9 + (3 - 3.1)^2/3.1 + (90 - 89.9)^2/89.9$$
$$= 0.38 + 0.013 + 0.39 + 0.014 + 0.003 + 0.0001$$
$$= 0.8$$

This value, when compared with the table for $(3 - 1)(2 - 1) = 2$ degrees of freedom, is not significant. We would need a χ^2 of at least 5.991 to be significant at $p < 0.05$ with 2 degrees of freedom.

Note: When comparing two proportions the confidence interval method described in Chap. 9, Sec. II can be used as an alternative to the chi-square test.

Correlation: A measure of the strength and direction of a linear relationship between two sets of measurements taken on the same subject. A linear relationship of two measures means that if the values of one measure are plotted against those of the other, the points will more or less approximate a straight line, depending on how strong the linear relationship is. Figures A-1 through A-3 illustrate various degrees and direction of correlation. In perfect positive correlation, all values lie on a straight line parallel to the diagonal (Fig. A-1). In perfect negative correlation, all values lie in a straight line opposite the diagonal (Fig. A-2). With no correlation, values do

Figure A-1. Positive linear correlation

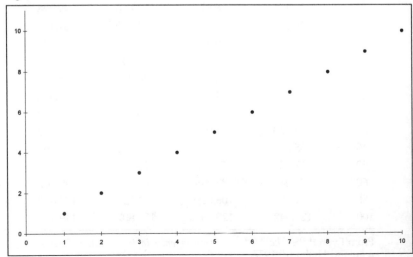

not create a straight line (Fig. A-3). See Pearson Product Movement Correlation Coefficient and Kendall/Spearman Rank Correlation Coefficient.

Figure A-2.   Negative linear correlation

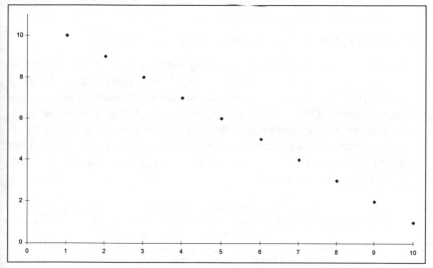

Figure A-3.   No correlation

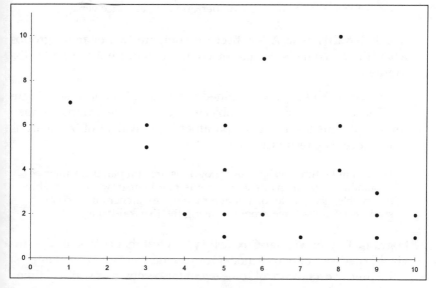

Degrees of Freedom (*df*): A number associated with a particular statistical test that is based on the sample size and number of groups compared. This measure is always reported along with the test statistic. The value of the test statistic and the degrees of freedom determine the *p*-value or level of significance of a test. Most statistical tests have one number to represent the degrees of freedom. The *F*-test, however, has two numbers.

***F*-Statistic, *F*-Ratio, or *F*-Test:** *See Analysis of Variance*

Kendall Rank Correlation (τ_b), or Spearman Rank Correlation Coefficient (r_s): A measure of the strength and direction of the relationship between two sets of ordinal measurements taken on the same subject. This statistic varies between −1 and 1. It is the nonparametric equivalent of the Pearson correlation. As with the Pearson correlation coefficient, we can derive a confidence interval for the Spearman rank correlation coefficient and test whether it is significantly different from 0.

> For example, researchers undertake a study to see if attending physicians' ratings of surgical residents on appearance are related to their ratings of the residents on performance in case presentations. They ask 10 attending physicians to rate a group of surgical residents on both attributes using a scale from 1, representing "very unsatisfactory," to 5, representing "very satisfactory." The Spearman rank correlation is 0.8, indicating a moderately strong positive relationship between the two sets of ratings (i.e., a resident receiving a poor rating on appearance is likely to receive a poor rating on performance, and vice versa).

Kruskal-Wallis Test: A test used to compare two or more groups when the outcome is ordinal or continuous but not normally distributed.

Computation: All subjects combined are ranked from lowest to highest. The sum of the ranks of subjects in each of the groups are then compared. This test is the nonparametric equivalent of the analysis of variance. The results are reported as a χ^2.

> For example, three weight loss programs are compared for their acceptability to participants. Participants rate their program as highly acceptable, acceptable, or not acceptable. Researchers then compare subjects from the three programs using the Kruskal-Wallis test.

Logrank Test, or Mantel-Cox Test (χ^2): A test that compares the survival experience of two or more groups when the outcome of interest is the time to occurrence of some event (also known as survival time).

Computation: The observed numbers of deaths in each group at each point in time is compared with the numbers expected if there were no differences in survival of the groups. Differences between observed and expected are then summed to obtain a χ^2 value.

> For example, a retrospective study is performed to determine if the presence of liver metastases at diagnosis affects survival in lung cancer patients. The logrank test compares survival time from diagnosis in patients with and without liver metastases.

McNemar's Test (McNemar's Chi-Square, Test of Symmetry) (χ^2): A test that compares two matched or paired groups when the outcome of interest is dichotomous.

Computation: The number of pairs that are "discordant," or dissimilar in one direction, is compared with the number of pairs that are discordant in the other direction. This test is reported as a χ^2 value.

> For example, in a study of the prevalence of *Klebsiella pneumoniae* in nursing home patients, investigators selected a sample of nursing home patients. For every patient in this group, they then selected an age-matched control from the community (noninstitutionalized). The pairs of subjects were compared on the presence of *K. pneumoniae*. McNemar's test shows whether a significant difference exists between the number of pairs in which the nursing home patient had *K. pneumoniae* and the community control did not, and the number of pairs in which the reverse was true. In the case of a significant test result, we would conclude that there was a significant difference between nursing home patients and age matched controls in the prevalence of K. pneumonia.

Mann-Whitney U-Test: *See Rank Sum Test.*

Mantel-Cox Test: *See Logrank Test.*

Mantel-Haenszel Test (χ^2): A test used with dichotomous outcomes to test whether odds ratios are similar across different strata of a confounding factor.

Computation: A pooled estimate of the odds ratio is obtained by combining the numerators and denominators of the odds ratios in each stratum, weighting by stratum size. To test if the pooled odds ratio is equal to 1, a chi-square statistic is computed by summing the squared difference of observed and expected values across all strata and dividing by the sum of the stratum variances.

For example, a randomized clinical trial is designed to test whether a new drug (Drug A) is better than the standard, cyclosporin, in preventing organ rejection in liver transplant patients. To control for confounding by age, patients are first stratified into three age groups (<50, 50-75, >75) and then randomized within strata to receive either Drug A or cyclosporin. Researchers use the Mantel-Haenszel test to estimate the risk of rejection for Drug A versus cyclosporin, for all strata combined, and to test whether the odds ratio is equal to 1.

Median Test (χ^2): A test used to compare two or more groups when the outcome is ordinal, or continuous but not normally distributed.

Computation: Compares the number of subjects above and below the median in each group. The results are reported as a χ^2.

For example, residents are judged on their performance on the oral examination. Scores range from 1, failure, to 4, strong pass. The median test is used to compare the median scores for residents who have taken an oral exam preparation course with those who have not taken the course.

Nonparametric Tests: Statistical tests that do not make assumptions about the distribution of the data. They are useful when outcomes are measured on an ordinal or discrete scale or when assumptions required for the usual parametric statistics cannot be met, often the case with small sample sizes. Examples are the rank sum test, Kruskal-Wallis test, logrank test, and Pearson chi-square test.

Odds Ratio: *See Relative Risk.*

Parametric Test: Statistical tests that are used to compare groups on a continuous characteristic when certain assumptions about the distribution of the data can be satisfied. Examples are the *t*-test, analysis of variance, and Pearson correlation coefficient.

Pearson Chi-Square Test: *See Chi-Square Test.*

Pearson Product Moment Correlation Coefficient (*r*). A measure of correlation of 2 continuous measurements. This statistic varies between −1 and 1. Values close to 1 indicate a strong positive relationship between the measurements (i.e., large values of one measurement are associated with large values of the other, and small values of one are associated with small values of the other). Values close to −1 indicate a strong negative relationship between the measurements, (i.e., large values of one measurement are associated with small values of the other). Values close to 0 indicate no pattern of relationship between the measurements. *See Correlation.*

Note: r is a point estimate for a population value, just like the mean or standard deviation, and thus we can also derive a confidence interval about r. Significance tests are also available to determine if r is different from 0.

> For example, researchers conduct a study to determine if height and weight are related. They measure the height and weight of 50 subjects. r is 0.9, indicating a strong positive relationship between the two measures: Tall people tend to weigh more than short people.

Rank Sum Test (Mann-Whitney U-test or Wilcoxon rank sum test [*U*]): A test that compares two or more groups when the outcome is ordinal, or continuous but not normally distributed. This test is the nonparametric equivalent of the two-sample *t*-test.

Computation: Measurements for all subjects are ranked from lowest to highest, and the distribution of ranks for the two groups are compared.

> For example, two analgesics are compared for their effect on pain from upper abdominal surgery. At 6 hours after surgery, subjects from the two analgesic groups use a pain scale to measure the amount of pain they feel. The scale ranges from 1 to 5, where 1 represents "no pain" and 5 represents "the most pain I ever felt." The rank sum test compares the amount of pain felt in the two groups.

Relative Risk, Risk Ratio, Odds Ratio: A measure of the strength of an association between a dichotomous risk factor and a disease. It represents the likelihood of disease occurring in subjects with the risk factor present versus absent, expressed as a ratio.

> For example, researchers design a cohort study to assess the relationship of jogging to stress fractures of the femur. They compare two groups of subjects, joggers and nonjoggers, to determine the incidence of stress fractures in a 1-year period and find that 10% of the joggers develop fractures, compared with only 1% of nonjoggers. The relative risk of stress fractures from jogging is thus 10:1.
>
> As another example, consider a cohort study to assess the importance of x-ray exposure in spontaneous abortions. A sample of pregnant hospital x-ray technicians is compared with a sample of pregnant hospital clerical workers on the incidence of spontaneous abortions. The incidence is 20% in the x-ray technicians and 5% in the office workers.

The relative risk is 20:5 or 4:1. This means that spontaneous abortions are four times more likely in x-ray technicians than in office workers.

Computation: Although relative risk and the odds ratio have the same interpretation, they are computed in different ways. Both can be calculated by setting up a table like this:

Risk factor	Disease Present	Disease Absent	Total
Present	a	b	a + b
Absent	c	d	c + d

Relative risk can be used only in cohort studies:

$$\text{Relative Risk} = \frac{\dfrac{a}{a + b}}{\dfrac{c}{c + d}}$$

When the proportion of disease is small in cohort studies, or in case control studies when cases are representative of all cases and controls are representative of all controls, the odds ratio or **cross-product ratio** is a good approximation of the relative risk. For this reason it is often called the "approximate relative risk" or simply "relative risk."

$$\text{Odds Ratio} = \frac{a \times d}{b \times c}$$

When n is small (<100), add 0.5 to each number in the formula for the odds ratio. Thus, the odds ratio formula for a small sample changes:

$$\frac{(a + 0.5) \times (d + 0.5)}{(b + 0.5) \times (c + 0.5)}$$

See Chap. 9 for help computing the confidence interval for the relative risk and odds ratio and testing whether they are equal to 1.

Risk Ratio: *See Relative Risk.*

Sign Test: A test used to compare paired measurements taken on the same subject or to compare matched subjects, when the measurements are ordinal, or continuous but not normally distributed. This test is especially useful when the important comparison is only whether one member of a pair is greater or less than the other, and when absolute ranking of all subjects is impossible. This test is a nonparametric alternative to the paired *t*-test.

Computation: The test compares the number of pairs in which the first member of the pair is greater than the second and the number in which the second is greater than the first. Pairs where both members are the same are not counted. The number of positive and negative differences is reported, and the probability of obtaining these by chance is calculated.

> Consider a study of the effect of a training course on ability to work with subordinates. One member of each of several pairs of workers in managerial positions in a large corporation were randomly assigned to receive the course, and the other member did not. Pairs were then compared to determine which member of the pair got along better with subordinates. The number of pairs in which the course trainee did better than the nontrainee was counted and compared with the number of pairs in which the nontrainee did better.

Spearman Rank Correlation Coefficient: *See Kendall Rank Correlation.*

t-test (*t*): A test used to compare the means for two sets of continuous measurements. A *two-group*, or *unpaired*, *t-test* is used when the same measurement is compared on two independent groups of subjects. A *paired t-test* is used when paired measurements are taken on the same subject (at two different times or under two different conditions) or on matched subjects.

Computation: To obtain the *t*-statistic, divide the observed difference in means by the standard deviation of the difference, as described in Chap. 9, Sec. I.

> For example, a randomized clinical trial was conducted to determine if a new type of angiography lowers the risk of mortality over the standard procedure. Patients were randomly assigned to receive either the new or standard procedure. Because age is known to be a factor in mortality, the new and standard groups were compared on age. A two-group *t*-test was used to compare the mean age of the groups.

> As another example, to determine the effectiveness of a new antihypertensive drug, the mzean blood pressure of a group of subjects was measured before and after administration of the drug. A paired *t*-test was used.

Wilcoxon Rank Sum Test: *See Rank Sum Test.*

Wilcoxon Signed Rank Test: A test used to compare paired measurements taken on the same subject or on matched subjects when the measurements are ordinal, or continuous but not normally distributed. This test is the nonparametric equivalent of the paired t-test.

Computation: Compares the relative size of the difference between pairs in which the direction of the difference is positive versus negative. Differences for all pairs are ranked in order of magnitude and the sum of the ranks of the positive differences is compared with the sum of the ranks of the negative differences. The sum of negative ranks and the sum of positive ranks are reported, and the probability of obtaining these by chance is computed.

> For example, a study tests the effect of an ophthalmic solution on visual acuity. Researchers administer a visual acuity test before and immediately after giving the solution to five subjects. Although visual acuity is measured on a continuous scale, the number of subjects precludes use of the paired *t*-test. The Wilcoxon Signed Rank Test is used to determine if visual acuity is significantly better or worse after giving the solution.

z-test (z): A test similar to the t-test that is used to compare the means of two independent groups when sample size is large (>25 per group). It can also be used instead of the t-test when group variances are unequal.

Multivariate Tests and Measures

Adjusted Odds Ratio: A ratio used in multiple logistic regression to indicate the degree of association of each risk factor to a dichotomous outcome. The adjusted odds ratio represents the likelihood of the outcome occurring with each risk factor present versus absent (expressed as a ratio), after adjusting for the presence of other significant risk factors in the logistic model.

> In a study on factors in postoperative complications, investigators obtain information on patient age, presence of previous surgery, anesthesia index at the start of surgery, and length of surgery. For the presence of previous surgery, an adjusted odds ratio of 2:1 means that the risk of postoperative complications is twice as great for patients with previous surgery as those with no previous surgery, after adjusting for the effects of patient age, length of surgery, and anesthesia index.

Table A-3. Summary of multivariate tests

Technique	Outcome	Associated statistics
Multiple logistic regression	Dichotomous (event)	Likelihood ratio
		Odds ratio
		Normal statistic
Cox regression	Time to event	Likelihood ratio
		Relative risk ratio
		Normal statistic
Multiple regression	Continuous	F-ratio
		Multiple R^2
		Normal statistic
Discriminant analysis	Discrete (group)	F-statistic
		Wilk's lambda
		Rao's v

Analysis of Covariance: A test that controls for the presence of confounding variables in comparing two or more groups on a continuous outcome.

Computation: The test computes adjusted means for the comparison groups, controlling for the effects of confounding variables or "covariates" and determines whether the difference in adjusted means is significant.

> For example, in a study on the effect of a treatment for high blood pressure, two treatment g.roups are compared on the mean change in blood pressure before and 6 weeks after treatment. To control for confounding by patient age, sex, and body weight, investigators use these variables as covariates in an analysis of covariance.

Chi-Square Goodness of Fit Statistic (χ^2): A statistic used in Cox regression or logistic regression to test how well the model fits the data (i.e., how well it predicts outcome). Unlike tests for the significance of individual risk factors, the **larger** the p-value for the goodness of fit statistic, the **better** the model fits the data.

Coefficient (β): The weighting factor for a risk factor in a regression formula or equation, indicating the relationship of the risk factor to the outcome. The sign of the coefficient indicates the direction of this relationship. Risk factors with **positive** coefficients **increase** the likelihood of the outcome occurring when the risk factor is present. Risk factors with **negative** coefficients **decrease** the likelihood of the outcome occurring. *See also Regression.*

Cox Regression: A type of regression used to assess the relationship of various risk factors to time to occurrence of an event (also known as survival time). In the Cox regression equation, a positive coefficient for a risk factor indicates an increase in the likelihood of the event occurring when the risk factor is present, and therefore a decrease in survival time. A negative coefficient for a risk factor indicates a decrease in the likelihood of the event occurring when the risk factor is present, and therefore an increase in survival time.

> For example, a study is designed to determine important factors in the length of survival from diagnosis for patients with lung cancer. Investigators record information on pathologic factors such as histologic type, grade, and stage; patient factors such as age, sex, and race; and treatment factors such as presence and type of radiation, chemotherapy, and surgery. They use Cox regression to examine the effect of these factors on length of survival from diagnosis.

Cross-Validation: When a model derived from one population is tested on a new population. This test usually involves substituting risk factor values for each individual in the new population into the regression model to derive a predicted value for a continuous outcome or a predicted probability of a dichotomous outcome for that individual. For continuous outcomes, the average difference between predicted and observed values in the new population is calculated. For dichotomous outcomes, the percent of correctly classified cases in the new population is calculated. When the outcome is time to some event (survival time), the actual distribution of survival times in the new population is compared to the predicted times.

Discriminant Analysis: Analysis used to classify individuals into one of two or more outcome groups on the basis of several risk factors. A formula or set of formulas is constructed to predict the group to which an individual belongs. Discriminant analysis can be used as an alternative to logistic regression but is most appropriate when all risk factors are continuous.

> For example, information on various growth hormones is obtained on normal height and growth-retarded subjects. Discriminant analysis determines if the two groups can be distinguished on the basis of growth hormone levels.

F-Statistic, or F-test (F): A test of the significance of an individual risk factor or a set of risk factors in discriminant analysis or multiple regression. This test can be used to determine whether a set of variables significantly predict outcome or whether an individual variable significantly affects outcome.

Likelihood Ratio Test (χ^2): A test of the significance of individual risk factors in logistic regression or Cox regression. This test is reported as a χ^2.

Multiple Correlation Coefficient (R^2): A statistic that indicates the fit of the model in multiple regression and represents the proportion of total variation in the outcome that is explained by the risk factors. This value ranges from 0 to 1. Values close to 1 indicate that the risk factors explain most of the variation. This statistic indicates the fit of the regression model, or how well it predicts outcome.

Multiple Logistic Regression: A type of regression used to assess the relationship of various risk factors to the probability of an event. In the logistic equation a risk factor with a positive coefficient increases the likelihood of the event occurring; a risk factor with a negative coefficient decreases the likelihood.

For example, a study is designed to determine what factors are important in the development of postoperative complications following upper abdominal surgery. All patients admitted for upper abdominal surgery at a particular hospital from June 1992 to December 1992 are included in the study. Researchers record information for all patients on age, American Society of Anesthesia index (ASA) admitting diagnosis, presence of previous surgery, length of surgery, estimated blood loss, and dose of anesthetic used. The effect of these factors on the likelihood of complications is assessed by multiple logistic regression.

Multiple Regression: A type of regression used to assess the relationship of various risk factors to a continuous outcome. *See Regression.*

For example, suppose we wish to identify important factors in postoperative blood pressure for patients undergoing cardiac surgery. We record information on length of surgery (hrs), estimated blood loss (ml), patient age (yrs), and total dose of anesthetic agents used (ml). Multiple regression describes the relationship of each factor to postoperative blood pressure and assesses its significance.

Rao's v: A measure of the difference between groups in discriminant analysis. Used as an alternative to the F-statistic in selecting variables for the discriminant model.

Regression: Any form of analysis in which a model or formula is derived relating one or more risk factors to an outcome. *See also Coefficient, Multiple Regression, Multiple Logistic Regression, Cox Regression, and Discriminant Analysis.*

For a more detailed explanation of regression analysis, see Chap. 8. Sec. II.

Relative Risk Ratio: A ratio used in Cox regression to represent the probability of an event occurring at any time for subjects with a risk factor present versus absent, after adjusting for the effects of other significant risk factors.

> For example, a study is designed to determine important factors in the length of survival from diagnosis for patients with lung cancer. Investigators record information on pathologic factors such as histologic type, grade, and stage; patient factors such as age, sex, and race; and treatment factors such as presence and type of radiation, chemotherapy, and surgery. A relative risk ratio of 2 for sex (maleness) would mean that the risk of dying at any time from diagnosis is twice as great for males as for females. A relative risk ratio of 0.5 for chemotherapy would mean that patients who receive chemotherapy have half the risk of dying at any time as those who do not receive chemotherapy.

Standardized Coefficient or Normal Statistic (Z): A coefficient that indicates the importance of a risk factor to an outcome, relative to other risk factors in the model.

Computation: The standardized coefficient is the regression coefficient divided by its standard error.

> For example, in a logistic model to predict the development of postoperative complications, if age had a normal statistic of 4.0 and estimated blood loss had a normal statistic of 2.0, age would be twice as important as blood loss in the development of postoperative complications.

Stepwise Procedure: A progressive process of choosing from multiple factors in a regression model. Risk factors are chosen for inclusion in a model according to some significance level set in advance. Factors that do not satisfy the significance criterion are not included in the model. **Forward stepwise regression** begins with no factors in the model and adds factors one at a time until no further significant factors are found. **Backward stepwise regression** starts with all factors in the model and discards factors one at a time until only significant factors are left. In both types of procedure, the significance of a factor at each step is assessed while accounting for other factors already in the model.

t-**Statistic:** An alternative to the *F*-statistic in testing the significance of individual risk factors in multiple regression.

Wilks' Lambda: A statistic used in discriminant analysis to test the significance of a set of predictors. Used as an alternative to the *F*-statistic or Rao's *V* for variable selection in the discriminant model.

Appendix B

Sample Protocol

EFFECT OF IONIC REARRANGEMENT OF IMPLANTABLE SILICONE INTRAVENOUS CATHETERS ON THE RATE OF CATHETER THROMBOSIS

Principal Investigator: William P Reed, MD[1]

Introduction[2]

Patients undergoing chemotherapy for treatment of cancer need a reliable route of entry into the venous system for administration of drugs, blood products, fluids, and salts and for the periodic removal of blood samples to assess the effects of treatment. The venous access port is one device that is commonly used to provide such a route of entry [1]. It consists of a reservoir covered with a silicone rubber septum through which a needle can be inserted for injection or blood withdrawal. This reservoir is attached to a catheter, which is threaded through a neck or chest vein into the superior vena cava. The reservoir is, in turn, placed in a pocket beneath the skin, so that no part of the device protrudes

---

[1]This protocol is reproduced with Dr. Reed's permission.
[2]Please see App. C for examples of forms similar to the ones mentioned in this protocol.

through the skin. Venous access is accomplished by piercing the skin over the reservoir with a special needle, which is then pushed through the septum and into the reservoir chamber. This chamber is in direct communication with the vena cava through the attached catheter. If thrombosis of the catheter lumen develops, as occurs in up to 25% of cases [2], venous access is lost unless the clot can be removed. Current methods of clot removal involve costly infusion of thrombolytic agents, such as urokinase, which may be effective in 30% to 90% of cases [3–4]. When the lumen cannot be opened by such infusion, replacement of the device may be necessary, requiring an additional operative procedure.

Ionic rearrangement of silicone material by electronic means (Spi-Silicone, Spire Corporation, Bedford, MA 01730) appears to reduce the amount of fibrin and thrombus that accumulates on the surface of implanted devices. This study will examine the effects of such treatment of standard venous access materials on the rate of catheter occlusion in a group of patients undergoing port insertion for chemotherapy. This treatment is not a coating but a physical alteration of the silicone molecules on the surface of the material. Silicone treated in this manner has been previously used for orthopedic prostheses.

Methods

Patients who are referred for venous access to facilitate chemotherapy will be eligible to participate unless they have platelet counts lower than 100,000; have hematologic malignancies such as leukemia, which are likely to produce thrombolic repair or disseminated intravascular coagulation (DIC); or are receiving therapeutic doses of anticoagulants. Patients with a life expectancy of less than 30 days will also be ineligible. Once patients agree to enter the study, they will be randomized by permuted block design [5] to one of two treatment groups: those receiving an untreated catheter or those receiving an ionically altered catheter. All catheters supplied will have nonattached portals.

Statistical Methods. The major outcome of the study will be the incidence of thrombosis. Other outcomes examined descriptively but not subjected to formal statistical analysis will be length of time until first thrombosis occurs, incidence of catheter dysfunction not related to tip migration, ease of restoring function by urokinase infusion, and frequency of premature discontinuation of catheter use. Two groups of 50 patients each will be required to provide power adequate to establish significance of a reduction in thrombosis from 25% to 5% [6].

The two treatment groups will first be compared on baseline characteristics such as age and disease severity, to establish adequacy of the randomization. Any differences between the groups at baseline will be controlled for in the analysis. The incidence of thrombosis in the two treatment groups will be compared using chi-square analysis if no baseline differences are found between the groups. Alternatively, multiple logistic regression (MLR) will be used to control for any baseline differences found [7]. A forward stepwise procedure will be used in the MLR with the maximum likelihood method used to calculate the regression coefficients. The likelihood ratio criterion will be used to determine the significance of individual factors in the regression model [8].

Patient Accession, Randomization, and Follow-Up

The process of enrolling and following study patients is graphically summarized in Fig. B.1. The following steps describe the process of implementing the study.

1. **Determine Eligibility.** Eligible patients include those with cancer and platelet counts greater than 100,000. Patients with leukemia or platelet counts less than 100,000 and patients on anticoagulants other than those contained in the flush solution will be ineligible.
2. **Obtain Consent.** Once a patient is deemed eligible to participate, obtain informed consent. Each participating institution should develop its own informed consent forms for this study, according to institutional requirements concerning informed consent.
3. **Randomize Patients.** After obtaining informed consent, randomize the patient by taking the next sequentially numbered catheter box. (See "Preparation of Study Materials" later in this appendix). Boxes should be available in a predesignated location so that patients may be enrolled at any time. **All eligible patients who consent should be enrolled.** Failure to do so may bias the study results from your institution. Enter each patient's name and date of entry on the randomization list next to the appropriate study number.

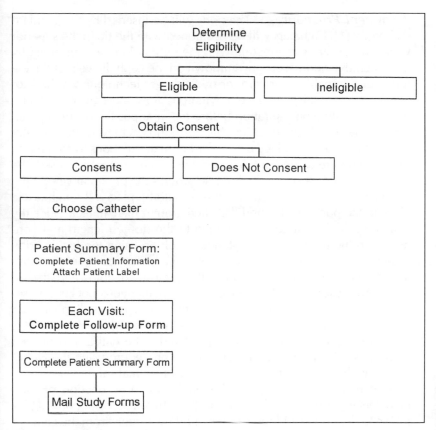

Figure B-1. Study procedure

4. **Complete Forms.** Place one of the prenumbered labels from in-
    side the catheter box on the Patient Summary Form. Complete
    all sections except the last two items and put the form in the pa-
    tient's study folder. Complete the Follow-up Form each time
    you access the port.
    See "Preparation of Study Materials" and "Instructions for
    Completing Study Forms" later in this appendix.
5. **Completion of the Study.** A patient is removed from the study
    when he or she dies or when the catheter is removed. Upon
    completion of the study for a particular patient, fill in the rea-
    son for discontinuing use of the catheter and the catheter re-
    moval date on the Patient Summary Form. Send all completed
    forms to Dr. William P. Reed, at the address listed on the forms.

Treatment Procedures.   The ports will be inserted by the standard technique [1]. Catheters will be positioned with the tip in the superior vena cava as far as its junction with the right atrium, as confirmed by intraoperative fluoroscopy, by cutdown on the cephalic vein or the external or internal jugular vein, or by Seldinger technique via the subclavian or internal jugular vein. Vigorous flow through the catheter must be possible on aspiration before the final position of the tip can be considered adequate. Once this position is achieved, the catheter should be secured in place before further manipulations to attach it to the reservoir are carried out. If a cutdown insertion has been used, the catheter should be secured with a tie around the proximal vein. If the Seldinger technique is used, a suture should be placed through fascia close to the puncture site and then tied around the catheter. Once the catheter is secure, it can be trimmed to the desired length and connected to the reservoir in the standard fashion using the locking ring provided. The locking ring is to be kept in a locked position with nonabsorbable suture passed through the preformed holes and tied in place. The reservoir is then placed in a subcutaneous pocket and secured in place with circumferential sutures to avoid its flipping over. Skin and subcutaneous tissues are then closed by whatever method is chosen (subarticular skin closure preferred). The catheter is flushed with heparinized saline at the end of the procedure using the Huber needle with 10 units of heparin per 1 cc of normal saline.

After patients recover from the procedure, the function of their catheters will be assessed at each visit for blood sampling or drug infusion to determine if blood can be withdrawn freely from the catheter and fluids infused. The status of patency to infusion and withdrawal will be recorded on the Follow-up Form. (Instructions follow for completing the Follow-up Form.) If no drug infusion or blood sampling is anticipated over an interval of time exceeding 30 days, a visit for flushing of the device with heparinized flush solution will be scheduled, as is currently standard for all patients with port access devices in place. Function will be assessed at the time of port access for flushing for patients not actively being treated. Each port will be filled with 6 mL standard flush solution (normal saline with 10 U/mL of heparin) at the conclusion of each flush, blood withdrawal, or access for infusion.

When catheters cease to function for blood withdrawal or infusion, a chest x-ray will be obtained to determine the location of the catheter tip. Under the unusual circumstances of tip migration, efforts to reposition the tip by endoluminal manipulation under fluoroscopic control will be carried out to restore function [1]. If no migration has occurred, standard procedures to restore patency by infusion of thrombolytic agents will be used. The standard infusion at our medical center consists of 15,000 units of urokinase in 250 mL D5W infused at a rate of 17 mL/hr for 12 to 14 hours.

Preparation of Study Materials

1. Each institution should make its own arrangements to receive equal quantities of treated and untreated catheters. The lot number of treated and untreated catheters will be supplied by the company. Only the person preparing the randomization materials, the person dispensing the catheters, or both should know which catheters are treated and which are untreated. All other personnel involved in the study who will be treating patients or completing study forms should be blinded to the type of catheter used on a given study patient.

2. The Materials Manager should obtain a Randomization List by mail from Ms. Jane Garb at Baystate Medical Center. She may be reached daily by phone. This list will contain study numbers and catheter types (treated or untreated) for 100 patients, as well as space for entering the lot number for each catheter used, patient name, and date of entry for each patient enrolled.

3. Separate the catheters received into treated and untreated stacks. For each study number on the randomization list, choose a catheter box of the appropriate type (treated or untreated) and mark the study number clearly in red pen on the outside of the catheter box and on all the labels that come inside the box. Enter the lot number printed on the outside edge of the catheter box on the randomization list.

4. Stack all the catheter boxes in numerical order according to study number. Place the boxes in a central location where appropriate study personnel will have access to them when a patient enters the study.

5. Copies of study forms can be found in the appendix of the protocol. Make multiple copies of the Patient Summary Form and Follow-up Form to keep on hand when a patient enters the study.

6. A manila folder labeled with the patient's name and ID number should be prepared for each patient entering the study. All study forms for this patient should be kept in the folder.

Instructions for Completing Study Forms

Patient Summary Form

1. Complete this form as soon as the patient has been randomized. Be sure to attach one of the inside labels from the patient's catheter box to the study form.
2. Obtain other information from the attending surgeon or from the patient's chart before the patient has been discharged.
3. Complete the last two items on completion of study.

Follow-Up Form   Complete the Follow-up Form each time you access the port.

1. Question 1: Ease of port access

   - Choose **Poor** if you have difficulty in palpating the location of the port or are unable to access the port on the first attempt.
   - Choose **Moderate** if you are able to access the port on first attempt, but with minor difficulty.
   - Choose **Excellent** if you are able to access the port on first attempt without difficulty.
   - Choose **NA** if the port is already accessed.

2. Question 2: Ease of infusion

   - Choose **Poor** if you are unable to infuse or flush the catheter.
   - Choose **Moderate** if the catheter flushes with some resistance.
   - Choose **Excellent** if the catheter flushes without resistance.

3. Question 3: Ease of blood withdrawal

   - Choose **Poor** if there is no blood return.
   - Choose **Moderate** if there is blood return only with intervention. Question 4 lists possible actions; check each action taken and check whether blood flow was restored as a result.
   - Choose **Excellent** if blood was aspirated without requiring any of the interventions listed in Question 4.

Institutional Assurances.   To ensure valid results of this clinical trial, all participating institutions must be consistent in carrying out all study methods according to the protocol. To ensure consistency, we are asking the principal investigator for each site to sign a copy of the agreement of participating institutions form in this protocol's appendix.

Personnel

The following study personnel should be identified and instructed in all study procedures.

- **Principal Investigator:** The principal investigator is responsible for accruing patients and administering study treatments as described in the protocol. He or she is also responsible for assembling a study team and overseeing the team's activities.
- **Nurse:** The study nurse is responsible for completing the Patient Summary Form and Follow-up Form. This job may be shared by any nurses responsible for catheter use. However, all persons filling this function must have read the study protocol and be familiar with the data forms.
- **Project Manager:** The project manager is responsible for preparing all randomization materials (i.e., for labeling and arranging catheters), photocopying and distributing all data forms, and keeping the randomization list updated. He or she is also responsible for making sure that all forms are completed on time and returned to Baystate Medical Center.

SAMPLE RANDOMIZATION LIST

Study #	Group	Lot #	Patient Name	Date Entered	Forms Received
1	Untreated				
2	Untreated				
3	Untreated				
4	Untreated				
5	Treated				
6	Treated				
7	Treated				
8	Treated				
9	Treated				
10	Untreated				
11	Treated				
12	Treated				
13	Treated				
14	Treated				
14	Treated				
15	Untreated				

References

This protocol was reproduced with the permission of Dr. William P. Reed, Director of Surgical Oncology, Baystate Medical Center, Springfield, MA.

1. Reed WP. Intravenous access devices for supportive care of patients with cancer. *Curr Opin Oncol* 3:634–642, 1991.
2. Tschirhart JM, Rao MK. Mechanism and management of persistent withdrawal occlusion. *Am Surg* 54:326–328, 1988.
3. Haire WD, et al. Obstructed central venous catheters, restoring function with a 12-hour infusion of low-dose urokinase. *Cancer* 66:2279–2285, 1990.
4. Monturo CA, Dickerson RN, Mullen JL. Efficacy of thrombolytic therapy for occlusion of long-term catheters. *J Parenter Enteral Nutr* 14:312–314, 1990.
5. Pocock SJ. *Clinical Trials, a Practical Approach.* New York: Wiley, 1991. pp 76–79.
6. Fleiss JL. *Statistical Methods for Rates and Proportion.* New York: Wiley, 1973. pp 176–194.
7. Cox DR. *Analysis of Binary Data.* London: Methuen, 1970.
8. Lee ET. *Statistical Methods for Survival Data Analysis.* New York: Wiley, 1992. pp 256–257.

Appendix  *C*

Sample Data Forms

GUILLAIN-BARRÉ STUDY   5/95
RANDOMIZATION FORM

Hospital Number ☐☐☐☐☐☐   Hospital Name _____

PATIENT INFORMATION

Last Name _____   First _____

D.O.B. ☐☐☐☐☐☐

Age   ☐☐ yrs   Grade on admission ☐

Weight ☐☐ lbs

Sex   ☐
   1 = Male 2 = Female
   9 = Unknown

Race   ☐
   1 = White
   2 = Black
   3 = Hispanic
   4 = Asian
   9 = Unknown

0 = Healthy
1 = Minor signs/symptoms
2 = Able to walk 5 meters unassisted
3 = Able to walk 5 meters with walker or equivalent support
4 = Bed or chair bound (unable to walk)
5 = Requires assisted ventilation
6 = Dead

ADMISSION DATA

Admit Date ☐☐☐☐☐☐   Est. Date of Onset ☐☐☐☐☐☐
      MO DAY YR   MO DAY YR

Referred by (MD) _____

ELIGIBILITY

Eligibility ☐   1 = Eligible   2 = Not eligible (check reasons below)

      ☐ < Grade III severity
      ☐ > 30 days duration
      ☐ Severe unrelated illness
      ☐ IGA deficiency
      ☐ Pregnancy
      ☐ Prior adverse reaction to IVIG
      ☐ Prior Rx w/immunosuppressives

CONSENT OBTAINED ☐   1 = yes   2 = no

RANDOMIZATION ID # ☐☐☐
Treatment Assigned ☐   1 = plasmapheresis   2 = IVIG

HEAD CT SCAN STUDY
Division of Trauma

Medical Record ☐☐☐☐☐☐   Date of Admission ☐☐☐☐☐☐
                                                    mo   day   yr

Patient Last Name _____   First _____

☐ **MECHANISM OF INJURY**

    1 = Vehicle   Vehicle ☐   1 = Car
                                                    2 = Motorcycle
                                                    3 = Pedestrian
                                                    4 = Bicycle

    2 = Assault/blunt   Weapon ☐   1 = Pipe
                                                    2 = Bat
                                                    3 = Wood
                                                    4 = Body
                                                    5 = Large animal
                                                    6 = Other: _____

    3 = Fall

CLINICAL/DEMOGRAPHIC DATA ON ADMISSION

Age ☐☐   Sex ☐   1 = Male
                                                    2 = Female

Amnesia Present ☐   1 = Yes   Intubated? ☐   1 = Yes
                     2 = No   2 = No

Glasgow Coma Score: ☐☐   Injury Severity Score: ☐☐

ETOH ☐☐☐

Drug Screen ☐   1 = Pos   Type of Substance ☐☐   1 = PCP
  Results   2 = Neg   #1#2   2 = Benzodiazepine
                 3 = Not done   3 = Cocaine
                                           4 = Amphetamines
                                           5 = Cannabi
OUTCOME   6 = Opiates
                                           7 = Barbiturates
Type of Injury Noted on CT (1 = Present)   8 = Other: _____

☐ Epidural   ☐ Brain Contusion
☐ Subdural   ☐ Localized Swelling
☐ Shear injury   ☐ Diffuse Brain Swelling

PRE-OPERATIVE RADIATION STUDY

PATIENT INFORMATION

☐☐☐☐ ID

☐☐ Age at Diagnosis

☐ Sex   1 = Male
            2 = Female

☐ Rx Group
      1 = Preop
      2 = Surgery Only

Patient Name

Last _____   First _____

Physician _____

Medical Record # _____

Birth Date _____   Date Dx _____

Check if: MP _____   RS _____   TR _____

Comments:

OPERATION

☐☐☐☐☐☐ Date of Surgery (Leave blank if unknown)
MO DAY YR

Procedure

☐ 1 = A-P   2 = Anterior   3 = Left Colectomy   4 = Hartmann's
   5 = Rectosigmoidectomy   6 = Extensive fulguration
   7 = Polypectomy   8 = Other: _____   9 = Unknown

Residual Disease at Time of Surgery (If none, leave blank)

☐☐ 1 = Pelvis   2 = Rectum   3 = Liver   4 = Lung   5 = Brain
       6 = Bone   7 = Other: _____   9 = unknown if residual
☐ Distance from Anal Verge   1 = < 8 cm   2 = 8–15 cm   3 = > 15 cm
☐ Purpose of surgery   1 = Curative   2 = Palliative   9 = Undetermined

Surgical Complications (If none, leave blank)

☐☐☐☐ See Attached Code Sheet
 #1   #2

PATH FINDINGS
Histology

☐ 1 = Adeno   2 = Mucinous Ad.   3 = Villous Ad.   4 = Epidermoid
   5 = Polypoid   6 = Small Cell   7 = Colloid Ad.   8 = Other_____
   9 = Unknown

Differentiation

☐ 1 = Well   2 = Moderate   3 = Poor   9 = Unknown

Stage

☐ Blank = No Residual Present   0 = In situ   1 = A   2 = B1   3 = B2
  4 = B3   5 = C1   6 = C2   7 = C3   8 = D   9 = Unknown

Nodal Status at Surgery

☐☐ # Positive Nodes   (99 = Unknown)
☐☐ # Nodes Taken   (99 = Unknown, or unknown if nodes taken)

RADIATION THERAPY

☐☐☐☐☐☐ Date Treatment Completed
MO DAY YR

☐☐☐☐☐ # Rads Given

Early Complications (Before Surgery): If none, leave blank

☐☐   1 = Diarrhea   2 = Nausea   3 = Vomiting   4 = Cramps
#1#2   5 = Frequency or Cystitis   6 = Dysuria   7 = Dermatitis
        8 = Rectal edema or bleeding   9 = Other: _____

FOLLOW-UP

☐☐☐☐☐☐ Date Last Seen Alive or Disease-Free
MO DAY YR

Date of Recurrence

☐☐☐☐☐☐
MO DAY YR

Site of Recurrence
☐☐☐   1 = Pelvis   2 = Rectum   3 = Liver   4 = Lung   5 = Brain
#1#2#3 6 = Bone   7 = Perineum   8 = Abdomen, generalized (inguinal
                                    nodes, peritoneum, gallbladder,
                                    kidneys, mesentery, pancreas)

        9 = UNKNOWN

Death

☐   0 = No   1 = Yes

☐☐☐☐☐☐ Date of Death
MO DAY YR

Appendix D

Determining Sample Size

To determine the sample size necessary to achieve adequate power for detecting a difference among your study groups, you need to know the following:

1. The estimated level of the outcome variable that you expect to find in your control or reference group. The reference group is the standard or control treatment in clinical trials, the control group in case control studies, or the group without the risk factor in cohort studies.

    You can estimate the outcome variable (usually a mean and standard deviation or a proportion) by using values from previous studies in the literature or from your own clinical experience. In the absence of any prior estimates of the outcome variable, you can conduct a pilot study.

2. The effect size (size of the difference between groups) that you would consider clinically meaningful or important
3. The significance level (*p*-value) you require for your study (usually 0.05 unless multiple comparisons will be performed)
4. The level of power you require (usually at least 0.80)

Using these values, you can obtain the required sample size for detecting a difference in two proportions or detecting a relative risk of some specified magnitude by referring to Tables D-1 or D-2, respectively. Refer to Table D-3 to obtain sample sizes for detecting a difference in two means. The computer program EPI INFO has a module to determine sample size and power. Some other statistics packages also have sample size modules.

Table D-1.   Sample size for comparing two proportions

Smaller probability, π_2	$\delta = \pi_1 - \pi_2$									
	0.05	0.010	0.15	0.20	0.25	0.30	0.35	0.40	0.45	0.50
0.05	621	207	113	75	54	42	33	27	23	19
	475	160	88	59	43	33	27	22	19	16
0.10	958	286	146	92	65	48	38	30	25	21
	726	219	113	72	51	38	30	24	20	17
0.15	1252	354	174	106	73	54	41	33	27	22
	946	270	134	82	57	42	33	26	21	18
0.20	1504	412	198	118	80	58	44	34	28	23
	1134	313	151	91	62	45	35	27	22	18
0.25	1714	459	216	127	85	61	46	35	28	23
	1291	349	165	98	66	47	36	28	23	18
0.30	1883	496	230	134	88	62	46	36	28	23
	1417	376	176	103	68	49	36	28	23	18
0.35	2009	522	240	138	90	63	46	35	28	22
	1511	396	183	106	69	49	36	28	22	18
0.40	2093	538	244	139	90	62	46	34	27	21
	1574	407	186	107	69	49	36	27	21	17
0.45	2135	543	244	138	88	61	44	33	25	19
	1605	411	186	106	68	47	35	26	20	16
0.50	2135	538	240	134	85	58	41	30	23	18
	1605	407	183	103	66	45	33	24	19	15

This table is used to determine the sample size necessary to find a significant difference (5% two-sided significance level) between two proportions estimated from independent samples where the true proportions are π_1 and π_2 and $\delta = \pi_1 - \pi_2$ is the specified difference ($\pi_1 > \pi_2$). Sample sizes are given for 90% power (upper value of pair) and 80% power (lower value). The sample size given in the table refers to *each* of the two independent samples. From Armitage P and Berry G. *Statistical Methods in Medical Research.* Blackwell Scientific Publications, ed 3, 1993, Oxford: p. 579.

Note: If $\pi_2 > 0.5$, work with $\pi'_1 = 1 - \pi_2$ and $\pi'_2 = 1 - \pi_1$.

Table D-2. Number of cases needed for detecting relative risk in a case control study

Proportion of controls exposed, p	OR (odds ratio)							
	0.5	1.5	2.0	2.5	3.0	4.0	5.0	10.0
0.05	1369	2347	734	393	259	150	105	43
	1044	1775	560	301	200	117	82	34
0.10	701	1266	402	219	146	87	62	27
	534	958	307	168	113	68	48	22
0.15	479	913	295	163	110	67	48	23
	366	691	225	125	85	52	38	19
0.20	370	743	244	136	93	58	43	21
	282	562	187	105	72	45	34	17
0.25	306	647	216	122	85	53	40	21
	233	490	165	94	66	42	32	17
0.30	264	590	200	115	80	51	39	22
	202	447	153	88	62	40	31	18
0.35	236	556	192	111	79	51	39	23
	180	421	147	86	61	40	31	18
0.40	216	528	188	111	79	52	41	24
	165	407	144	85	61	41	32	20
0.45	203	533	189	112	81	54	43	26
	155	403	145	87	63	43	34	21
0.50	194	538	194	116	85	58	46	29
	148	407	148	90	66	45	36	23

This table is used to determine the sample size necessary to find the odds ratio statistically significant (5% two-sided test) in a case control study with an equal number of cases and controls. The specified odds ratio is denoted by OR, and p is the proportion of controls that are expected to be exposed. **For each pair of values, the upper figure is for a power of 90%, and the lower, for a power of 80%.** The tabulated sample size refers to the number of *cases* required. From Armitage P and Berry G. *Statistical Methods in Medical Research.* Blackwell Scientific Publications, ed 3, 1993, Oxford: p. 580.

Note: If $p > 0.5$, work with $p' = 1 - p$ and $OR' = 1/OR$.

Table D-3.   Sample sizes per group for testing the difference in 2 means
$d' = \text{difference}/\sqrt{2} \times SD$

d' \ $1 - \beta$	$\alpha = 0.01$; $z_{.995} = 2.576$					
	0.30	0.50	0.70	0.90	0.95	0.99
0.1	422	664	961	1,489	1,782	2,403
0.2	106	166	241	373	446	601
0.3	47	74	107	166	198	267
0.4	27	42	61	94	112	151
0.5	17	27	39	60	72	97
0.6	12	19	27	42	50	67
0.7	9	14	20	31	37	50
0.8	7	11	16	24	28	38
0.9	6	9	12	19	22	30
1.0	5	7	10	15	18	25
1.2	3	5	7	11	13	17
1.4	3	4	5	8	10	13
1.6	2	3	4	6	7	10
1.8	2	3	3	5	6	8
2.0	2	2	3	4	5	7
2.2	1	2	2	4	4	5
2.4		2	2	3	4	5
2.6		1	2	3	3	4
2.8			2	2	3	4
3.0			2	2	2	3

Continued

Table D-3.   *(continued)*

d'	$\alpha = 0.05$					
$1 - \beta$	0.30	0.50	0.70	0.90	0.95	0.99
0.1	207	385	618	1,052	1,300	1,837
0.2	52	97	155	263	325	460
0.3	23	43	69	117	145	205
0.4	13	25	39	66	82	115
0.5	9	16	25	43	52	74
0.6	6	11	18	30	37	52
0.7	5	8	13	22	27	38
0.8	4	7	10	17	21	29
0.9	3	5	8	13	17	23
1.0	3	4	7	11	13	19
1.2	2	3	5	8	10	13
1.4	2	2	4	6	7	10
1.6	1	2	3	5	6	8
1.8		2	2	4	5	6
2.0		1	2	3	4	5
2.2			2	3	3	4
2.4			1	2	3	4
2.6				2	2	3
2.8				2	2	3
3.0				2	2	3

From Dixon WJ and Massey FJ. *Introduction to Statistical Analysis,* 4th ed. New York: McGraw-Hill, 1980.

For example, suppose we wish to conduct a randomized clinical trial to study the effects of drug X on blood coagulation in patients with coagulopathy. Patients with drug X (treatment group) and those given placebo (controls) will be compared on mean prothrombin time (PTT). From previous clinical studies we know that average PTT in such patients is 17 seconds, with a standard deviation of 4 seconds. We would like to see at least a 1.7-second drop in PTT with drug X before we consider it to be clinically effective, at a power of 90% and significance level of 5%. To use Table D-3, we first need to define the quantity d' that appears in the table. This is merely the difference in means we wish to detect (i.e., the effect size), divided by $\sqrt{2}$, times the expected standard deviation (SD).

$$d' = \frac{\text{difference}}{\sqrt{2} \times \text{SD}}$$

From our example,

$$d' = \frac{1.7}{\sqrt{2 \times 4}}$$

$$= 0.3$$

Looking up $d' = 0.3$ in Table D-3 for $p = 0.05$ and power = 0.90, we find that the required minimum sample size to detect a difference of this magnitude would be 117 patients per group. (Note that in the table, power is referred to as "$1 - \beta$.")

As another example, suppose we wish to determine whether a causal association exists between estrogen use and breast cancer. Using a case control design, we plan to compare the proportion of women who have used estrogen in cases and controls. Related studies in the literature report the prevalence of estrogen use in nondiseased women to be between 10% and 15%. We would require an odds ratio of at least 2.0 to conclude that there is causal evidence for an association of estrogen and breast cancer. Using Table D-2, which gives sample sizes for p of 0.05 and power of 0.80 or 0.90, we find that a sample size of 307 cases would be required for 80% power and 402 cases for 90% power to detect an odds ratio of 2.0 when the proportion of controls is 0.1. If we were concerned with odds ratios of 3 or higher, the resulting sample sizes needed would be only 113 and 146, respectively.

Appendix E

Randomization Methods

Researchers usually randomize an equal number of subjects to each study group. The two most common ways to achieve this are random allocation and restricted randomization (also called permuted block design).

In random allocation, numbers can be randomly generated by a computer or selected in sequence from a table of random numbers. If two treatments are used, numbers from 1 to n are selected in sequence from a table of random numbers, where n is the total sample size. When an odd number is chosen, the first treatment is assigned next. When an even number is chosen, the second treatment is assigned. If three treatments are used, numbers with a first digit of 1 through 3 can represent the first treatment; those with a first digit of 4 through 6 can represent the second treatment, 7 through 9 the third treatments, and 0 is ignored. If four treatments are used, beginning digits of 1–2, 3–4, 5–6, and 7–8 can be used, and 9, 0 ignored. Using this method allows generation of a list of all treatment assignments for the total number of study subjects.

Although this method of randomization results in approximately equal sample sizes per group, there is the slight possibility of very unequal numbers among the groups. This possibility is increased with small sample sizes. If this occurs, the investigator may want to generate an entirely new randomization list. This is known as replacement randomization, and is preferable to selectively replacing individual treatment assignments, which destroys the randomness of the list. An alternative is to use a permuted block design.

A permuted block design is used to ensure an equal number of subjects for each treatment group at specified intervals throughout the study. Subjects are assigned in blocks of a specified number, with an equal number of subjects in each treatment group within each block. For example, if the block size were set at 20, then after every 20 subjects, each treatment group would have an equal number of subjects. This method is used to avoid treatment group imbalances in size if the study is stopped prematurely, before the total predetermined sample size is reached.

The persons responsible for randomizing subjects should be unaware of the randomization scheme used, as well as the block size, to avoid any possibility of predicting a particular subject's treatment assignment. With a random number table, the method used for random allocation can be adapted to the permuted block design by allocating treatments in blocks of the desired size. For example, if block size is 30, the first block of 30 numbers in the random number table can be allocated to two treatments by choosing odd and even numbers. The next block of 30 numbers can then be similarly assigned, and so on.

Pocock [1] describes additional randomization methods. Tables E-1 and E-2 provide random numbers, and random permutations of various block sizes are given. EPI INFO and many other computer programs generate random numbers.

After completing one of the above procedures, prepare a randomization list to record the results of randomization. This should consist of a list of sequential study numbers and treatment assignments, as well as space for recording the name and date of patients entered into the study. A sample randomization list is given at the end of Appendix B.

Table E-1. A table of random numbers

```
0 5 2 7 8 4 3 7 4 1 6 8 3 7 4 1 6 8 5 0 0 6 1 1 8 0 5 6 9 1 6 9 8 8 7 4
5 9 7 2 4 3 2 8 0 6 1 5 5 6 3 9 9 9 0 8 2 9 6 2 8 1 9 6 4 2 6 5 3 0 7 9
2 5 9 8 4 8 9 1 4 5 8 6 6 5 9 5 4 8 9 8 2 8 0 9 4 8 4 5 5 1 4 7 3 9 3 2
3 0 3 1 3 1 0 8 7 3 0 6 6 7 3 7 1 7 0 9 5 0 2 6 8 9 5 6 1 5 6 0 5 5 2 4
6 8 6 7 6 8 7 7 3 8 8 3 4 9 0 7 2 6 8 9 2 1 5 9 5 9 8 6 8 5 6 6 8 1 9 9
7 3 3 5 8 3 5 8 1 5 7 1 9 4 8 5 6 0 7 8 3 6 3 9 5 9 7 9 5 3 6 7 5 3 8 5
7 0 0 8 5 0 4 2 0 1 8 9 7 2 6 6 0 9 0 2 2 5 9 9 5 0 6 3 7 9 5 7 1 4 5 3
2 8 1 0 3 2 6 0 1 3 5 0 9 0 2 6 2 9 0 5 6 7 1 5 7 1 9 7 1 1 4 5 5 2 4 4
1 5 6 7 5 1 9 3 0 8 6 5 2 9 6 0 1 7 5 3 0 3 5 9 5 3 9 0 6 5 5 1 7 1 3 3
0 5 6 2 9 6 3 9 0 0 4 0 1 2 0 4 6 2 8 4 2 4 3 7 0 9 7 4 5 9 1 9 7 8 9 6
9 0 2 6 0 8 2 3 0 0 5 3 8 2 1 5 3 6 0 3 5 3 9 0 8 3 9 7 3 9 0 5 9 5 3 4
3 9 6 8 9 3 5 1 4 2 0 7 2 3 2 1 0 4 1 5 7 5 5 9 4 0 6 9 5 4 7 7 2 9 0 7
2 6 1 1 9 6 2 9 3 3 2 8 6 0 1 4 8 8 4 7 8 4 0 6 0 1 3 5 7 9 0 5 1 4 9 0
5 9 6 3 1 6 2 7 6 0 6 7 3 8 0 6 6 6 5 7 9 2 6 4 6 2 8 4 0 1 2 9 6 8 7 6
0 4 2 7 7 5 4 4 4 6 9 9 0 6 9 2 4 2 2 9 0 1 0 4 9 9 5 7 6 5 6 1 2 3 4 4
7 2 3 5 9 8 5 9 8 1 7 6 6 9 4 2 9 0 6 1 4 8 3 3 2 9 6 2 6 1 1 3 4 6 6 0
9 3 0 2 6 3 1 1 8 3 0 5 5 8 5 7 0 3 2 5 3 4 2 9 7 7 6 4 0 2 9 7 5 4 5 9
6 0 7 2 3 0 0 3 6 4 3 2 9 0 4 4 0 8 4 7 6 8 3 7 5 4 9 1 3 3 7 1 0 5 1 2
7 1 7 6 5 4 9 2 1 6 2 1 0 6 8 9 3 2 1 2 9 0 2 3 4 0 9 9 8 6 4 9 5 8 8 0
8 3 4 2 1 7 7 1 3 5 9 3 0 9 3 2 8 4 8 7 2 4 4 6 2 4 5 6 3 7 1 3 9 7 1 3
7 3 2 3 8 6 2 0 5 2 4 3 0 6 0 4 5 2 6 8 1 5 5 3 5 8 9 0 3 3 0 6 3 9 0 6
```

7 6	6 3	0 0	8 8	7 4	2 3	9 5	8 1	2 6	7 1	4 8	6 9	7 1	9 6	9 9
4 3	2 8	9 0	4 5	7 9	0 5	2 3	5 8	7 9	1 6	4 2	7 5	6 2	4 3	8 4
0 5	6 6	0 1	5 1	7 2	8 7	3 5	1 6	8 9	9 6	2 4	5 5	0 9	2 5	6 6
0 6	1 4	3 7	7 4	1 2	8 9	1 6	2 7	7 5	2 0	4 0	4 8	3 6	3 9	2 7
6 9	7 7	8 5	1 4	9 6	1 8	4 0	6 3	4 3	8 3	5 2	2 5	9 5	5 7	6 8
2 1	4 8	6 3	9 7	7 9	2 0	3 1	2 1	5 6	0 3	1 9	2 3	4 3	8 4	6 2
4 7	6 9	5 6	1 7	5 8	6 8	2 9	2 5	9 5	3 1	0 9	8 9	6 8	6 0	5 9
2 5	5 7	7 5	8 3	3 1	9 1	4 3	7 9	7 7	0 3	5 5	8 8	7 5	6 9	2 0
5 6	5 2	8 8	7 4	5 1	6 3	2 4	0 1	6 5	6 9	2 0	7 3	8 6	7 3	2 1
4 8	3 6	7 3	7 5	3 9	5 9	9 8	2 5	7 2	5 8	9 4	1 3	1 7	2 7	5 5

From Pocock SJ. *Clinical Trials, a Practical Approach.* New York: Wiley, 1983, p. 74.

Table E-2. Random permutations of 20 numbers (each row represents a random ordering of the numbers 0 to 19)

11	19	15	5	9	0	6	13	7	2	16	1	12	18	4	17	10	8	3	14
14	12	0	1	19	8	7	17	11	18	2	15	5	9	4	16	10	6	13	3
5	17	2	4	16	19	10	11	14	7	12	15	1	18	6	9	0	3	13	8
8	13	3	12	10	5	17	2	6	7	16	19	0	1	4	11	14	15	18	9
11	6	8	0	1	10	13	18	12	14	17	7	4	5	3	9	19	16	2	15
17	18	3	6	9	15	14	5	4	19	2	1	0	8	11	13	7	12	10	16
14	19	13	16	1	9	18	0	5	15	4	12	10	11	2	3	8	6	7	17
0	3	2	13	7	8	19	12	5	9	16	6	4	17	15	14	1	11	18	10
11	19	2	6	12	15	17	0	10	3	4	14	7	5	16	13	1	8	9	18
13	18	9	6	5	17	19	0	8	10	15	7	11	3	12	4	16	1	2	14
9	3	4	17	18	2	13	14	15	11	0	8	1	7	6	19	16	12	10	5
2	9	17	12	6	19	14	4	1	7	5	3	10	13	0	18	8	15	11	16
14	8	11	2	13	6	5	0	10	12	19	4	16	15	9	17	7	18	1	3
5	9	11	3	7	14	19	15	0	17	2	12	18	4	13	16	10	1	6	8
3	19	11	17	18	10	6	4	14	2	1	16	9	5	7	8	12	13	0	15
13	3	9	11	2	7	0	15	19	4	14	10	12	6	5	1	17	16	18	8
0	5	18	12	3	11	8	15	6	16	9	4	7	2	19	17	14	10	1	13
10	15	0	16	7	5	4	13	12	1	17	3	9	14	11	8	6	18	2	19
2	16	13	19	8	6	17	9	14	4	12	3	1	11	5	15	0	10	7	18
18	15	5	11	6	3	14	13	7	0	9	17	2	1	8	10	12	19	4	16
9	14	3	6	16	1	0	11	4	2	10	12	19	13	7	15	18	8	17	5
15	18	4	12	1	7	11	10	5	17	14	8	2	0	3	6	9	19	13	16
12	1	7	13	19	8	6	4	10	14	0	18	15	9	17	16	11	2	5	3
15	11	3	10	14	9	16	2	5	17	18	19	4	6	13	1	8	0	7	12
1	17	16	10	15	18	0	7	11	9	2	14	3	5	13	12	6	4	19	8
5	9	16	12	6	17	19	15	2	14	11	0	3	10	8	18	1	4	7	13
9	8	0	7	4	17	19	3	5	6	13	15	16	10	11	12	1	14	2	18
9	2	17	7	16	14	5	15	19	8	13	6	0	4	18	3	10	11	1	12
9	4	14	1	5	0	6	10	15	17	8	16	19	18	7	2	11	13	3	12
6	4	17	14	16	2	1	8	15	11	3	0	10	18	5	13	19	7	12	9
11	6	14	13	10	4	7	18	19	12	15	2	8	5	17	3	1	16	9	0
17	2	14	8	4	11	9	12	3	18	6	13	1	19	7	0	16	5	10	15
1	11	5	9	4	17	14	7	6	12	0	10	19	15	8	16	3	13	2	18
8	19	5	15	9	14	4	1	18	16	11	0	3	12	17	13	7	10	2	6
12	11	6	18	7	13	3	2	14	19	10	9	16	0	4	15	5	8	17	1

Continued

Table E-2. (continued)

17	7	11	4	3	15	16	9	8	0	5	18	10	19	2	13	12	14	1	6
7	11	18	0	17	19	15	12	10	5	8	3	9	13	4	14	1	2	16	6
5	8	0	2	3	13	15	19	6	18	1	10	9	12	14	16	4	7	17	11
15	11	1	12	7	14	13	19	2	16	10	6	18	8	3	17	0	5	4	9
8	1	9	10	6	15	4	19	0	18	2	7	16	13	5	3	11	14	17	12
13	1	17	14	11	16	3	5	7	9	0	15	19	6	18	12	4	10	8	2
3	12	9	4	6	15	5	16	17	18	7	2	19	11	14	8	1	13	10	0
10	3	8	15	2	16	19	4	1	5	13	14	6	7	11	0	17	12	18	9
16	5	9	1	15	18	17	12	10	19	8	13	6	11	4	14	7	3	0	2
19	1	9	16	3	11	8	15	4	13	12	18	0	10	7	6	2	14	5	17
0	10	3	5	13	17	19	8	7	16	14	9	11	12	4	6	2	18	15	1
3	16	15	13	7	9	0	2	18	14	5	10	17	4	19	11	12	1	8	6
14	16	15	7	4	17	2	10	3	1	8	11	18	0	19	12	6	13	5	9
3	1	17	18	19	0	5	9	14	10	8	2	15	4	12	6	16	7	13	11
11	17	13	19	16	18	2	15	1	8	7	10	14	6	0	9	4	5	3	12

From Pocock SJ. *Clinical Trials, a Practical Approach.* New York: Wiley, 1983, p. 78.

Once researchers have prepared a treatment assignment list, they must select the method of implementing the randomization assignment. The following are two common techniques:

1. **Sealed Envelopes.** Using the randomization list, prepare a card for each treatment assignment and study number and place it in a sealed envelope. Put the study number on the outside of the envelope, and place the envelopes in sequential order. Each time a patient is enrolled in the study, choose the next sequentially numbered envelope. This technique is not completely immune to tampering, because the person responsible for randomization may peek inside the envelope to determine the randomization assignment before the patient consents. However, this method is still acceptable if a coordinator can oversee the randomization process and monitor it for tampering.

2. **Central Randomization Center.** Designate a central phone number as a randomization center, and assign one or two people not otherwise involved in the study as "randomization coordinators." The phone number will need to be available 24 hours a day if patients can be randomized at any time of the

day. Otherwise, specify certain hours during which randomization can occur. This method is particularly suited to multi-center clinical trials to coordinate randomization from several different sites but can also be used for a single-center trial.

References

1. Pocock SJ. *Clinical Trials, A Practical Approach.* New York: Wiley, 1983, pp. 73-89.

Index

Questions for Screening Tests*

1. What is the primary purpose of the test?

   a) Is it early detection of people with the disease?
      (1) What will be gained by early detection?
      (2) Are facilities available for referral and definitive testing of people who screen positive?

   b) Is it to rule out people with the disease?
      (1) What are the risks for false negatives?
      (2) What are the costs of false positives?

2. How was the presence of disease established? Was it definitive?

3. Are the operating characteristics good enough to satisfy the primary purpose of the screening test?

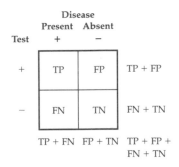

   a) What is the sensitivity? *Calculate TP/(TP + FN)*

   b) What is the specificity? *Calculate TN/(FP+ TN)*

4. On what population was the test based? Was it broad enough that the test's operating characteristics will apply to other populations? Is the sample unbiased? Is the sample size large enough to give precise estimates?

5. Is the test fast and easy to apply? Is it reproducible?

6. Is it relatively inexpensive?

7. Could a different cutoff have been used to improve sensitivity or specificity?

8. With estimates of the positive or negative predictive value and the aim of the test specified in Question 1, was the screening test useful for its major purpose **in this population?**

*For a more detailed explanation of questions, refer to Chap. 11, Sect I. in Garb JL. *Understanding Medical Research: A Practitioner's Guide.* Boston: Little, Brown, 1996.

Questions for Hypothesis Testing*

A. Identify the Study Design
1. What are the groups to be compared?
2. On what basis are the groups being compared?
3. What is the study design?

B. Rule Out Bias
4. Was bias present in the design of the study?
   a) For cohort studies and clinical trials,
      (1) Were all subjects taken from the same pool?
      (2) In assessing outcome, were observers blinded to the risk factor status of the subjects?
      (3) Was information on outcome obtained in a similar manner for all groups?
      (4) Was there differential attrition from the study groups?
      (5) For clinical trials, was randomization used?
   b) For case control studies,
      (1) Were all subjects taken from the same population?
      (2) Were controls chosen from an appropriate group?
      (3) Were multiple control groups chosen?
      (4) Were deceased cases included?
      (5) Were observers blinded to the disease status of subjects in assessing risk factor status, or did they have information on risk factor status before knowledge of outcome?
      (6) Was information for risk factor status obtained in a similar manner for cases and controls?

C. Rule Out Confounding
5. Were the groups similar at baseline (e.g., by demographics or clinical characteristics)?
   a) If the groups were not similar, was the possibility of confounding controlled for in the study design (by restriction, stratification, or matching) or in the analysis (by stratification or regression analysis)?

D. Rule Out Chance
6. Was a statistically significant difference found between the groups?
   a) If results were not significant,
      (1) Was the sample size adequate to detect a difference of clinical interest?
      (2) Could bias or confounding be masking real differences between groups?
   b) If the results were significant, did researchers account for multiple statistical tests in interpreting the p-value, and did they perform appropriate multiple comparisons procedures?

E. Establish a Causal Association
7. Was there evidence of a causal association according to the following criteria?
   a) Strength
   b) Consistency
   c) Biological plausibility
   d) Temporal correctness
   e) Specificity

F. Establish Clinical Significance
8. Were the results clinically significant? What is the effect size and its 95% confidence interval?

---

*For a more detailed explanation of questions, refer to Chap. 12, Sect I. in Garb JL. *Understanding Medical Research: A Practitioner's Guide.* Boston: Little, Brown, 1996.

Questions for Estimation[1]

1. To what types of people should the results of this study be generalized (i.e., what are the characteristics of the population from which this sample was chosen)?

2. Was there bias in the selection of subjects for the sample so that resulting estimates are not valid?

3. Were confidence intervals reported for the estimates given?

4. Does the size and variability of the sample chosen result in precise or imprecise estimates, i.e., narrow or wide confidence intervals?

Questions for Meta-Analysis[2]

1. What methods were used to locate and include studies?

2. Was the quality of the studies considered?

3. What were the risk factor and outcome(s) evaluated? Was the same outcome evaluated for all studies?

4. Were the studies included homogeneous with regard to treatment (e.g., dose), patient population, sample size, and other study characteristics?

5. Were the studies homogeneous with regard to outcome (i.e., the magnitude or direction of treatment effect)?

6. Was bias possible in the selection of studies for inclusion?

[1] For a more detailed explanation of questions, refer to Chap. 10, Sect. I. in Garb JL. *Understanding Medical Research: A Practitioner's Guide.* Boston: Little, Brown, 1996.
[2] For a more detailed explanation of questions, refer to Chap. 12, Sect. VI. in Garb JL. *Understanding Medical Research: A Practitioner's Guide.* Boston: Little, Brown, 1996.

Fig. 15-2. Choosing a test*

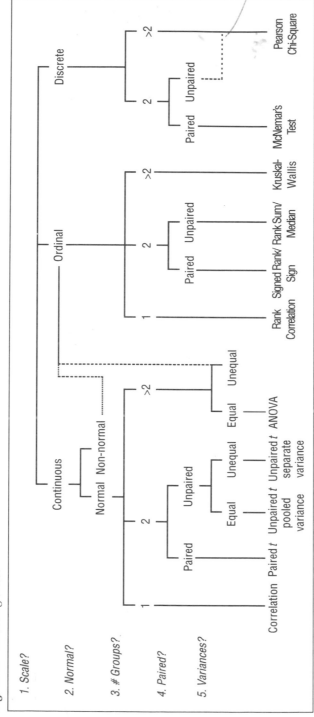

*For a more detailed explanation of choosing a test, refer to Chap. 15, Sect II. D.2. in Garb JL. *Understanding Medical Research: A Practitioner's Guide.* Boston: Little, Brown, 1996.